CHILDREN'S

A TO Z

ENCYCLOPEDIA

First published in 2003 by Miles Kelly Publishing Ltd

This edition published in 2006 by Bardfield Press

Bardfield Press is an imprint of Miles Kelly Publishing Ltd
Bardfield Centre, Great Bardfield, Essex, CM7 4SL

British Library Cataloguing-in-Publication Data
A catalogue record for this book is available from the British Library

ISBN 978-1-84236-472-7

Printed in China

Editorial Director
Belinda Gallagher

Art Director
Jo Brewer

Project Management
Amanda Learmonth, Nicola Sail

Copy Editors
Sarah Doughty, Ann Kay, Sarah Ridley

Designers
David Gillingwater, Debbie Meekcoms, Robert Walster, WhiteLight

Picture Research
Liberty Newton

Production
Elizabeth Brunwin

Indexer
Jane Parker

Reprographics
Anthony Cambray, Liberty Newton, Ian Paulyn

www.mileskelly.net
info@mileskelly.net

CHILDREN'S

A TO Z

ENCYCLOPEDIA

BARDFIELD
PRESS

Contents

How to use this book

Your *Children's A to Z Encyclopedia* is bursting with information, colour pictures and fun activities. The pages run from A to Z with a new subject on every page. This will help you find information quickly and easily. There are cartoons to bring amazing facts to life, and puzzles and games to tease your brain. The index at the back of the book will help you look for more specific information.

Colour bands
Your encyclopedia has six subject areas. The coloured bands along the top of each page tell you which subject area you are in.
• The Natural World has green bands.
• People and Places has orange bands.
• Planet Earth has blue bands.
• Universe has yellow bands.
• Science and Technology has red bands.
• History has purple bands.

Pictures
Illustrations or photographs accompany each caption. Many illustrations are labelled to explain the different parts in more detail.

Activity and puzzle boxes
Some pages will have activities, games or puzzles for you to do. Look for the green, blue or purple panels.

Alphabet strip
Your book is alphabetical. This means it runs from A to Z. Along the bottom of every page is an alphabet strip. The letter that starts the main heading is in bold. Above the letter there's a small arrow to highlight where you are in the alphabet.

Jobs

Teacher, truck driver, dentist, sales assistant, builder and banker are kinds of job. A job is the work you do to earn money. Some people do outdoor jobs working on the land or at sea. Other jobs involve making things in factories and workshops, such as cars and computers. Some jobs provide help and information for others, for example in shops, hospitals, offices and banks.

Word box

assemble
to put together

natural resource
something useful from the land or the sea

▲ By hand
This potter is workin... hands. He uses ma... in his job, such as a... called a kiln to bake...

▲ Helping others
Jobs in offices, banks, hotels and shops are called service jobs. These jobs involve organizing and helping instead of working with natural resources or making goods.

◀ Healing
People who work i... profession such as... and surgeons, hav... Surgeons carry ou... operations on their... the latest technolo... having laser treatm... correct his eyesight...

◀ Dangerous jobs
Fire-fighting can be a dangerous job. Fire-fighters have to be fit and strong and ready to risk their lives for other people. They also have to know about preventing fires, rescuing people and giving first aid in an emergency.

Job search
The names of five jobs are hidden in t...
Can you find them?

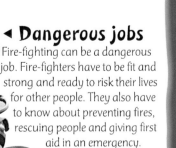

C		R		O		L		I		T
H	E	S	K	D	A	A	R	R	T	M
E	F	K	Z	A	G	R	I	T	O	I
F	P	L	W	G	A	I	W	O	Y	N
P	U	W		S	S	L	A	Y	L	E
U										R

Answers: vet lawyer miner chef artist

Cross-references
Within the colour band are cross-references to other subjects.
These tell you where you can find out more information about
your chosen topic. Follow the arrows to turn backwards or
forwards to the correct page.

Kangaroos and wallabies

Find out more:
Mammals ▶

Main text
Every page begins
with a paragraph
introducing each
subject.

**One of the world's speediest animals bounds
along on its huge back feet at more than
50 kilometres an hour – the red kangaroo.**
At almost 2 metres tall, it is the largest of about 50 kinds
of kangaroos and smaller wallabies. These marsupial
mammals live in Australia, with a few in Papua
New Guinea.

◀ Boomers and fliers

A big male red kangaroo, or 'boomer', can
clear a fence 3 metres tall. Many
red kangaroos vary in colour from
cream to rusty brown. They live in
groups in the outback and gather
at waterholes during drought.

Captions
Captions give
you detailed
information
about all the
photographs
and illustrations
in your book.

Wow!

Some kangaroos live in trees! Tree
kangaroos dwell in forests in
Papua New Guinea and northeast
Australia and have grasping
hands and padded feet.

▲ Wallaby

There are many kinds of wallabies,
with names such as wallaroos,
pademelons, bettongs and
prettyfaces. Some live in forests,
while others prefer rocky scrub or
grassy plains. Like kangaroos,
they use their tail for balance when
bounding and to lean on at rest.

▼ Boxing kangaroos

Male kangaroos push, pull and
wrestle with their arms, and may
kick out with their great feet, using
the strong tail for support. They are
battling for females at breeding time.

**Orange wow
boxes**
Look for the
orange panels
to read amazing
true facts – the
funny cartoons
will make
you laugh!

Word box

drought
a long, dry period with
little or no rain

marsupial
pouched mammal

▲ Mother and joey

A newborn kangaroo is smaller
than your thumb. It stays in its
mother's pouch for up to six
months, feeding on milk and
growing fast. Then the youngster,
or joey, hops out for a short while,
dashing back if frightened.
It finally leaves at one year old.

**Yellow word
boxes**
New or difficult
words are
explained in the
yellow panels.

a b c d e f g h i j **k** l m n o p q r s t u v w x y z **133**

Africa

Africa is the second largest continent in the world, after Asia. It is a land of great contrasts, with hot deserts, thick forests and grassy plains. Most places are either hot and wet, or hot and dry. The world's longest river, the Nile, flows through North Africa to the east of the biggest desert in the world, the Sahara.

▶ Amazing sights

Africa is a land of spectacular sights, including the Great Rift Valley and the towering Mount Kilimanjaro, shown here, which is the remains of an extinct volcano.

▼ Victoria Falls

The Victoria Falls are situated on the border between Zambia and Zimbabwe. Local people call them the 'smoke that thunders' because they make a deafening noise and produce a smokelike spray of mist.

▶ Hunters and hunted

Animals such as giraffes and antelopes roam across the African grasslands, followed by hunters such as lions. They all share the same watering hole.

elephant

giraffe

buffalo

antelope

lion

hippopotamus

warthog

Air is the mixture of gases that you breathe. You cannot see, smell or taste air but it is all around you. Layers of air surround our planet Earth, too, making up the Earth's 'atmosphere'. Oxygen is a gas found in the air. All animals, including humans, need it to stay alive.

▶ Oxygen-makers

Animals take in oxygen from the air and breathe out a waste gas called carbon dioxide. Plants do the opposite. They take carbon dioxide from the air and turn it into oxygen. The oxygen is given off through their leaves.

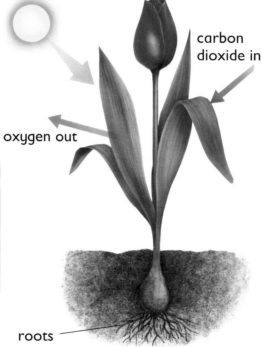

energy from the Sun

carbon dioxide in

oxygen out

roots

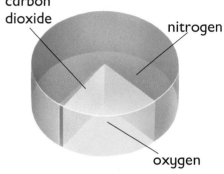

carbon dioxide

nitrogen

oxygen

▲ Gases in air

Nitrogen and oxygen are the two main gases found in the air. About one-fifth of the air you breathe is oxygen. Air also contains very small amounts of a gas called carbon dioxide.

▲ Moving air

When the wind blows it is really air on the move. If you stand outside on a windy day you can feel this flowing air as it rushes past you.

Wow!

On calm days a thick, yellow fog called smog hangs over the American city of Los Angeles. It is mainly caused by exhaust gases from traffic.

▶ Less air!

There are tiny particles in air called molecules, which are always bumping into each other. The more they do this, the greater the air pressure. Gravity pulls the molecules closer to Earth, so this is where there is greater air pressure. At higher altitudes there is less pull by gravity, giving lower air pressure and less oxygen. This is why mountaineers often wear breathing equipment.

Air travel

The first flying machine, or aircraft, to carry people through the air was a hot-air balloon. It was built by the French Montgolfier brothers, and in 1783 it flew for about eight kilometres. Two hundred years later, people could fly at supersonic speeds (faster than the speed of sound) in specially designed jet aircraft.

◀ Hot air

Two passengers travelled in the Montgolfier balloon in the skies above Paris, the capital of France. The linen balloon was filled with air heated by burning straw and wool.

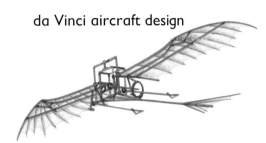

da Vinci aircraft design

▲ Early plane

An Italian artist and inventor called Leonardo da Vinci (1452–1519) produced one of the first aircraft designs, in the 1500s. The aircraft's wings flapped like a bird's wings.

▶ War planes

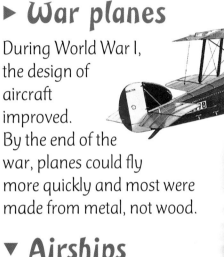

During World War I, the design of aircraft improved. By the end of the war, planes could fly more quickly and most were made from metal, not wood.

▼ Airships

Like balloons, airships are filled with gas, but they also have engines and steering equipment. Travel by airship was popular until 1937, when the *Hindenburg*, a huge airship filled with hydrogen gas, exploded near New York, USA. Thirty-six people on board were killed.

flying boat

▲ Flying boats

In the 1920s and 1930s a few people travelled abroad in large aircraft that landed on water. These seaplanes were called flying boats. They made regular flights across the Atlantic Ocean between Europe and North America.

the *Hindenburg*

▶ The first flight

Orville and Wilbur Wright, were the first people to make a powered, heavier-than-air aircraft fly. In 1903 their *Flyer* aeroplane flew over Kitty Hawk in North Carolina, USA, for 12 seconds.

Aircraft

Aircraft fly through the air, supported by their wings, and allow us to travel at high speeds to distant places. Aircraft are lifted into the air by the force of air flowing over their curved wings as their engines push them forwards.

flap

rib

spar

aileron

tip

▲ On the wing

The wing of an aircraft is curved to provide lift. It is very strong but also light, because it is made of special alloys. Hinged flaps and ailerons can be moved to change the wing's shape and move the aircraft.

▶ Jumbo jets

A modern 'Jumbo' jet can carry up to 500 passengers for thousands of kilometres without stopping for more fuel. These huge aircraft have two decks, like a ship. Their weight is supported by a complicated set of wheels.

▲ Fast fighter

The Spitfire was a graceful fighter plane that played an important part in World War II. It became one of the fastest propeller-driven aircraft. It was replaced by newer jet-powered fighters.

Wow!

Some fighter aircraft can fly so fast that they could catch up with their own bullets!

Word box

aileron
surface on a plane's wing used to control the plane's direction

alloy
a mixture of metals

▶ How does it fly?

Planes fly by balancing opposite forces. Gravity pulls the plane down, while lift pulls it up. Thrust propels the plane forwards, but drag, caused by air resistance, holds it back.

lift

thrust

drag

gravity

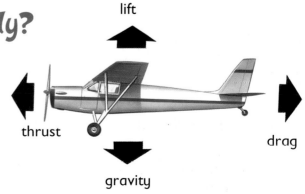

American Revolution

How did the USA begin?

During the 1600s and 1700s, many people from the British Isles settled in North America. The places where they made their new homes were called colonies. These were ruled by Britain. In the 1770s, people living in the colonies rose up against the British. They wanted their freedom.

▲ What a tea party!

The people of Boston were fed up with paying money to the British government and getting nothing in return. They even had to pay a tax on tea. In 1773, in protest, some colonists crept on board three British ships, wearing disguises. They threw the cargoes of tea into the harbour!

▼ First president

The rebel army had been led by a soldier called George Washington. In 1789 he became the first president of the United States.

◄ A free country

In 1776, the American rebels declared that the colonies were independent from British rule. The war continued but by 1781 the British had lost. A new country called the United States of America had been born.

▲ The war begins

In 1775, a man called Paul Revere discovered that British soldiers were marching to a village called Lexington to capture rebels there. He rode all night to warn them. When the British finally reached the village, the rebels were ready for them. The battle that followed sparked off the War of Independence.

Word box

independence
freedom from rule by another country

tax
money which people have to pay to a government, so that it can run the country

Amphibians

Frogs, toads, newts and salamanders are amphibians. Most amphibians are small animals with soft, smooth skins. They can live on land as well as in water and are found near ponds, streams and lakes. Amphibians usually breed in water.

▶ Lots of amphibians

There are more than 3,500 different kinds of amphibian. The largest is the Japanese giant salamander, shown here, which is more than 1.5 metres long. Newts are very like salamanders, but in general, they spend more of their lives in water.

Japanese giant salamander

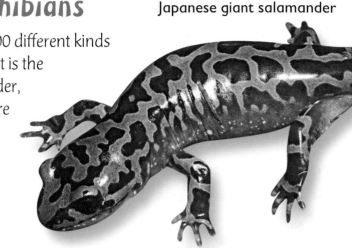

◀ Poisonous frogs

Frogs and toads make up the biggest group of amphibians. This poison arrow frog lives in the rainforests of South America. Its poisonous skin helps to protect it from enemies.

▼ From egg to frog

Tiny tadpoles hatch in water from the eggs of a female frog. As they grow, tadpoles develop four legs and a frog-like body. After a few months the tadpole has changed into a frog.

▼ Greedy toad

The cane toad is a pest. It was introduced to Australia in the 1930s to eat beetles. Unfortunately it also began to eat other frogs, lizards and birds living in the area!

cane toad

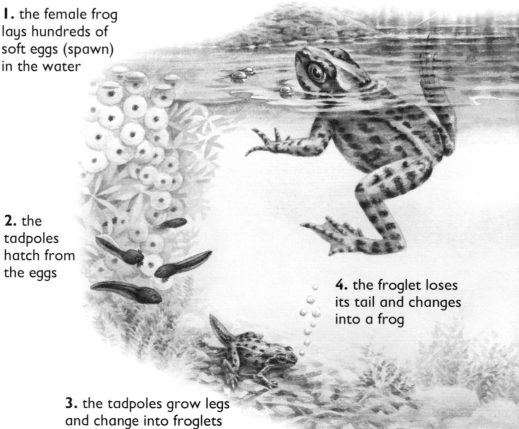

1. the female frog lays hundreds of soft eggs (spawn) in the water

2. the tadpoles hatch from the eggs

3. the tadpoles grow legs and change into froglets

4. the froglet loses its tail and changes into a frog

Ancient Egyptian life

Find out more:
Ancient Egyptian tombs ▶

Egypt became a powerful kingdom about 5,000 years ago. Its rulers were called pharaohs. The ancient Egyptians built great cities, pyramids, statues and temples. Some of them can still be seen today. The ancient Egyptians used a kind of picture-writing and made paper called papyrus from reeds.

▲ **Marvellous mud**

Floods from the river Nile left behind thick, black mud. This was the perfect soil for growing wheat, barley and vegetables. Egyptian farmers also raised cattle, sheep, pigs and geese.

▶ Water works

This machine is called a *shaduf*. The ancient Egyptians used it to lift water from the river Nile. They needed water for their crops, because there was hardly any rainfall. Egypt is a baking-hot land with sandy deserts.

◀ Fashion and beauty

Ancient Egyptian women wore eye make-up and lipstick. Both men and women wore jewellery and wigs. Men wore a simple tunic or kilt, while women wore long dresses of white linen.

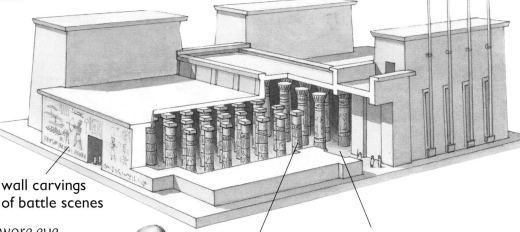

wall carvings of battle scenes

decorated columns

hypostyle hall where processions took place

▶ Pharaoh power

This pharaoh was called Rameses II. He ruled Egypt over 3,000 years ago. People believed that the pharaohs were gods living on Earth.

▲ Praise to Amun-ra!

The temple of Karnak is massive. Its priests worshipped a god called Amun-ra around 4,000 years ago. Each New Year they held a big festival there. They killed oxen and offered them to the god.

Ancient Egyptian tombs

Magic spells and curses were used to protect ancient Egyptian tombs. At first, the pharaohs were buried inside huge stone tombs called pyramids, which pointed up to the sky. Later, they were buried secretly in rock tombs, hidden in the Valley of the Kings, near the ancient city of Thebes.

▲ World wonders

Three huge pyramids can still be seen at Giza, near Cairo. The biggest one is made of over two million heavy blocks of stone! It was built for a pharaoh called Khufu, who died in 2566BC.

Osiris   Horus

Isis

Wow!
The Egyptians made mummies of animals, including cats, birds and crocodiles.

▲ King Tut's tomb

A young pharaoh called Tutankhamun died in 1327BC. He was buried in the Valley of the Kings. His tomb was packed with gold and all sorts of fantastic treasure. This was for him to use in the next life, or afterlife.

▲ Gods and death

The ancient Egyptians worshipped thousands of different gods and goddesses. Three of the most important ones were Osiris, the god of death and his wife Isis, maker of the first mummy. Horus was their son, and protector of the pharaoh.

▶ Making mummies

Egyptians wanted their bodies to stay whole after they died, so that they would be able to travel to the next world. Trained people removed the internal organs first. Then they dried out the body, rubbed it with oils and wrapped it in bandages. The body was placed inside a wooden coffin.

Ancient Greek beginnings

Dolphins leap through sparkling blue seas. Women shake their black, curly hair. Servants carry jugs of wine. All these scenes appear in wall paintings found in ancient palaces on the Greek island of Crete. They show us what it was like to live in Greece between about 3000BC and 1100BC.

▼ Stone cities

Kings in the south of Greece built stone forts called citadels. This one was at a place called Mycenae. It contained a royal palace, as well as houses for soldiers and craftsmen. It was surrounded by a stone wall.

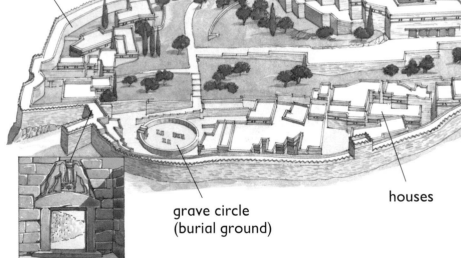

store rooms for food

royal palace

city walls

houses

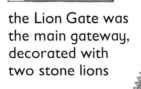

the Lion Gate was the main gateway, decorated with two stone lions

grave circle (burial ground)

▲ Monster in the maze

Greek myths tell how a terrifying monster lived on Crete in an underground maze called the labyrinth. He was believed to be half-man, half-bull and was called the Minotaur.

▼ The Wooden Horse

For years the Greeks tried to capture the city of Troy, in what is now Turkey. Finally, they came up with a plan. They built a big wooden horse, and left it outside the city walls. A few of the Greek soldiers hid inside, while the rest sailed away. Puzzled, the people of Troy hauled the horse into the city. Little did they know what was hidden inside! The Greek soldiers burst out and attacked everyone.

▲ Thrills and spills

The king of Crete was called the Minos. The nobles at his palace liked to watch acrobats. These young people would somersault over the backs of fierce bulls and leap between their sharp horns.

Ancient Greek cities

Find out more:
Ancient Greek beginnings ◄

After about 800BC, cities began to grow up all over Greece. Each city had its own ruler. In 508BC, the people of Athens decided to be ruled by a group of locals, or citizens. This new idea was called democracy, meaning 'rule by the people'.

Wow!

Alexander the Great used soldiers on elephants to charge at the enemy.

▲ City of the goddess

Athens was named after the goddess of wisdom, Athena. Her temple, the Parthenon, stood on a high rock above the city. The Athenians were great thinkers, poets, artists and craftsmen.

◄ Tough ones

In Sparta, both men and women were trained to be really tough. When a huge Persian army invaded Greece, Spartan soldiers like this one fought to the last man.

▼ To the east

In 334BC, Alexander led a Greek army to capture lands to the east. His soldiers were extremely well-trained. The Greeks conquered Persia and marched on to India. They conquered Egypt, too, where the city of Alexandria is named after him.

▼ A great leader

Alexander the Great, a brilliant soldier, came from Macedonia, in northern Greece. All of Greece came under his rule.

Black Sea
Macedonia
Caspian Sea
GREECE
PERSIAN EMPIRE
Alexandria   Babylon
EGYPT
Red Sea
INDIA

Ancient Roman Empire

Find out more:
Ancient Roman life ▶

Rome was the centre of the world.
Or this is how it seemed to people in Europe 2,000 years ago. From small beginnings, this Italian city grew and grew. It became the centre of a huge empire. Roman power lasted until AD476, when the city was captured by German warriors.

▶ Julius Caesar

Julius Caesar was the most famous Roman soldier of all time. He conquered Gaul (France) and attacked Britain. He became the leader of the Romans, but some people were jealous of his power and they murdered him, in 44BC.

▲ The power of Rome

The Romans conquered Greece and Egypt. Soon they ruled all the lands from sunny Spain to the deserts of Syria, from rainy Britain to the mountains of North Africa.

▲ High arches

Roman cities had paved streets with gutters and drains. Pipes and channels called aqueducts carried fresh water into the cities.

◀ On the march

The Roman army was divided into legions. The soldiers wore iron armour and helmets and fought with spears and short swords.

▼ Straight roads

Roman engineers built the best roads. They were made of stone and followed a straight line from one city to the next.

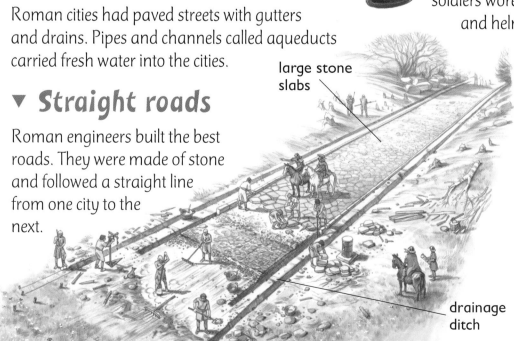

large stone slabs

drainage ditch

Word box

empire
many different lands that are ruled by one country

legion
a unit of the Roman army, made up of about 5,500 mounted troops and foot soldiers

Ancient Roman life

Find out more:
Ancient Roman Empire ◄

The city of Rome had bustling streets, crowded blocks of flats, markets, theatres, public baths and stadiums for horse-racing. Out in the country, rich people lived in fancy houses called villas. Some of these even had central heating! Roman farmers grew crops such as wheat, olives and grapes.

◄ At the baths

Every town in the Roman Empire had public baths. These ones in Bath, England, can still be seen. People came here to meet their friends, to have a hot or a cold dip, or perhaps a massage with oil.

▲ Cruel combat

The Colosseum was a big arena in Rome. Up to 50,000 people could pack into the stands. They loved to watch trained fighters called gladiators battle to the death.

Jupiter   Juno

► Gods and thunderbolts

The Romans worshipped many different gods. Jupiter was the father of them all. He could send thunderbolts whizzing across the sky. Juno, his wife, was goddess of marriage. Their son was Mars, god of war.

▼ Dinner time

The Romans' main meal was in the evening. Diners lay on couches around a low table. Pork, veal or goose might be on the menu — or, for a special treat, fat little dormice or flamingo tongues!

Make a mosaic

The Romans made floor pictures called mosaics from many little coloured tiles.

1. Cut out small squares of brightly coloured paper.

2. Arrange them to make a picture and stick them on to a large piece of card.

Anglo-Saxons

Find out more:
Britain and Ireland ▶

Who were the Anglo-Saxons? Their ancestors (relatives from long ago) were people from northern Germany, called Angles, Saxons, Frisians and Jutes. Groups of them invaded southern Britain about 1,500 years ago and set up small kingdoms. Over time, the language they spoke developed into much of the English spoken today.

▼ Life in a Anglo-Saxon village

The Anglo-Saxons built villages of timber houses with thatched roofs. They farmed the land and raised cattle and sheep. During the AD600s and AD700s many of them became Christians and built stone churches.

▶ Face of war

In about AD625, one Anglo-Saxon warrior was buried in his finest rowing ship, under a big mound of earth. It is thought the warrior may have been Redwald, king of East Anglia. He was buried with his gold coins, his finest jewellery, his prized weapons and this scary-looking helmet made from iron and bronze.

▲ King Alfred of Wessex

In the AD800s the most powerful of the Anglo-Saxon kingdoms was called Wessex. Its wisest king was called Alfred. He built new towns and a fleet of ships. His warriors fought against the Danes, who were invading the north and east of England.

Animal behaviour

Find out more:
Apes ▶ Birds ▶ Mammals ▶
Mammals and their babies ▶

Behaviour describes what an animal does – its actions and movements. Some animals, like worms and slugs, have very simple behaviour. A worm does little except try to avoid light, dryness and being touched, and will just eat its way through soil. Other animals, especially birds and mammals, have complicated behaviour.

▶ Clever behaviour?

Some animals can use tools. The Egyptian vulture picks up a stone in its beak to use as a hammer. It then smashes open an egg so it can eat what is inside. But if we replace the real egg by a painted wooden one, the vulture still keeps trying to smash it. So maybe this bird is not so clever after all! The cleverest birds are probably members of the parrot and crow families.

Wow!

Some gorillas 'talk' to the human guards who protect them from poachers (thieves), using the sign language they have invented themselves.

▼ Learned and not learned

An orb-web spider can make its intricate web without watching or learning from other spiders. Its behaviour is 'built in' from the start, rather than learned later. This is called instinct. Many animals, including spiders, insects and frogs, have instinctive behaviour.

▼ Breeding behaviour

In the breeding season, male mammals like impalas, deer and goats clash heads and fight each other. This behaviour is called rutting. The strongest, healthiest male wins the contest and is able to mate with the females. This means his offspring are likely to be strong and healthy too.

Shape puzzle

Can you put these shapes in an order that makes sense? Some chimps can!

answers
The shapes in order are triangle, square, hexagon (six sides) and decagon (ten sides). Their number of sides increases in this order.

strongest male wins pushing contest

horns locked

Animal camouflage

Find out more:
Arctic ▶ Insects ▶

Why are a baby deer, a plaice flatfish, a polar bear and a vine snake all similar? They are all camouflaged – coloured and patterned to blend in with their surroundings. This is common in all kinds of animals, from worms to whales. It helps them to stay unnoticed by predators, or if they are predators themselves, to stay unnoticed by prey (hunted animals)!

▲ Tawny frogmouth

This nocturnal (night) bird rests by day out in the open, relying on its camouflage. It stays perfectly still on a tree or log, its feathers patterned to look like an old, rotting branch stump. It watches through narrow eye-slits – opening its big eyes would get it noticed.

▼ Find the flounder

The sea bed can be made up of pale sand, speckled stones or grey mud. Many flatfish have good camouflage. As this flounder swims about, it slowly changes its colours and patterns to match the sea bed. This prevents its wide body showing up clearly to any of its enemies such as sharks.

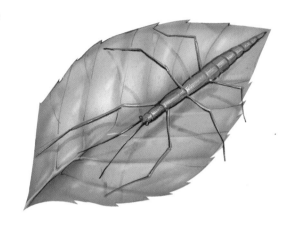

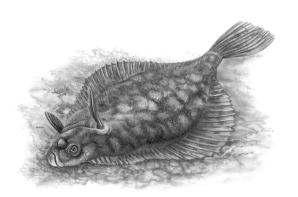

▲ Looks and actions

A creature is often shaped like objects in its surroundings, such as a forest leaf, or seaweed on the shore. The stick insect looks like twigs in trees and bushes, and when the breeze blows, it also sways from side to side, just like them.

Wow!

The fastest quick-colour-change animal is the cuttlefish (cousin of the squid). In a second its whole body can go from almost white to black – or yellow, blue-grey, reddish, even striped!

▶ Spot the chameleon

The chameleon lizard is famed for its camouflage. Its eyes see the colours around it. They send a message to the brain, which sends signals along nerves to the skin. This makes tiny grains of pigment (coloured substances) spread out or clump together and change the skin colour.

Animal kingdom

Find out more:

Amphibians ◄ Animal life ► Birds ► Fish ► Insects ►
Mammals ► Reptiles ► Spiders and their relatives ►

Animals live in almost every corner of the world. They swim in the oceans, walk or run across the land, and fly through the air. The biggest animal on land, the African elephant, weighs as much as a farm tractor. You would need a microscope to see the smallest animals.

there are five main kinds of **vertebrates**:

birds

amphibians

mammals

reptiles

fish

► Animal groups

We divide animals into two main groups: vertebrates (animals with backbones) and invertebrates (animals without backbones). Within each group there are many kinds of animal. For example, roundworms and sponges are two different kinds of invertebrate, and lions and pelicans are two different kinds of vertebrate.

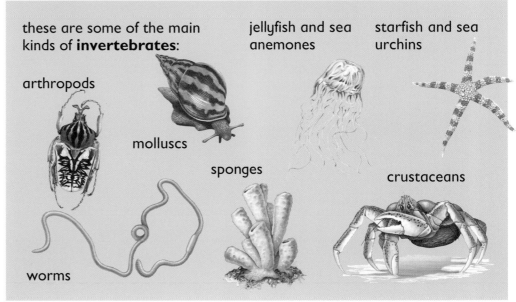

these are some of the main kinds of **invertebrates**:

jellyfish and sea anemones

starfish and sea urchins

arthropods

molluscs

sponges

crustaceans

worms

▼ Biggest of all

The blue whale is the biggest animal on Earth. A male can weigh as much as 120 tonnes and be up to 26 metres in length.

◄ Lots of insects

Insects are the biggest group of animals. There are more than one million different kinds. All insects have six legs, and most can fly.

Wow!

Some large land tortoises can live to be around 200 years old.

Animal life

Find out more:
Amphibians ◄ Animal kingdom ◄ Birds ► Fish ► Insects ►
Mammals ► Reptiles ► Spiders and their relatives ►

Animals live in hot deserts and on snowy mountain-tops, in thick jungles and on wide, open grasslands. Where an animal or group of animals lives is called a habitat. For example, the hot, steamy rainforest of South America is the habitat of jaguars, monkeys and parrots. The frozen landscape of Antarctica is the habitat of penguins.

►▼ Working animals

Across the world, people and animals work together to do different jobs.

in Asia, elephants carry loads

sheep dogs are used all over the world to round up sheep

in India, oxen pull ploughs

▼ In the cold

Polar bears can survive on the frozen land and in the icy cold waters of the Arctic. Their thick coat of fur protects them from the cold. A thick layer of fat below the skin also helps to keep them warm.

a large surface area from which body heat is lost

▲ Hot and dry

Animals that live in very hot places, such as the fennec fox, often have long ears and tails to help their bodies lose heat.

▼ Animal travellers

Some animals travel huge distances to look for warmer weather or food supplies each year. Usually to the same place and back again. This journey is called a migration. In North America, caribou travel thousands of kilometres to find food in winter.

▼ Animals and sport

For thousands of years, people have trained horses to take part in races. Races between horse-drawn chariots were held in ancient Rome. Horse races have been held in Europe since the early 1600s.

Antarctica

Antarctica is the world's coldest continent. This bare, icy land lies around the South Pole, the most southerly place on the Earth. Most of Antarctica is covered with a huge sheet of ice which is up to three kilometres thick in places. During winter, Antarctica is completely dark because the Sun never rises there.

• South Pole

◀ Big chunks of ice

Huge chunks break off the ice around the South Pole to form icebergs, which float out to sea. Icebergs are a danger to ships.

Roald Amundsen

◀ The South Pole

Many explorers tried to reach the South Pole after people first sighted Antarctica in 1820. In 1911 two teams of explorers, one from Norway and one from Great Britain, began a race to the South Pole. The team led by Norwegian Roald Amundsen arrived first.

▶ A cold life

Only a few land animals, such as penguins, can survive the freezing conditions of Antarctica. Yet the waters of the Antarctic Ocean are filled with seals, fish, squid and tiny, shrimp-like creatures called krill. Several kinds of whale spend the summer months in Antarctica.

young emperor penguins rely on their parents for food and warmth

Apes

Find out more:
Monkeys ▶

Our closest animal cousins are apes. Their body shape is similar to ours. They are clever and use tools, and most live in groups called troops. The smaller apes are gibbons of Southeast Asian rainforests. The larger apes are chimpanzees and gorillas, from Africa, and orang-utans, from Southeast Asia. All apes are rare and need our protection.

◀ Grooming friends

Chimps form large troops, of 100 members or more. Friends in a troop groom each other's fur and sleep in tree-nests at night. They eat plants, small animals and birds. Males can form a 'gang' to hunt monkeys or attack wandering chimps from other troops.

Word box

territory
an area where an animal lives, feeds and defends itself or its group against other animals or danger

▲ The biggest ape

A full-grown male gorilla, or silverback, stands almost 2 metres tall and weighs over 200 kilograms. He defends his small troop of 5 to 15 against other gorillas and predators, such as leopards. But most of the time, gorillas just munch plants, sleep, groom or play.

▶ The lonely ape

There are two kinds of orang-utans: Bornean and Sumatran. Unlike other apes, they live mainly alone, except for a mother and her baby. Like most apes, orang-utans are mostly vegetarian, eating fruits, shoots, buds, flowers and leaves. They rarely leave their trees.

▲ Noisy gibbons

Gibbons, such as the white-handed or lar gibbon, live in small family groups. They whoop and holler at dawn and dusk to defend their territory. They can make 10-metre swings through the treetops.

Arabs

The Arabs came from the burning hot deserts of Arabia, in southwest Asia. They lived in tents and herded camels. They also built towns and cities. Between the AD600s and AD900s, Muslim Arabs conquered areas of the Middle East, Africa and Spain. They built beautiful palaces and mosques.

▲ Dome of the Rock

Muslim Arabs captured Jerusalem in AD638. They built this mosque with the golden roof in AD691. Jerusalem remains a holy city to Jews, Christians and Muslims.

▲ Sailing the seas

The Arabs built big wooden sailing ships called dhows. These carried bales of silk and cotton, spices and coffee beans. The Arab merchants traded with East Africa, India, Southeast Asia and China.

▼ Holy words

Arab design and Arab script, or way of writing, were often very beautiful. This is a copy of the *Qur'an* (the Koran), the Muslim holy scriptures.

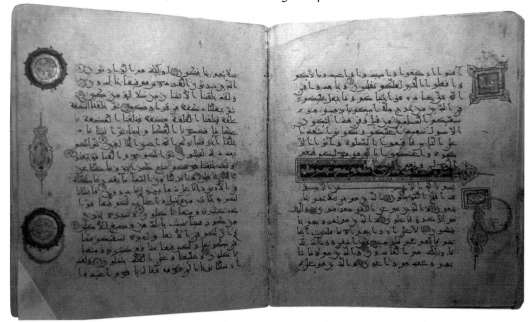

Word box

mosque
a place of worship for Muslims

Muslim
a follower of Islam, the religion of the Prophet Muhammad

Arctic

The Arctic Ocean, in the far north of the world, is almost totally covered in winter by a huge floating ice sheet. The land around is frozen, yet animals still thrive. Fish, seals and whales swim in open water. Polar bears, musk ox, Arctic foxes and hares roam the land. Snowy owls swoop around above the icy ground.

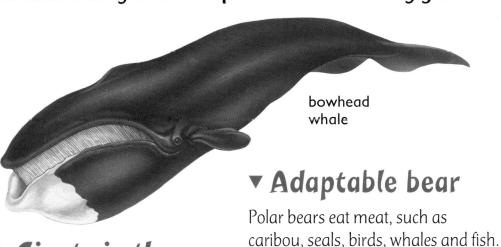

bowhead whale

▲ Giants in the sea

Some great whales, like the 20-metre-long, 60-tonne bowhead, stay in Arctic waters all year. Others, such as blue and minke whales, arrive only for summer. Like seals, they have a thick layer of blubber to keep them warm.

▼ Adaptable bear

Polar bears eat meat, such as caribou, seals, birds, whales and fish. The female digs a snow den in early winter. Without eating any food, she stays here and gives birth to two or three cubs, feeding them on her milk.

▲ Musk ox

Large herds of musk oxen roam the tundra. Their long fur keeps out the cold. They scrape away snow with their large hooves to find plants to eat. If a predator appears, oxen stand in a circle, facing outwards, to protect their young in the middle.

◀ Winter white

Many Arctic animals, like snowy owls, are white in winter, to blend in with snow and ice. This camouflage makes them less noticeable to predators and prey.

Wow!

The bowhead whale has the largest mouth of any animal, almost 10 metres around the lips!

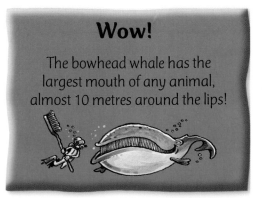

Art

Early humans first painted pictures of animals on cave walls about 30,000 years ago. A great deal of early art was created for gods and religion. Since that time, people everywhere have produced all kinds of painting, sculpture, carving and pottery – we call them works of art.

▲ Kinds of paint

Different kinds of paint produce different effects. Oil paints are thick and textured. Watercolours (above) are much thinner and softer.

▼ Decorative art

Peter Carl Fabergé was a Russian jeweller, whose decorative art skills became popular with the Russian tsars in the 1880s. He is most famous for his beautifully decorated Easter eggs. Fabergé also made picture frames, clocks and other traditional items.

Fabergé egg

Wow!
Some paintbrushes are so fine that they are made from just one or two hairs. The artists work with a magnifying glass to see what they are doing!

▲ Pablo Picasso

Pablo Picasso was born in Spain in 1881, but he mostly lived in France. In many of his paintings, people and objects are turned into shapes and patterns.

▶ Looking at art

You can visit an art gallery to look at paintings and sculptures. This is the Guggenheim Gallery, in New York, USA.

Asia

Asia is the biggest continent in the world. It stretches from the Mediterranean coast of the Near East, to the islands of Japan, off Asia's eastern coast. A range of mountains called the Himalayas separates the warmer, wetter countries of southern Asia from the rest of the continent.

▶ Highest place on Earth

The world's highest mountain is in Asia – Mount Everest. It is 8,848 metres high. Mount Everest is part of the Himalayas, a mountain range on the border between Nepal and Tibet.

◀ Heavy rain

In southern Asia, winds called monsoons blow at certain times of the year. These winds bring very heavy rains.

▼ Sandy desert

Deserts cover most of southwest Asia. Little rain falls there and water is scarce in most of the region. The dry lands are no good for farming.

▼ Rare wildlife

In the rainforest areas of Borneo and Sumatra lives the orang-utan, the only great ape to live in Asia. It is now a protected species.

Word box

monsoon
strong winds and heavy rains

tropical
hot, wet conditions

range
a line of mountains

Asia: Southeast

Find out more:
Religion ▶

Southeast Asia is a region of tropical forests and islands. For thousands of years people grew rice and traded with India, China and Arabia. Some became Hindus, Buddhists or Muslims. Powerful kingdoms grew up in Southeast Asia between 1,500 and 700 years ago.

cinnamon

cloves

pepper

▲ Angkor Wat

The world's biggest religious site is called Angkor Wat. This temple was built in honour of the Hindu god Vishnu. It dates back to the 1100s, when the Khmer Empire ruled Cambodia.

▼ Ancient dances

Beautiful dances like these have been seen on the island of Java for hundreds of years. They were first performed at the royal court.

▲ Spice islands

The islands of Southeast Asia produced precious spices. These included pepper, cinnamon bark and the dried flower buds of the clove tree. After the 1500s, merchants from Portugal, Britain and the Netherlands seized control of the trade in spices.

▼ Early cinema

Puppets like this one were being used on Java over 900 years ago. They were placed behind a cotton screen and lit from behind. When moved by sticks, they made shadows across the screen. Shadow puppets are still in use today.

▶ Countries of Southeast Asia

A hundred years ago, most of Southeast Asia was ruled by European countries. About 50 years ago, Southeast Asian countries began to win back their freedom.

CHINA

MYANMAR

THAILAND VIETNAM

CAMBODIA

PHILIPPINES

BRUNEI Pacific Ocean

MALAYA

Singapore BORNEO

SUMATRA

JAVA Bali

Assyrian Empire

The Assyrians were a mean bunch. Their soldiers were famous for skinning enemies alive! But they were clever scholars, too. They were carvers of stone and builders of roads and cities. Between about 1700BC and 612BC, the Assyrians built up a mighty Middle Eastern empire.

▲ The last king

Ashurbanipal came to the throne in 668BC and set up a great library in the city of Nineveh. He was the last great Assyrian king. After his death there were revolts all over the empire. Nineveh was destroyed in 612BC.

▲ Chariots and bows

Big chariots pulled by three horses were used in war. Some had sharp, whirling knives fixed to the wheels. Assyrian soldiers carried deadly bows and arrows and iron spears and swords.

Wow!

Assyrian soldiers used inflated animal skins to cross deep rivers.

▲ Winged gods

Like the people of Babylon, the Assyrians worshipped gods of earth, fire, wind and water, and winged spirits or genies. The chief god of the Assyrians, shown in this stone engraving, was called Ashur.

◄ Many peoples

The great empire stretched from Egypt and Cyprus in the west to the Persian Gulf in the east. Many different peoples came within its borders.

Astronomy

Find out more:
Moon ▶ Planets ▶ Stars ▶ Universe ▶

Do you like looking at the stars in the night sky? Astronomy is the study of these stars. It is also the study of our Moon, the planets in our Solar System and all kinds of objects found in the Universe. In ancient times, people studied the Moon's movements to make the first calendars. Now astronomers use amazing technology to see farther into space than ever before.

Make a star mural

Have stars twinkling on your own bedroom wall!
1. Cut out star shapes from shiny sweet wrappers. Glue the stars onto a large sheet of black paper.
2. Brush some PVA glue onto the paper and sprinkle glitter over it. Shake off any loose glitter.
3. Stick your star mural up on the wall with multi-purpose tac.

▶ Seeing by radio

The light from the stars you can see has taken millions of years to reach us. Some stars are so far away that we can't even see them. However, they produce faint radio waves that we can measure. Huge metal dishes called radio telescopes collect these radio waves. Some scientists think they have found radio waves left over from when the Universe began.

sliding roof

spare mirrors

focus cage

mirror in base

control room

▶ Watching the sky

Modern astronomers use huge telescopes with giant mirrors and lenses. These help them to see objects millions of kilometres away. The telescopes are kept in buildings called observatories. Parts of the roof slide back so that the telescope can be pointed at the sky. The telescope slowly moves around as the Earth turns, to watch the same patch of sky.

Atoms and molecules

Find out more:
Solids, liquids and gases ▶

Atoms are some of the smallest objects that exist – so small that they are invisible. Everything around us is built from billions of them. Atoms do not usually exist on their own, but join together to make molecules. Two or more atoms joined are a molecule.

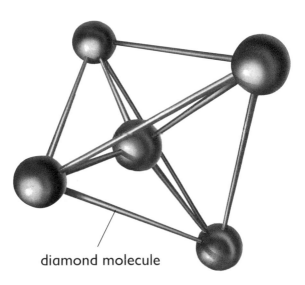

diamond molecule

▲ Coal or diamond?

It seems odd to compare a precious diamond with a lump of common coal, but they are, in fact, very similar! Both contain carbon atoms. In coal, the atoms of carbon are joined up in one particular way. In a diamond, they are joined up in a different way, to form the hardest substance known.

▼ Inside an atom

An atom is made up of different types of tiny particles. It looks like a small version of our Solar System. The central part – called the nucleus – is like our Sun. The electrons are arranged like the planets that fly around the Sun.

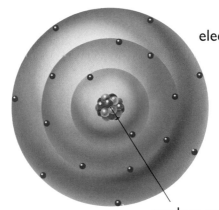

chlorine atom

carbon atom

electrons

nucleus made up of protons and neutrons

◀ Water-works

One drop of water is made up of millions of molecules. Each of these molecules consists of one atom of oxygen and two atoms of hydrogen. Hydrogen and oxygen are themselves gases, but when they combine, they form water.

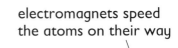

electromagnets speed the atoms on their way

tunnels

atoms speed round and round the tunnels, and are then directed by the magnets into the detector

particles collide here in the detector
▼

◀ Atom-smasher

The only way to study atoms is to smash them open. To do this, scientists use a huge machine called a particle accelerator. The accelerator shoots atoms at each other very rapidly so that they collide.

Word box

collide
crash into each other

particle
tiny object that the eye cannot usually see

The first Australians are called Aborigines. They came to Australia from Southeast Asia over 50,000 years ago. They fished and hunted animals, such as kangaroos and wombats. Dutch explorers sailed along the coasts of Australia in the 1600s. Then, in 1788, British people arrived at Botany Bay and began to settle the land.

◀ Ned Kelly

The 1870s were wild and lawless times in Australia. Ned Kelly and his gang of bushrangers stole cattle and robbed banks. When Ned was captured, he was wearing a home-made suit of armour.

◀ Ancient sounds

This Aborigine is playing an ancient instrument called a didgeridoo. Music, dance and storytelling recall the ancient history, beliefs and traditions of the Australian Aborigines.

▶ A new nation

The British used Australia as a place to send prisoners and to settle free people. They divided the land into separate colonies. Australia became a united country in 1901. This flag, which dates back to 1909, became the official flag of Australia in 1954.

Australia's flag

stars of the Southern Cross

Word box

bushranger
an escaped convict or gangster who lived in Australia in the 1800s

colony
a settlement created in a foreign land by people who have moved away from their own country

◀ Gold and sheep

In the 1800s, more and more Europeans arrived in Australia. They often attacked the Aborigines and forced them off their land. Many of the newcomers were sheep farmers. Others were miners — shown here at a gold mine in Western Australia in 1910.

Aztecs and Mayans

In the 1840s, explorers discovered ruined cities deep in the jungles of Mexico and Central America. They had been built by the ancient peoples of the region, such as the Mayans, whose history stretches back 5,000 years. The Aztec people built the city of Tenochtitlán in the middle of a lake in 1325. It was the capital of a great empire.

▶ Chichén Itzá

The Mayans built a city at Chichén Itzá over 1,100 years ago. It had massive stone temples like this one. When the Toltec people conquered the Mayans, they built a new city nearby. Chichén Itzá fell into ruins and the jungle grew up around it.

▲ Score!

The Central Americans loved to play a ball game called *tlachtli*. The players on the court had to get a small rubber ball through a stone hoop. The game was fast, rough and very exciting.

Wow!

The peoples of Central America invented chewing gum. It was made from the sap of a tree and was called *chicle*.

▶ Steps to heaven

The Great Temple towered over Tenochtitlán. It was 60 metres high. Steps led up to two shrines at the top. Here priests worshipped the rain and Sun gods.

Great Temple

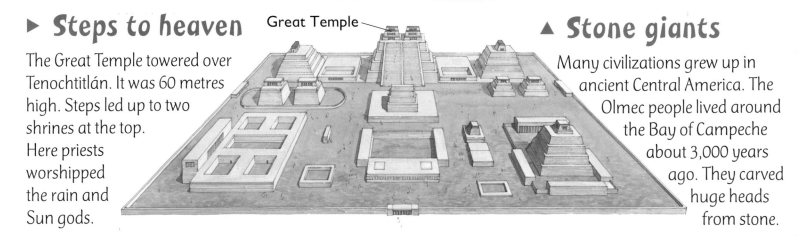

▲ Stone giants

Many civilizations grew up in ancient Central America. The Olmec people lived around the Bay of Campeche about 3,000 years ago. They carved huge heads from stone.

Babies

A human baby spends about nine months inside its mother's body before being born. It takes about 40 weeks for a baby to grow from a tiny egg to a small human being – with eyes, ears, a nose, fingers and toes.

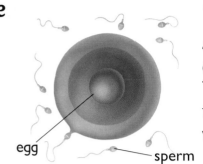

egg

sperm

◀ Life begins

A baby starts out as a tiny egg inside its mother's body. This egg has joined with a tiny cell called a sperm, which comes from the father.

▶ From egg to baby

The egg begins to grow inside its mother's body and it divides quickly into lots of other cells. These cells group together to form different body parts.

at 6 weeks the egg develops quickly and is called an embryo

at 8 weeks the growing embryo is called a foetus

at 12 weeks the foetus looks like a very tiny baby

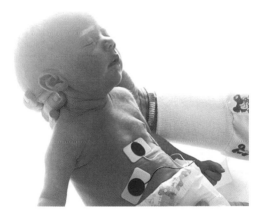

▲ A newborn baby

Newborn babies cannot walk, talk or feed themselves. At first the baby feeds only on milk, either from the mother or from a bottle.

▼ Getting around

In Africa, many mothers carry their babies on their back. The mother has both hands free while the baby is held safely against her body.

at 6 months the baby is well developed but not yet ready to live outside its mother's body

at 9 months the baby is ready to be born. A newborn baby is about 50 centimetres long

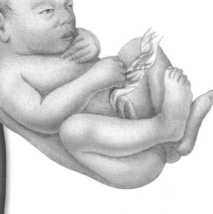

▼ Learning to move

Babies can crawl by eight months. They take their first steps and usually say their first word at about one year old.

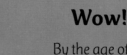

Wow!

By the age of six a child knows more than 2,500 different words.

Baby animals

Find out more:
Birds ▶ Eggs ▶ Mammals and their babies ▶
Nests ▶ Reptiles ▶

Many kinds of baby animals survive without help from their parents. Insects, and most fish and amphibians, hatch from eggs and survive on their own. But some reptile parents, and almost all birds and mammals, care for their babies.

▼ Helpless baby

Like all baby mammals, the young baboon feeds on its mother's milk. It clings to its mother for warmth. As with most other large mammals, baboons usually have just one baby.

▲ Big baby

A young elephant is a 'baby' longer than almost any other animal. It feeds on its mother's milk for two years, and stays near her for another three. Many females in the herd help to protect the baby.

▲ Mother duck

After hatching, ducklings will follow the first moving thing they see — nearly always their mother. This behaviour is called imprinting. Ducklings use sounds when in trouble, cheeping loudly if they are lost.

▼ Help with hatching

The female of nearly all crocodiles and alligators makes a caring mother. She guards her eggs and babies fiercely. The babies squeak loudly in their eggs. The mother helps them to hatch, carries them gently to a quiet pool, and guards them for several weeks.

American alligator

Baby quiz

What animal will each of these babies grow up to be?

1. foal **2.** cub
3. leveret **4.** calf **5.** kid

Choose from:
a. tiger **b.** goat
c. whale **d.** horse **e.** hare

answers
1d 2a 3e 4c 5b

Bats

Bats are the only mammals that can fly.
There are almost 1,000 kinds of bat (nearly one-fifth of all mammals) and most live in tropical forests. They are tiny, and flit about at night after flying insects. Bigger, more powerful bats hunt fish, small birds and owls. Most bats rest by day in dark, sheltered places like caves, hollow trees and the roofs of buildings.

flying foxes

high-pitched sounds echo off the moth

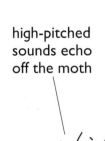

common pipistrelle

▲ Squeaks in the night

Most bats find their way in the dark helped by both eyes and ears. Bats make high-pitched sounds that bounce off nearby objects as echoes. The bat hears the echoes and can work out the position of objects as small as a gnat.

▶ Fruit bats

About 190 kinds of bats are fruit bats, called 'flying foxes' due to their long-snouted faces. They eat fruits, seeds, shoots and plant juices but can be pests and ruin farm crops.

Wow!

Bats have strong muscles to power their wings. Some can fly at more than 50 kilometres an hour!

▲ Bat roosts

Bats usually rest or roost by day in groups. They hang upside down by their clawed feet, wrapped up in their wings. The wings are the bat's 'arms', designed for flight. They are made of a thin, light, tough membrane, which is held out by extremely long finger bones.

Word box

echo
sound that has bounced, or has been reflected, off an object

membrane
a thin layer of skinlike substance, on or inside the body of an animal or plant

Bears

Bears are big, powerful mammals. They have a large head, wide body, massive legs, huge paws and claws and a tiny tail. Most live in forests and eat mainly plant foods. The biggest is the polar bear, which is white and eats meat, and the brown bear or grizzly.

▼ Sun bear

The sun bear lives in the trees of Southeast Asia. It stands about 1.4 metres tall and weighs around 50 kilograms, making it the smallest bear. Its tongue can stick out 25 centimetres to lick honey from bees' nests, grubs from wood holes and termites from their nests.

▲ Spectacled bear

The only bear of South America, the spectacled bear has pale eye rings and rarely leaves the trees of upland forests. It bends branches over to make a rough nest, to rest and sleep.

Bear senses

Do bears find their food and their way around using mainly their eyes, ears or nose? Put these bear senses in order, from the strongest to the weakest:

**ears and hearing
eyes and sight
nose and smell**

answers
1. nose and smell. 2. ears and hearing. 3. eyes and sight.

▼ Fishing for salmon

Like most bears, grizzlies eat many foods – roots, nuts, berries, grubs, birds' eggs, honey and occasionally meat. In autumn, grizzlies gather along rivers to catch salmon. A grizzly then sleeps for much of the winter in a cave or den.

Wow!

The grizzly bear is the largest land-based carnivore (meat-eater), standing 3 metres tall and weighing up to 1 tonne.

A-Z of bears

American black bear – middle of North America
Asiatic black bear – south and east Asia (mainland)
Brown bear (grizzly) – northern Europe, Asia and North America
Giant panda – west and south China
Polar bear – all around the Arctic
Sloth bear – southern Asia
Spectacled bear – uplands of western South America
Sun bear – Southeast Asia

Beetles

Beetles are the largest single animal group on Earth. There are more than 350,000 kinds. These insects live in every habitat, from icy mountains to deserts and deep lakes (but not the sea). A beetle has two hard, curved wing-cases over its body, which are really its toughened front pair of wings. Underneath, folded up, are the second pair of large flying wings.

▲ Lady beetle

A ladybird's colourful spots warn other animals: 'I taste horrible, don't touch me!'. They are a gardener's best friend. Ladybirds protect garden plants by eating huge numbers of caterpillars and aphids (greenfly and blackfly).

▼ Ferocious beetle

The male rhinoceros beetle is one of the longest in the world, at 18 centimetres. The male uses his huge head horn to fight off other males and attract the smaller-horned female for breeding.

▲ Beetle lookalike

Cockroaches have a tough body covering and look similar to beetles. But they belong to a different insect group (*Blattodea*). Most kinds live in tropical forests. A few invade buildings, coming out at night to eat scraps of food.

▶ Great diving beetle

Most beetles eat plants or scraps, but the great diving beetle hunts tadpoles, pond snails, small fish and even baby frogs. It does this as a larva, too. It has to come to the surface for air, which it traps as tiny bubbles under its wing-cases.

Pest beetle quiz – who eats what?

A few beetles cause great damage, usually in their fast-eating grub or larval stage, often called a 'worm'. Can you match these beetle pests with what they eat?

1. Colorado beetles
2. woodworms
3. larder beetles
4. mealworms
5. death-watch beetles

a. potato crops
b. oak beams
c. wooden items such as furniture
d. meat or animal products
e. stored grains (wheat, flour)

answers
1a 2c 3d 4e 5b

Bird life

Birds are the only animals with feathers. All birds have wings too, but not all birds can fly. Penguins cannot fly but they are good swimmers. The ostrich cannot fly but it can run at speeds of more than 60 kilometres an hour, faster than any other bird.

▼ Making nests

Most birds lay their eggs in nests made inside trees and bushes, on cliff ledges, in riverbanks, or in holes in the ground. The weaver bird makes a complicated nest by knotting strips of leaves together.

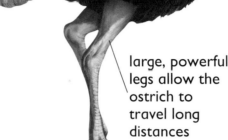

large, powerful legs allow the ostrich to travel long distances

the male weaver twists strips of leaves around a branch or twig

he makes a roof and an entrance

the finished nest has a long entrance, and provides safety and shelter for the eggs

▼ Breaking out

Many baby birds are blind and helpless when they break out of their shells. They are cared for by their parents for several weeks.

the chick chips at the egg

the egg begins to crack

the egg splits open

the chick wriggles out

◀ Fast and big

Ostriches are the only birds with two toes. This means that less of their foot makes contact with the ground, which makes them fast runners.

▼ Different bills

Birds use their bills, or beaks, to get food and to protect themselves. The bill of the grosbeak is short and fat — ideal for eating berries and seeds.

▼ Long-distance traveller

Some birds leave their home during winter to find food in warmer places. This journey is called migration. The Arctic tern flies more than 17,000 kilometres from its summer home in the Arctic to the Antarctic in the south.

Birds

Find out more:
Animal kingdom ◄ Bird life ◄
Seashore life ►

There are more than 9,000 different kinds of bird. The largest is the African ostrich, which can grow to be taller than a man. The smallest is the bee hummingbird, which could easily fit in the palm of your hand. Birds live in every corner of the world, from hot deserts to the icy lands of Antarctica.

bee hummingbird

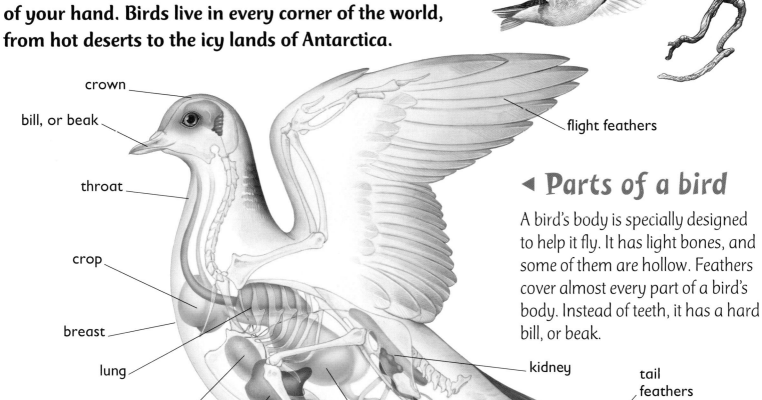

crown
bill, or beak
throat
crop
breast
lung
heart
liver
flight feathers
kidney
tail feathers
stomach
toes

◄ Parts of a bird

A bird's body is specially designed to help it fly. It has light bones, and some of them are hollow. Feathers cover almost every part of a bird's body. Instead of teeth, it has a hard bill, or beak.

▼ Water birds

Puffins live on cliffs by the sea. They dive into the water to catch fish. Their large beaks enable them to hold many fish at once

► Birds of prey

Birds that are fierce hunters of other animals are called birds of prey. They include eagles, vultures, hawks and owls. They have sharp claws and strong, sharp bills. This owl is hunting a mouse.

Blood

Find out more:
Cells ▶ Human body ▶
Solids, liquids and gases ▶

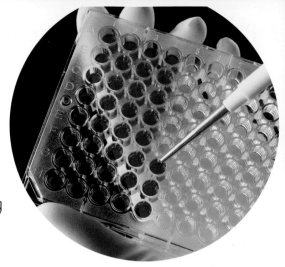

Blood is the life support system for our bodies. It carries the vital oxygen and goodness from food that we need for life and growth. It also helps to collect dangerous waste products from around the body.

Word box

plasma
clear, yellowish liquid that makes up most of blood

transfusion
putting blood from a healthy person into someone who is sick or injured

▼ Under pressure

Blood is pumped under pressure round the body. Doctors often check this pressure, as it can cause problems if it is too high or low.

▼ Blood cells

Blood contains several types of living cell, floating in a liquid called plasma. Red blood cells are tiny, flattish discs that take oxygen round the body. White cells fight infection. Tiny platelets help to stop bleeding.

red blood cells   white blood cell

white blood cell   white blood cell   platelets

▲ Which group?

People who have lost a lot of blood through injury or disease may need a blood transfusion. It is vital that patients get blood from someone who has blood of the same group (type). To check this, small drops of blood from the person who is giving it are tested carefully beforehand.

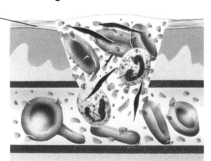

skin   sticky clot blocks the cut

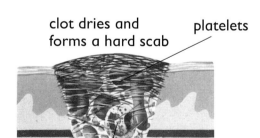

clot dries and forms a hard scab   platelets

white blood cell   red blood cell

▲ Stopping the flow

If you cut yourself, tiny structures called platelets release sticky substances. These block the cut with a mass of fibres to form a clot. White cells swarm into the cut to kill any germs, and repair begins. The mass of fibres and trapped red cells dry to form a scab. Underneath this, fresh skin develops.

Books

Millions of new books are created every year.
Some, like this encyclopedia, have both words and
pictures in them. Some books have only
words, some have mainly pictures and
very few words. We read books to give us
information as well as for enjoyment.

▼ Book beginnings

Authors are the starting point for
most books. Some authors write
out their work by hand, but many
use a computer.

▼ Writing books

Charles Dickens (1812 to 1870) wrote
some of the most famous books in
world literature. His characters were
brought to life in classics such as
Oliver Twist, *A Christmas Carol* and
David Copperfield.

Wow!

A Chinese book called the
Diamond Sutra is the oldest
printed book – it was made over
1,100 years ago.

▲ Religious writing

The main scripture of the Sikhs is called *Adi Granth*, or 'First Book'.
It is a collection of nearly 6,000 hymns of the Sikh gurus, or religious
teachers. They were written down between 1604 and 1704.

▼ Book characters

We all have favourite
characters from the
books we have read.
How many of these
famous book
characters do
you recognize?

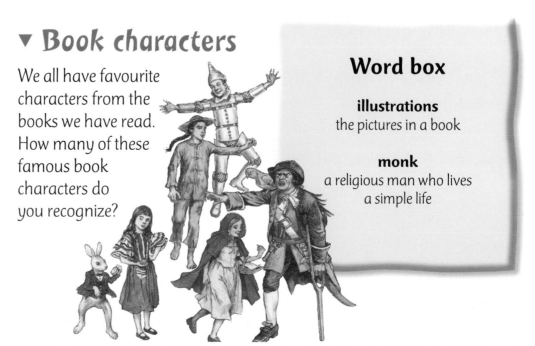

Word box

illustrations
the pictures in a book

monk
a religious man who lives
a simple life

Britain and Ireland

Find out more:
Anglo-Saxons ◀ Celts ▶
Empires and colonies ▶ Normans ▶

Celts, Anglo-Saxons, Vikings and Normans settled on the islands of Britain and Ireland long ago, and founded small kingdoms. These later grouped together into Ireland, Wales, Scotland and England, and eventually joined to form the United Kingdom (or UK). During the 1800s, people from Britain and Ireland settled in many other parts of the world.

▲ Scotland's might

Parts of Edinburgh Castle are nearly 1,000 years old. Its high walls guarded the kingdom of Scotland from attacks by the English. From 1603 the Scottish king became king of England, too. Scotland and England were fully united in 1707.

▲ For England!

England became very powerful in the Middle Ages. It fought many wars against its neighbours. This fierce battle took place at Agincourt, in France, in 1415. It was a victory for Henry V (Henry the Fifth) of England.

▲ Welsh uprising

The Welsh battled with the English, too, but were conquered in 1283. In 1400, the Welsh rose up against English rule, under a leader called Owain Glyndwr. The English were back in control by 1413 and the two countries were united in 1542.

◀ Irish freedom

England tried to rule Ireland for centuries, and it did become part of the United Kingdom from 1801. In 1916, there was an uprising in Dublin against British rule. The country won independence after 1922, but the North remained within the United Kingdom.

Buildings and bridges

Since earliest times, we have needed buildings to protect us from the weather – and sometimes from enemies. The first buildings were made of straw, sticks and mud. Now we use much stronger materials such as concrete and steel.

Wow!
Many castles were built in India between 1500 and 1700. The gateways had iron spikes in the doors to stop war elephants breaking them down.

▲ The longest steel-arch bridge

The longest steel-arch bridge, with a span of 518 metres, is the New River Gorge Bridge in West Virginia, USA. Another steel-arch bridge, Sydney Harbour Bridge in Australia, is the world's widest long-span bridge.

▼ Reaching for the sky

Modern buildings, such as these skyscrapers, are built around a steel skeleton. Cranes are used to lift sections of the buildings into place.

▲ Super suspension

Suspension bridges span the greatest distances – the longest is the Akashi-Kaiko Bridge in Japan. It spans 1,990 metres.

Butterflies and moths

Most butterflies are colourful and beautiful. Moths are mainly small, grey or brown – but there are exceptions. There are more than 160,000 kinds of these insects, mostly moths, living mainly in tropical forests and grasslands. They all have two pairs of wide, flat wings covered with tiny scales, and eat plants.

1. butterfly egg

2. caterpillar hatches

3. when fully grown, the caterpillar is ready to turn into a pupa

4. the adult butterfly pushes its way out of the pupa

5. the butterfly spreads and dries its wings

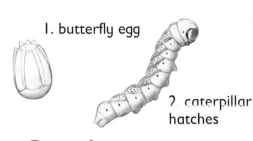

▲ Growing up

All butterflies and moths begin as tiny eggs. These hatch into larvae or caterpillars. When the caterpillar is fully grown it forms a hard body case called a pupa or chrysalis. Eventually, the case splits open and the adult butterfly crawls out. It then dries its wings and can fly after about an hour.

▼ Death's head hawk moth

Most moths hide by day. Their wings are patterned so they blend into their surroundings. But this big, powerful, fast-flying moth has scary markings on its back that look like a human skull!

▲ Bright moth

Most moths are small, have hairy bodies, feathery antennae and fly at night. But the zodiac moth of New Guinea is big and bright, with slim antennae and flies by day.

Word box

antennae
feelers found on an insect's head, they are also used to smell

nectar
sweet, sugary liquid made by flowers, to attract insects and other animals

◀ Pest butterflies and moths

Most adult butterflies and moths sip sweet nectar from flowers. But some of their caterpillars feed on farm crops and cause great damage. White butterfly caterpillars eat cabbages and other vegetables.

Byzantine Empire

Find out more:
Russia ▶

In AD324, the Romans decided to make the city of Byzantium, in the east of their empire, every bit as grand as Rome. Byzantium was renamed Constantinople. The city survived long after Rome itself had fallen, ruling large areas of southern Europe and western Asia. In 1453, it was captured by the Turks, who called it Istanbul.

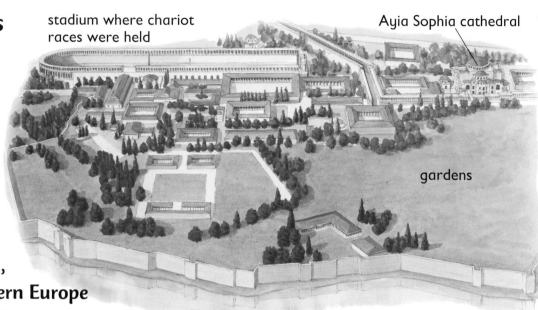

stadium where chariot races were held

Ayia Sophia cathedral

gardens

▲ Constantinople

The city was a rich seaport with high walls. It had markets, workshops, gardens and a beautiful cathedral. The people who lived there were mostly Greeks.

▼ Holy wisdom

The city of Constantinople was an important centre of the Christian faith. It was full of churches and monasteries. The great cathedral, Ayia Sophia (meaning 'holy wisdom'), can still be visited today.

Wow!
Theodora was the daughter of a circus bear-tamer. She married the emperor Justinian in AD525, and became the most powerful woman in the world.

▲ Man of law

The emperor Justinian lived from about AD482 to AD565. Under his rule the Byzantines recaptured many lands of the old Roman Empire. He was a great law-maker.

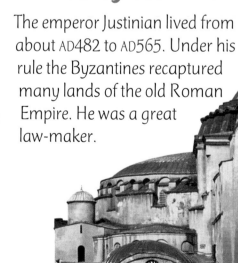

Canada

The first Canadians were hunters.
They may have crossed into Canada from Asia over 30,000 years ago. After about 3000BC, new people came from Asia to settle the frozen north, hunting polar bears and seals. Their descendants (family) are called Inuits.

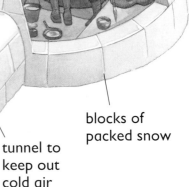

animal skins and fur to help keep the ice house warm inside

blocks of packed snow

tunnel to keep out cold air

▶ Arctic survival

The Inuit built houses of stone and turf to keep out the bitter cold of winter. On hunting trips they made shelters out of ice blocks. These were surprisingly cosy.

◀ European Canada

French and British explorers and settlers moved into Canada in the 1500s and 1600s, trading in fish and furs. In 1534, Jacques Cartier became the first European to explore the St Lawrence River.

▲ Mohawk warrior

The Mohawk people settled in southeast Canada and around the St Lawrence River. They lived in wooden houses and grew beans, maize, squash and tobacco.

Jacques Cartier

◀ Canadian Pacific Railway

In 1885, a new railway was opened. It linked the eastern city of Montreal with Canada's Pacific coast. More and more Europeans travelled westwards and settled the land.

Cars

Today, there are more than 500 million motor cars on the world's roads. They come in many different shapes and sizes, from small three-wheeled ones to large four-wheel drive cars for travelling over rough ground. Most cars are powered by an engine, which burns either petrol or diesel fuel.

Wow!

The longest car in the world is so long, it has a swimming pool inside it!

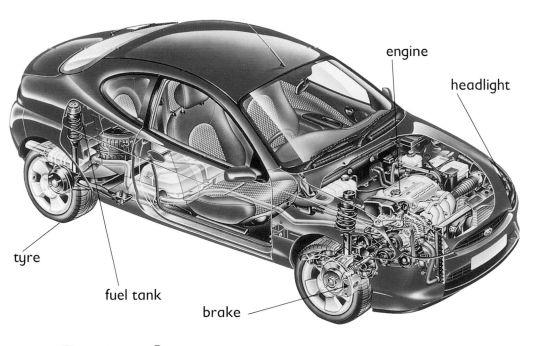

engine

headlight

tyre

fuel tank

brake

▲ Parts of a car

A car has thousands of different parts. This cutaway view shows some of the most important ones.

▼ Motor racing

Racing cars have a sleek shape to help them go faster. This Formula One racing car can reach speeds of up to 320 kilometres an hour.

Word box

mass-produced
made in large numbers

pollute
make dirty

sleek
smooth and shiny

▲ Cleaner cars

Electric cars are cleaner because they do not produce waste gases like cars that use petrol or diesel. Waste gases from motor cars pollute the air.

▲ Early cars

One of the earliest mass-produced cars was the Model T, built by the Ford company in the United States. For about 20 years it was the most popular car and over 15 million of them were sold during this time.

Castle life

A castle was the home of an important and powerful person, such as a king, a lord or a knight. Castles were also places where soldiers were stationed, wrong-doers imprisoned, weapons and armour made and great banquets and tournaments held.

▶ Life in a castle

The centre of castle life was the keep, where the lord of the castle and his family lived. Castles were usually surrounded by a high outer wall, and often a ditch filled with water called a moat.

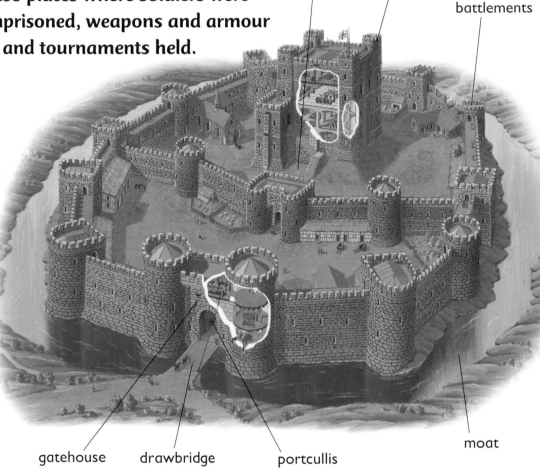

bailey   keep

battlements

gatehouse   drawbridge   portcullis

moat

▲ Lord and lady

The lord of a castle controlled the castle itself, as well as the lands and people around it. The lady of the castle was in charge of its day to day running.

▼ Who worked in the castle?

Many servants lived and worked inside the castle. They cooked, cleaned, served at the table, worked as maids and servants and ran errands. A man called the steward was in charge of all the servants.

steward

Castles

A castle was a kind of fortress home for kings, queens, lords and ladies. It had high towers and massive walls to keep out the enemy. Soldiers guarded the castle and controlled the surrounding countryside.

► The first castles

The first castles looked like this. They had a wooden tower, called a bailey, on top of a high mound of earth, called a motte. They were built by the Normans over 1,000 years ago.

motte-and-bailey castle

▲ Knock it down!

This giant catapult was called a trebuchet. It hurled rocks at castle walls in order to knock them down.

◄ Stronger and stronger

By 700 years ago, castles were being built with more and more round towers and walls. Around them were ditches filled with water, called moats. The walls of this castle, built at Conwy in Wales, went right around the town as well.

► Digging underneath

Enemy soldiers would surround a castle and cut off its supplies. This was called a siege, and it could go on for months, or even years. Sometimes the enemy tunnelled underneath the castle walls to make them fall down.

Word box

catapult
a weapon of war, designed to fire rocks and boulders

fortress
a building or town that has been specially built to protect it from attack

Cats, lions and tigers

Cats are deadly hunters, fast and silent, with strong legs and sharp claws and teeth. All 38 kinds of cat are very similar, differing mainly in size and fur colour. Lions and tigers are the largest cats. Lions live in groups called prides; tigers usually live alone. Most wild cats live in forests, have spotted or patched coats and climb trees well. Some survive in deserts.

▲ Big cats

The seven big cats are the lion, tiger, cheetah, jaguar, leopard, snow leopard and clouded leopard. The leopard stores a large kill in a tree, away from hyenas and jackals, to eat over several days. It also hunts in towns and raids rubbish for leftover food.

Word scramble

Unscramble these words to find the names of five types of cat:

a. TACLIWD
b. MUPA
c. REGIT
d. TOLECO
e. HATEECH

answers
a. wildcat b. puma
c. tiger d. ocelot e. cheetah

▲ Fast cats

Most cats run fast in bursts, but cannot keep going as dogs do. The cheetah is the world's fastest runner, reaching up to 100 kilometres an hour, but for less than 30 seconds.

▲ Male or female?

The lion is the only big cat where the female and male look different. The male (see above) is bigger and has long, shaggy neck fur called a mane.

Wow!

The smallest cat is the black-footed cat of southern Africa, which is half the size of many pet cats.

▶ The biggest cat

The Siberian tiger is not just a big cat — it's the biggest cat. It measures 3.5 metres long, from nose to tail-tip. This tiger prowls the cold, snowy lands of eastern Asia and is the rarest kind, with less than 200 left in the wild.

Cells

Your body is made from billions of tiny living units called cells. **Different types of cell are grouped together to carry out particular jobs. Cells divide and multiply as we grow. They are replaced as they wear out.**

lysosomes are like recycling centres, breaking up old and unwanted substances so their parts can be used again

cell membrane is the 'skin' around the cell and controls what comes in and goes out

mitochondria change food into energy to power the cell's processes

◀ Oxygen-carriers

This microscope photo of blood shows hundreds of red cells, which take oxygen around the body. The darker specks are white blood cells, which fight infection. They have been stained a dark colour to make them easier to see.

nucleus is the cell's control centre and contains the genetic material, DNA

ribosomes are ball-shaped factories that make useful substances or products

golgi layers wrap up the cell's products so they can be sent to where needed

Word box

plankton
tiny organisms that float in water

▲ Looking inside

All cells have the same basic form, although there are many different types. The nucleus controls how the cell works. It contains DNA, a material that contains a pattern for the development of the whole body.

axon

axon

signals jump gap

◀ Pass it on

Nerve cells carry messages round the body, in the form of electrical signals. These signals pass along the long, thin axon and then jump to the next nerve cell. Our brain, spinal cord and nerves are packed with millions of these cells.

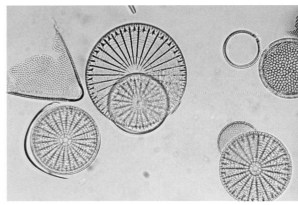

▲ Pond life

Have you seen green haze on a pond? This contains millions of microscopic plants, each made from a single cell. These are diatoms, and they live inside a hard, protective shell. Diatoms are also found at sea, floating in plankton.

The ancient Celts were farmers and iron workers. Their homeland was in central and western Europe. Between about 700BC and 300BC, Celtic warriors swarmed across Europe, bringing their languages and ways of life to many regions. Celtic peoples included the Gauls of northern Italy and France, the Gaels of Ireland and the Britons of Great Britain.

▲ Charioteers

A Celtic charioteer practises his skills. His job was to drive a fully-armed warrior into the thick of battle at high speed.

◄ Furious fighters

Celtic tribes often fought against each other. Many also went to war with the Romans, Greeks and Germans. Their warriors were armed with iron swords, daggers, spears and long shields.

◄ Mirror, mirror

This beautiful bronze hand mirror was used by Celts in southern Britain over 2,000 years ago. The Celts also loved wearing gold jewellery. The Romans complained that they liked showing off too much!

▼ The hill fort

Maiden Castle, in southern Britain, was the chief town of a Celtic tribe. It was on a high hilltop, defended by fences and steep ditches. It was attacked and captured by the Romans after they invaded Britain in AD43.

timber gates

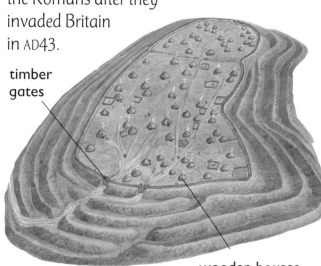

wooden houses

► Later Celts

The Celts worshipped various gods and spirits, but during the AD300s and AD400s they turned to Christianity. Ireland became a centre of the faith and produced beautiful religious books, stone crosses and silver work.

Chemicals

Most of what is around us is made up of chemicals.
Plastic, soap, even water, are a mix of chemicals. Some chemicals
are dangerous – chlorine for example. However, when chlorine
is mixed with another chemical called sodium, salt is
formed, which is harmless.

acidic substance, such
as citric acid in
lemons, turns red

neutral substance

alkaline substance
turns purple

Fun and froth!

Make your own chemical reaction.
You will need: vinegar and
washing soda
Add a few drops of vinegar to a
spoonful of washing soda in a
saucer. They will react with each
other by frothing and giving off a
gas called carbon dioxide.

▶ Chemical groups

Acids and bases are 'opposite'
types of chemicals. They can be
tested by using indicator paper,
which changes colour when it
touches different substances.

▶ Petroleum products

Petroleum, or crude oil, is a
natural material that is used
to make many different
chemicals. Plastics, fuels,
paint and soaps all come
from crude oil. They are
made in an oil refinery,
where crude oil is heated in
a huge tower. The oil is
separated into different
substances by boiling it at
different temperatures.

oil refinery tower

cooking and
heating gases

petrol and
vehicle fuels

kerosene for jet fuel,
heating and lighting

diesel oils for truck
and train fuel

crude oil turns
to gas and
rises up tower

▼ Chemical colours

Fireworks use chemicals to make
wonderful displays. Inside them are
tiny metal particles, or chemicals that
contain metal. They also contain
substances that produce oxygen.
When these burn together, each
metal produces a different coloured
flame – and exciting sparks!

crude oil is
heated in a
furnace

waxes, tars
for road
surfaces,
polishes

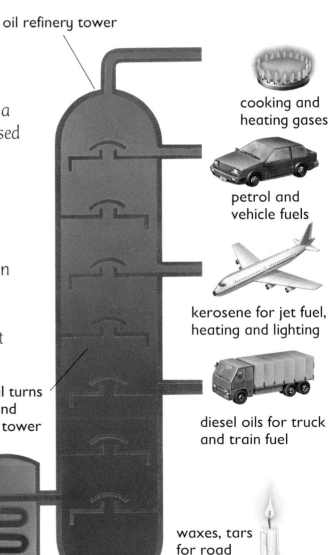

China: beginnings

Find out more:
China: Empire and Republic ▶

The ancient Chinese believed that they lived at the centre of the world. They built great cities and canals and learned how to make beautiful silk, paper and pottery. Many of the world's most useful things were invented long ago in China.

meeting house in centre of village

hole in roof to let out smoke

thatched roof

wooden wall plastered with mud

supporting poles

▼ Ghostly army

By 221BC, China was a united empire. The first emperor (Qin Shi Huangdi, pictured left), was a powerful man. Only one thing scared him – death. Just before he died, he arranged for an army of life-sized terracotta (clay) soldiers to stand guard around his tomb.

◀ First farmers

This is what a northern Chinese village would have looked like over 5,000 years ago. The farmers living there grew millet and kept pigs and dogs. They made pottery. Rice was grown in central and southern China.

▶ The Great Wall

The first emperor sent hundreds of thousands of workers north to build a great wall. It was meant to stop fierce tribes from invading China. Work on the wall carried on for hundreds of years. When it was finished, it measured over 6,000 kilometres in length.

China: Empire and Republic

Find out more:
China: beginnings ◄

For 2,000 years the Chinese Empire grew bigger and bigger. Its merchants traded with India, the Middle East and distant Europe. The Empire survived wars and invasions until it came to an end in 1911, when it became a republic.

◄ A golden age

During the period AD618 to AD907, China became extremely wealthy. It made the first ever printed books and produced the world's finest pottery, such as this horse figurine.

▶ Forbidden City

Twenty-four emperors made their homes in this splendid palace at Beijing, between 1423 and 1911. It included 800 separate buildings. Ordinary people were never allowed inside its high red walls, so it became known as 'the Forbidden City'.

▲ Silk robes

The emperors of China ruled over a glittering court. They wore robes of silk, such as this one decorated with dragons.

▶ Power to the people

After 1911, there were many wars. The Japanese invaded China during the 1930s. Different political groups fought each other, too. The Communists, led by Mao Zedong, aimed to give power to poor working people. They ruled China after 1949.

Mao Zedong

Make a Chinese fan

1. Take a sheet of A4 paper.
2. Use colour felt-tip pens to make a Chinese dragon design.
3. Fold the paper into pleats.
4. Staple the bottom end of the fan together.

Cities of ancient times

Find out more:
Cities of modern times ▶

When people lived by hunting, they had to follow herds of wild animals in order to survive. Only when they began farming could people settle down in one place, with a sure supply of food. Villages grew into towns and cities where people traded goods. The world's first towns were built in western Asia about 10,000 years ago.

▲ A town with no streets

Çatal Hüyük was built by farmers in about 7000BC, beside a river in Turkey. Its houses were made of mud bricks and flat roofs. They were all joined up, with no streets in between.

▲ Walls and gates

The city of Babylon was built beside the Euphrates river, Iraq, about 3,800 years ago. It was protected by massive walls. Nine gates led into the city. The Ishtar Gate was covered with blue tiles, decorated with bulls and dragons. Through it, a paved highway led to temples and royal palaces.

▼ Gardens of Babylon

A thousand years after it was built, Babylon was still a great city. It was famous for its beautiful terraces and gardens, made for a queen called Seramis.

How many people?
See how the number of people in each ancient city grew over time:

3000BC	Uruk (Iraq)	50,000
2200BC	Ur (Iraq)	250,000
600BC	Babylon (Iraq)	350,000
200BC	Patna (India)	500,000
100BC	Rome (Italy)	1,100,000

Cities of modern times

In the 1800s, country people began to pour into the cities around the world to work in new factories and offices. Some cities now housed as many as four million people. Numbers doubled and doubled again in the 1900s. Today, one in three people in the world lives in a town or a city.

◀ City of London

London, the capital of the United Kingdom, became the world's biggest city in the 1880s. Roads, railways and houses soon swallowed up farmland around the city. Factory and household smoke made cities dirty places to live.

How many people?

See how the number of people in each modern city has grown:

AD900	Angkor (Cambodia)	1,000,000
1279	Hangzhou (China)	1,500,000
1890	New York City (USA)	1,500,000
1939	London (England)	8,600,000
1990	Tokyo-Yokohama (Japan)	27,200,000

▲ The Eiffel Tower

This 300-metre-high tower was put up in Paris, France, in 1889, to mark a big exhibition. At that time it was the world's highest building.

▶ Reach for the sky

During the 1890s, skyscrapers were built in the centres of New York City and Chicago. They took up very little space at ground level. They were made possible by new ways of building and by the invention of the lift. These buildings are the Petronas Towers in Kuala Lumpur, Malaysia.

▲ Under the ground

Cities built underground railways from the 1860s onwards. The Moscow Metro, built in the 1930s, has very grand stations, like this one.

Wow!

Siberia, in eastern Russia, has the biggest difference between summer and winter. Temperatures vary from 15° Celsius in July to -51° Celsius in January!

The Earth moving around the Sun causes certain weather patterns that are repeated regularly. These patterns are called climate. A region's climate is affected by many factors such as distance from the Poles or Equator, distance from the ocean, nearby mountains, ocean currents and height above sea level.

▼ All kinds of climate

Earth has several climate regions. Tropical areas around the Equator generally have a hot, rainy climate throughout the year. The lands around the Poles are cold for most of the year. The area between the tropical and polar regions has a temperate climate with warm summers and cool winters.

look at the coloured rings to match the different climate scenes to the main map

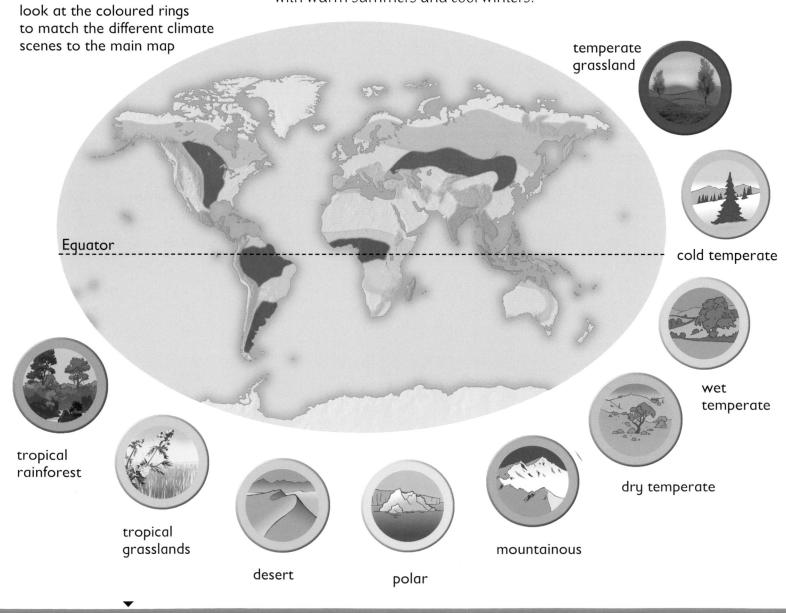

temperate grassland

cold temperate

Equator

wet temperate

dry temperate

tropical rainforest

tropical grasslands

desert

polar

mountainous

Climate change

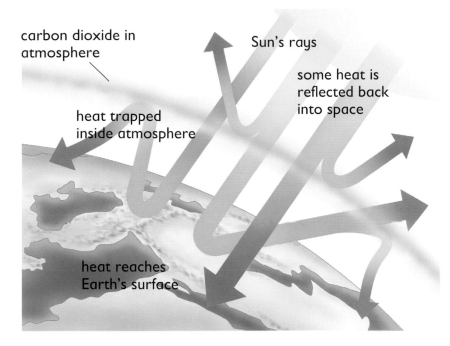

carbon dioxide in atmosphere

Sun's rays

some heat is reflected back into space

heat trapped inside atmosphere

heat reaches Earth's surface

Climates can change. This may be caused by a warm ocean current changing position. Humans also cause change, by doing things such as cutting down tropical forests. This may reduce rainfall over a wide area, turning it into desert.

▲ Getting warmer

The Earth's surface absorbs sunlight and turns it into heat. Some of this heat escapes into space. When we burn fuels such as coal and oil a gas called carbon dioxide is released into the air. Large amounts of this gas trap the Sun's heat – the 'greenhouse effect'. This raises the air temperature, just as glass on a greenhouse traps heat inside. This is known as 'global warming'.

▼ Rising waters

As the climate changes with global warming, polar ice is melting. This makes the sea level rise. Some coral islands in the Pacific Ocean have already vanished, and others may follow.

Word box

coral
hard, stony material produced by tiny animals in tropical seas

hurricane
giant storm with high winds

▶ Ice Ages ago

The 'Ice Age' was made up of several cold and warm periods, each lasting many thousands of years. During the last Ice Age, around 15,000 years ago, ice sheets covered the land. Early humans were well adapted to the cold conditions.

▲ Wild winds

Changes in climate may increase the number of hurricanes that sweep in from the sea. These hurricanes can cause huge amounts of damage to buildings and homes, due to the enormous power of the wind and the great floods that usually follow.

Clothes around the world

Find out more:
Clothes in history ▶

We choose our clothing to suit what we do each day. To play sport we wear hard-wearing but comfortable clothes that let us move freely. In cold weather we wear clothing to keep us warm. In some parts of the world, people still wear traditional clothes that they have worn for centuries, particularly in country areas.

Wow!

In ancient Rome, only the emperor was allowed to wear an all-purple toga. A toga was a loose piece of cloth worn by men.

▼ Clothes for the job

Some workers have to wear special clothing for their job. Fire-fighters wear protective suits made of a material that stops their bodies from being burned.

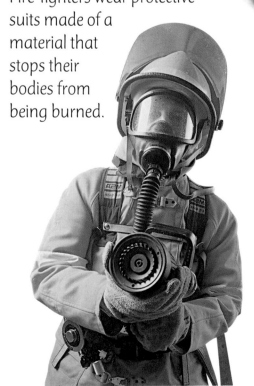

▼ Keeping cool

In hot countries, people wear loose-fitting clothing to keep cool. Their clothes are made of cotton or linen. They are usually light-coloured to reflect the Sun's rays.

▶ Keeping warm

People who live in cold climates, such as Inuits in the far north, often wear thick layers of clothing made from natural materials such as wool, fur or leather. Scientists have developed new synthetic materials made from chemicals, which are also extremely warm.

▶ Uniforms

A uniform tells you that a person does a certain job, or belongs to an organization. You notice doctors in hospitals from what they are wearing.

Word box

climate
the usual weather of a place over a long period of time

linen
cloth made from the flax plant

reflect
to make light bounce back

synthetic
not natural

Clothes in history

Find out more:
Ancient Roman life ◄

The first humans made simple clothes from animal skins, furs and plant fibres. By about 7000BC, people had learned to weave cloth on looms. Wool, linen and cotton were often used for keeping warm or staying cool. Different styles of clothes were worn around the world.

Word box

breeches
trousers that reach only as far as the knees, where they are fastened

fibre
threads of wool, hair, flax, straw, cotton or silk used to make clothing

loom
a frame used for weaving cloth

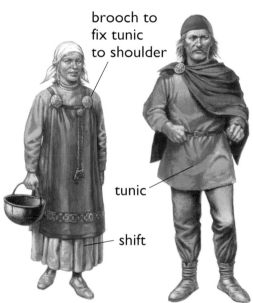

brooch to fix tunic to shoulder

tunic

shift

long dress, or *stola*

toga

thick cloak, or *palla*

▲ Viking dress

Viking women wore a shift with a long woollen tunic over the top. The men wore a knee-length tunic over trousers, with a cloak for warmth.

▲ Roman togas

In ancient Rome, important men wrapped themselves in a heavy white robe called a toga. Senators who passed the laws wore a toga with a purple stripe. Most women wore several layers of cloth.

▼ A true gentleman

This is how European men dressed in the 1700s. They wore long 'frock-coat' over a waistcoat, knee-length breeches and a three-cornered hat. Both men and women wore white wigs, over their own hair.

▲ In the Middle Ages

In Europe during the Middle Ages, most poor children wore simple clothes woven from home-made wool. Boys wore short tunics and girls long ones. Hoods and cloaks kept off the rain.

◄ Paris fashions

The French were famous for fashion as long ago as the Middle Ages. In the 1800s and 1900s, women all over Europe and North America searched magazines for the very latest Paris designs. These ones date from 1913.

Colour

Colour is all around you – in the clothes you wear, in the flowers in the park, in a rainbow in the sky and on your TV screen. Even the light from the Sun, which seems to have no colour at all, is filled with colour.

► Colours of the rainbow

When white light passes through a glass prism, it breaks up into the different colours of the rainbow: red, orange, yellow, green, blue, indigo and violet. The whole range of bands of colour is called a spectrum.

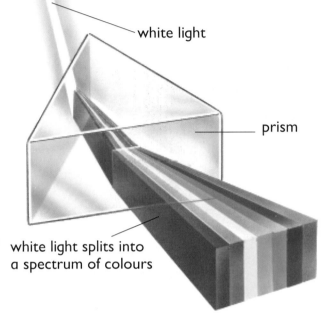

white light

prism

white light splits into a spectrum of colours

Word box

primary
most important

prism
a specially shaped piece of glass

spectrum
bands of colours

a rainbow occurs when raindrops in the air act like prisms

▲ Warning colours

Some animals use colour to warn off their enemies. The bright markings on this butterfly's wings tell its enemies that it tastes nasty!

► Mixing colours

We mix colours together to create different ones. Only three colours of light – red, blue and yellow – are needed to make all the other colours. These three colours produce all the pictures that you see on your television screen.

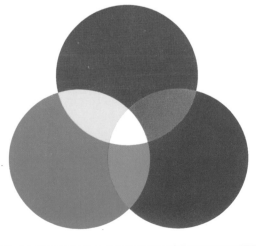

Colour mix

Red, blue and green are the primary colours of paint. All other paint colours are made from them. Can you fill in these gaps with the correct colours?

a. red + . . . = orange
b. . . . + red = purple
c. blue + yellow = . . .

answers
a. yellow b. blue c. green

Colour in use

Try this!

Have fun mixing lots of colours with your paints. Blue, yellow and red are the primary paint colours (these are different from the primary light colours – see 'Mixing light'). See how many different colours you can come up with. You'll be amazed!

When we look at an object, we do not actually *see* its colour. Instead, we see the light that the object reflects, or bounces off. White light (a mix of all colours) falls on the object, but most of its colours are soaked up or absorbed. The colours that are reflected reach our eyes and give the object its colour. So, we see a leaf as green because it absorbs all other coloured light except green.

▶ Colour wheel

On a colour wheel, one primary colour (red, yellow or blue) will appear opposite the mixture of the two other primary colours. For example, red will appear opposite green, which is a mixure of yellow and blue. These opposites are called complementary colours.

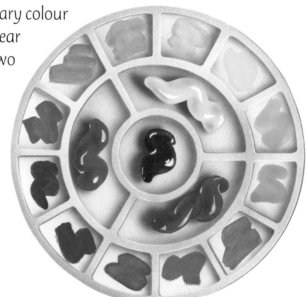

tiny dots of colour

▲ On the page

Colour pictures in magazines and books and on TV screens are actually made up of thousands of tiny dots of colour. Our eyes naturally mix these colours together.

yellow plate

magenta plate

cyan plate

black plate

roller

cylinder

▶ Colour in printing

Lithography is a printing process, used for creating colour pictures. An image is transferred to a surface called a plate. Four of these plates are used to print a full colour picture (see right). Each plate is placed on a cylinder. A roller then wets all of the plate except the image. Another roller spreads ink that only sticks to the image. The inked image is then transferred to paper.

Communication

Find out more:
Computers ▶ Internet ▶
Sound and hearing ▶ Technology ▶

Our whole lives are is based on communication.

Communication is the sharing of information. People communicate mainly by speaking and writing. We also communicate by facial expressions, gestures and even body language. Animals communicate with each other in a variety of ways.

◀ Noisy monkey

The noisiest land animals are the red and black howler monkeys of South America. They live in troops of 10 to 30 animals, the monkeys howl to define their territory or to send alarm signals to others. The sound comes from the echo chambers beneath their chins, and can be heard 5 kilometres away.

▶ Let's communicate!

As well as words, we use a lot of 'body language' to communicate with people – often to say hello or goodbye. Hand gestures, facial expressions, body positions and eye contact are all ways of communicating with others.

Wow!

One of the longest phone calls ever recorded lasted for 550 hours – nearly a whole month!

Find out more:
Computers ▶
Sound and hearing ▶

Did you write a letter today, make a phone call or send someone a message by e-mail? All these are different ways of communicating with people. Modern technology lets us communicate at very high speeds across the world – by telephone, radio, television or the Internet.

Wow!

There are more telephones than people in the city of Washington D.C., capital of the USA.

Word box

e-mail
short for electronic mail (sending letters by computer)

remote
far away

satellite
a spacecraft that circles the Earth

▲ Faraway places

In remote parts of Australia, the only way to communicate with others is by radio. Some children do their schoolwork by talking to their teacher over a two-way radio.

▼ First telephone

The first telephone was made in 1876 by a Scottish-born inventor called Alexander Graham Bell.

▼ Up in space

When you telephone someone in a distant country, the signal from your call is beamed up to a satellite above Earth. The satellite then sends the signal through space, back down to the Earth and into the other person's phone.

satellite

telephone exchange sends messages along the phone network

▼ On the move

With the help of mobile phones, people can keep in touch with each other, wherever they are. These phones are small enough to fit in your pocket – or even in the palm of your hand.

Computers

Computers are complicated machines that can process huge amounts of information in a very short time. They are not intelligent themselves, but they help us to do clever things that we would not be able to do on our own. For example, computers can now beat humans at chess.

Wow!

Special computers are used to calculate the weather forecast. Some can work out a six-day global forecast in just 15 minutes!

▲ Early computers

One of the first proper computers was called *Colossus*. It was built in 1943 to decode (work out) complex messages used by Germany during World War II.

Word box

circuit
a loop of electricity

microchip
tiny slice of a substance called silicon, containing millions of electronic parts

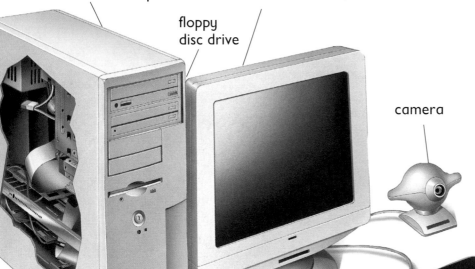

CD-ROM drive reads information from a compact disc

monitor (screen) displays information from the computer

floppy disc drive

camera

mouse

the microprocessor is the computer's main microchip and controls the computer

keyboard

▲ What goes where?

Computers have a keyboard, a screen, a mouse and a main box that contains electronic circuits that control computer processes. Some of the latest computers have a flat screen. The mouse is a hand-held device that allows you to control the computer quickly and conveniently.

Conservation

Many animals and plants are in danger of dying out, or becoming extinct. Their habitat may have been destroyed by pollution or deforestation, while some animals may have been hunted for their fur or meat. Conservation is important for protecting all of these living things.

Word box

deforestation
cutting down large areas of forest

habitat
home

▼ Empty seas

For thousands of years, the sea has provided fish for us to eat. But now modern fishing boats are able to catch more fish than can be replaced. Fish that were once very common, such as cod, are in danger of being wiped out.

◀ Saving the panda

China is trying to preserve its giant pandas by breeding them in captivity. Farming is destroying the places where the pandas live. They are also hunted for their skins.

▼ National parks

To try and conserve wild parts of the world, large areas have been set aside as national parks. Here, building, tourism and other activities are strongly controlled.

▶ The last orchid

Human actions have made some wild plants so rare that they need to be protected. The rare lady's slipper orchids grows only in one place — in Yorkshire, England. Its location is kept secret in order to protect it.

Crabs and other crustaceans

Find out more:
Seashore life ▶

Crustaceans are 'insects of the sea'. Like insects on land, they swarm in the oceans in billions. There are over 40,000 kinds including crabs, lobsters, prawns, shrimps, krill (which look like shrimps) and barnacles on seashore rocks. Copepods and branchiopods are smaller and more rounded, and even more numerous. They include a few freshwater types like the pond 'water flea', daphnia.

Wow!

The largest crustacean is the giant spider crab. Its body is as big as a dinner-plate and its long legs and pincers would hang over the edge of a double bed!

▶ On the march

Some crustaceans migrate (travel) with the tides or seasons. These spiny lobsters are marching to deeper water to breed.

▼ Crustaceans on land

A few crustaceans, like the wood-louse (sowbug), survive on land, far from the sea. Even so, they need to stay in cool, damp places, such as under bark or logs, or they dry out and die.

▼ Tough customer

The robber crab is big, strong and fierce, with pincers the size of your hands. Like many crabs and other crustaceans, it feeds by scavenging on old, rotting bits and pieces of almost anything. This crab lives mainly on the shore, and can even climb trees.

◀ Non-crusty crustacean

Most crustaceans have a hard outer body casing, one or more sets of antennae (feelers), at least four pairs of legs, and perhaps strong pincers. The hermit crab is unusually soft-bodied. It finds an empty whelk or similar shell and hides safely inside it.

Crocodiles and alligators

Find out more:
Baby animals ◄ Reptiles ►
River and lake animals ►

Crocodiles have survived from the age of dinosaurs – but in some cases, only just. There are 23 types of crocodiles and their cousins – alligators, caimans and gharial (gavial). All are powerful meat-eaters, catching prey or scavenging on dead meat. But some have been hunted by people for meat and skins, or because they threaten us or our animals.

Word box

estuarine
in or from an estuary (river mouth), where a river widens and flows into the sea

hibernate
sleep very deeply for weeks, usually to survive a long winter

▼ Biggest reptile

The largest crocodile, and biggest reptile, is the saltwater or estuarine crocodile. Most crocodiles live in fresh water along rivers, lakes and swamps, but this massive beast swims along coasts and even out to sea. It lives along the shores of South and Southeast Asia and Australia.

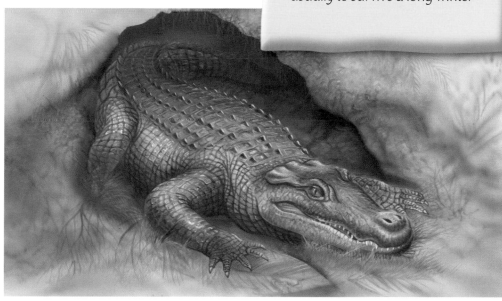

▲ Chinese alligator

One of the smallest and rarest types, the Chinese alligator is only 2 metres long. Its prey is also small – water snails, worms and the occasional water rat or duck. During the winter it hibernates out of water, in a cave or den, waking up in the warmth of spring.

Wow!

Crocodiles are among the longest-lived animals. Some survive to well over 100 years of age.

► Teeth and scales

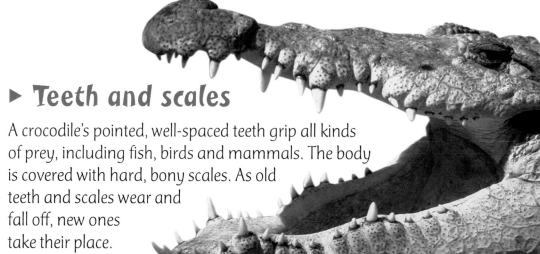

A crocodile's pointed, well-spaced teeth grip all kinds of prey, including fish, birds and mammals. The body is covered with hard, bony scales. As old teeth and scales wear and fall off, new ones take their place.

Crusades

In 1075, Turkish Muslims captured the holy city of Jerusalem. In 1096, after the Muslims declared that pilgrims could no longer visit Jerusalem, Christian knights living in Europe began a series of religious wars called the Crusades. Most of these were fought against Muslims in the Near East, but others took place in Spain and Central Europe.

▶ Sword on sword

Terrible wars were fought in the Near East until 1291. The Christian knights wore heavy armour, even in the heat of the desert. Their Muslim enemies were armed with steel swords, round shields and bows and arrows. The Europeans called them 'Saracens'.

▶ Saladin

One Saracen leader was admired and respected even by his enemies. His name was Saladin, or Saleh-ed-din Yussuf, and he lived from 1137 to 1193.

Word box

Crusades
'wars of the Cross', the Cross being the badge of the Christian knights

Near East
the lands of southwest Asia, today occupied by Turkey, Syria, Lebanon, Israel and the Palestinian Territories

Crystals

Most crystals are formed from minerals – natural substances found in the Earth's crust. They come in different shapes, but all have straight edges and flat surfaces. Some crystals, such as salt, are simple cubes. But other substances produce crystals with more complex shapes.

▼ Sugary crystals

The sugar you use at home is actually tiny crystals. Water is slowly made to evaporate (disappear into the air) from sugar syrup, so that solid sugar is left lumpy as crystals.

▲ Inside snow

Snow is made up of millions of tiny ice crystals. These form inside cold clouds, where they collide and stick together to produce snowflakes. Some snowflakes have star shapes with six sides like this, others look like long needles of ice.

▲ Spiky shapes

Amethyst crystals are formed from a mineral called quartz. With its many different surfaces and angles, this is a good example of crystals with a complex shape.

◄ Liquid crystal

The LCD (liquid crystal display) screen of this hand-held television is made up of 'liquid' crystals. These are crystals that have been heated up so they become cloudy. Thousands of liquid crystals build up to make the image you see on the screen.

Try this!

Put hot tap water (careful!) in a jam jar. Now pour in salt, stirring until it has all dissolved. Let the water cool. Tiny salt crystals will slowly form on the bottom of the jar. Use a spoon to remove most of the crystals, leaving just one or two of the largest. Put the jar somewhere warm and check it every week. As the water evaporates, the salt crystals will grow in size.

Deep sea animals

At the bottom of the sea, every day is the same – and night too. It's always dark, cold and still, with huge pressure. Below about 500 metres there is no light, and so no plants. Animals survive on bits of food sinking down from above – or eat each other. There are glow-in-the-dark fish, squid, strange-shaped crabs, shellfish, starfish, sea urchins, sea cucumbers, sea lilies and giant worms galore!

▲ Big-mouthed eel

The gulper eel, about 60 centimetres long, is also called the black swallower. Its flexible mouth can swallow an animal twice its size. Many deep-sea creatures are black. Colours and patterns are of no use in the darkness. Some have no eyes at all.

▶ Fanged fish

The deep sea is the world's biggest habitat. But food is quite scarce, so relatively few animals live there. Most are small – the viperfish is hardly longer than your hand. It has long fangs, like a snake, to grab any possible passing meal.

◀ Deep-sea anglerfish

This wide-mouthed, sharp-toothed hunter 'fishes' for prey with its long front fin spine, which has a glowing tip. Small creatures are lured by this light in the darkness, and the angler swallows them whole.

Word box

fang
a long, thin, sharp-pointed tooth

pressure
a pushing or pressing force, measured over a certain area such as a square centimetre

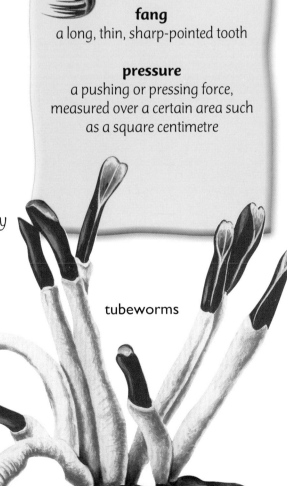

tubeworms

▶ Deep-sea tubeworms

Here and there on the sea bed, hot water rich in minerals, from deep in the Earth, spurts out through cracks. Microbes and tiny creatures thrive on the minerals, and they become food for bigger crabs, blind fish and tubeworms larger than your arm. It is a warm, food-rich 'island' on the vast, cold, muddy ocean floor.

Deserts

Deserts are dry places where very little rain falls each year. Sometimes heavy rains in one year are followed by no rain at all for the next few years. Life for desert people can be very difficult. Many, such as the San people of Africa's Kalahari desert, are nomads. They move from place to place in search of water.

Wow!

The Atacama Desert in Chile, South America had no rain for 400 years. The rains finally arrived in 1971.

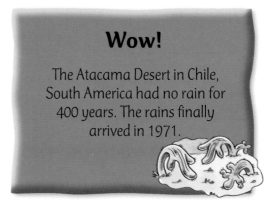

▲ Clever plants

Most deserts are near the Equator, the imaginary line that runs around the centre of the Earth. These deserts are hot and dry and few plants can survive. One type of desert plant, the cactus, stores water in its thick, fleshy stems.

► Keeping cool

Animals in hot deserts try to avoid the extreme daytime heat by hiding beside rocks or underground. They come out in the cool night-time air to look for food.

► Desert water

Oases lie near sources of water, such as springs or underground streams. Plants can grow here, so people often settle in these areas.

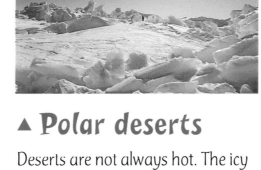

▲ Polar deserts

Deserts are not always hot. The icy lands around the North and South Poles are known as cold deserts.

Key

1 - kangaroo rat
2 - rattlesnake
3 - tarantula
4 - ringtail
5 - chuckwalla
6 - fennec fox
7 - long-nosed bat
8 - mule deer

Dinosaur ages

Find out more:
Dinosaurs ▶ Reptiles of the world ▶

Dinosaurs lived between 230 million and 65 million years ago. This vast length of time is called the Mesozoic Era. Dinosaurs were around for about 80 times longer than people have been on Earth!

▼ Timeline

This timeline shows some of the animals and dinosaurs that lived between 286 million and 2 million years ago.

MILLIONS OF YEARS AGO

PALAEOZOIC ERA	MESOZOIC ERA	
PERMIAN PERIOD	**TRIASSIC PERIOD**	**JURASSIC PERIOD**

PERMIAN PERIOD — The reptiles, including the ancestors of the dinosaurs, are becoming more important than the amphibians.

Erythrosuchus

Thrinaxodon

TRIASSIC PERIOD — The first proper dinosaurs appear. These are small two-legged carnivores, meat-eaters, and larger herbivores, or plant eaters.

Riojasaurus

Plateosaurus

JURASSIC PERIOD — Many different dinosaurs lived at this time, including the giant plant-eaters like *Barosaurus*.

Barosaurus

Heterodontosaurus

Apatosaurus

MILLIONS OF YEARS AGO

286   248   208   144

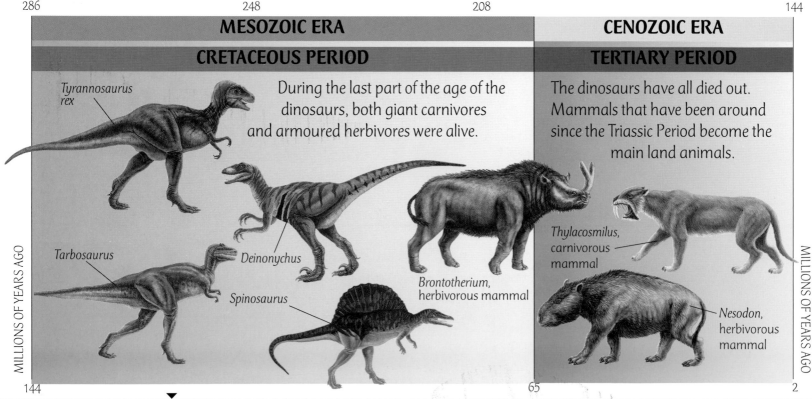

MILLIONS OF YEARS AGO

MESOZOIC ERA	CENOZOIC ERA
CRETACEOUS PERIOD	**TERTIARY PERIOD**

CRETACEOUS PERIOD — During the last part of the age of the dinosaurs, both giant carnivores and armoured herbivores were alive.

Tyrannosaurus rex

Tarbosaurus

Deinonychus

Spinosaurus

Brontotherium, herbivorous mammal

TERTIARY PERIOD — The dinosaurs have all died out. Mammals that have been around since the Triassic Period become the main land animals.

Thylacosmilus, carnivorous mammal

Nesodon, herbivorous mammal

MILLIONS OF YEARS AGO

144   65   2

Dinosaurs

Dinosaurs were reptiles that roamed the Earth millions of years ago. The giant ones were the largest creatures ever to have lived on land. The smallest dinosaur, *Compsognathus*, **was the same size as a chicken. Some dinosaurs were fierce meat-eaters and some only ate plants.**

Compsognathus

Wow!

Argentinosaurus, the heaviest dinosaur, weighed over 100 tonnes — that's 20 times heavier than a fully grown African elephant.

► Fierce hunters

Tyrannosaurus Rex was one of the fiercest, largest meat-eating dinosaurs. It was 12 metres long and hunted large, plant-eating dinosaurs.

▲ Flying reptiles

Pterodactyls were large prehistoric flying lizards, not dinosaurs. They had enormous wing spans of up to 12 metres, and were very good fliers. Their wings were made of skin and their bodies were usually furry.

▼ Finding fossils

Everything we know about dinosaurs comes from fossils, the hard remains of animals and plants found in rocks. People began to study dinosaurs after an English woman found a huge tooth buried in rock. Her husband realized that the tooth probably came from a giant reptile that looked like an iguana.

Word box

iguana
a kind of lizard

prehistoric
a very long time ago

▲ Dinosaur defences

Stegosaurus was a plant-eating dinosaur that walked on all four legs. A row of bony plates along its back protected it from attack. These plates may have helped to cool the dinosaur's body too.

Disasters

In the past, life was much less certain.
If the harvest was bad, everyone went hungry.
People suffered, as we do today, from floods,
fires, volcanoes and earthquakes, but in those
days they had no fire engines or
rescue teams. There was little
understanding of disease and
no modern medicine.

▲ The plague

Between 1347 and 1351, a terrible illness
called the Black Death raged across Asia
and Europe. It was passed on to humans
by rat fleas and killed about 75 million
people. This deadly disease, or plague,
returned again and again. It killed tens
of thousands of people in London in 1665.

▲ Great Fire of London

When houses were mostly built of wood, there was a great
risk from fire. In 1666, a fire at a London bakery spread
across the city, destroying over 13,000 homes.

Wow!

In AD472, so many ashes erupted
out of the volcano Vesuvius that
they were carried as far away
as Turkey!

▶ Volcano disaster!

Almost 2,000 years ago, the entire
Roman town of Pompeii was buried
under hot ashes when the volcano
Vesuvius erupted in AD79. Since then,
it has erupted several more
times, with equal force.

Dogs and wolves

Wolves, wild dogs, foxes and jackals form a group known as canids. Most are predators but they can also survive on fruits, berries and scraps. Wolves and wild dogs form groups called packs. Foxes and jackals usually live as female and male parents with their young.

▲ Small cub, big ears

The African bat-eared fox is one of the smallest foxes. It uses its huge ears to detect insects. The cubs (young) like this one grow up with their parents and then leave to set up a family in their own area.

Word scramble

Unscramble these words to find the names of five types of canid:

a. DILW OGD
b. KLACAJ
c. OXF
d. GINOD
e. REYG FLOW

answers
a. wild dog b. jackal
c. fox d. dingo
e. grey wolf

▶ No escape

Once African wild (hunting) dogs start to chase a victim, there is little escape. They speed along at 40 kilometres an hour, bringing back meat for females with cubs, and for sick or injured pack members.

▶ Maned wolf

The maned wolf lives in South American grasslands. In some areas it is kept as a tame pet, but in other places it is killed as a night-time attacker of farm animals.

▶ Leader of the pack

Grey wolves live in packs of about ten members in most northern lands. Only one pair breed – the rest help by bringing food such as smaller mammals for the cubs in their den (home).

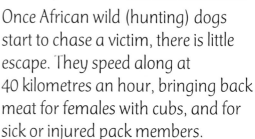

Dolphins

Find out more:
Mammals ▶

Dolphins seem to have great fun as they swim, leap and play among the waves. But each year millions get caught in fishing nets and drown. There are 32 types. These include pilot whales and six river dolphins, which live in fresh water. The six types of porpoises have much blunter snouts. They all have teeth and hunt fish or squid. Most live in schools or pods (groups), and communicate with squeals and clicks.

Wow!

Hector's dolphin is sometimes called the Mickey Mouse dolphin, because its dorsal (back) fin is shaped like this famous cartoon character's ears!

◀ The largest dolphin

The largest dolphin is one of the world's biggest predators – the killer whale, or orca. A big male is almost 10 metres long and 10 tonnes in weight. Some pods of orcas hunt mainly fish in one area, while others wander and prefer seals.

▲ Blunt-beaked dolphin

Risso's dolphin is one of the larger types, measuring about 4 metres in length. Like most dolphins it has smooth, sleek skin, two flippers, a dorsal fin and curved tail flukes. It also has an unusually short beak.

▶ Baby dolphins

Dolphins are mammals and breathe air through the blowhole on the top of their head. A baby dolphin is born underwater and nudged to the surface by its mother, for breaths of air. A calf, like this spinner dolphin, swims close to its mother.

Eagles and hawks

Find out more:
Birds ◄

Eagles, hawks and falcons are the great predators of the skies. There are more than 300 kinds of birds of prey, or raptors, from huge American condors with 3-metre wings to tiny falconets and kestrels hardly bigger than blackbirds.

Wow!

The peregrine falcon moves faster than any other animal when it power-dives or 'stoops' onto prey at 220 kilometres an hour.

▲ International hunter

The osprey or fish-eagle is the most widespread raptor, found on all lands except the far north and Antarctica. Like most raptors, it hunts by day using its incredible eyesight, soaring and gliding until it spots a fish just under the surface. It is about 61 centimetres long with a wingspan of nearly 1.8 metres.

osprey talon

▼ Gyrfalcon

The largest falcon is the gyrfalcon, which hunts over Arctic ice and snow. It swoops low and catches mainly birds, such as ptarmigan and willow grouse, plus occasional lemmings and voles. As with many raptors, the male and female make amazing courtship flights as they dive, climb, roll and loop in the air.

► Feet for fishing

All birds of prey have sharp, hooked beaks and sharp, curved talons (claws). The osprey's talons are especially sharp, and its toes are spiny underneath, to grip slippery fish as it hurls itself feet-first into the water.

◄ Golden eagle

The female and male golden eagle build a big, untidy nest of twigs, high on a tree, cliff or crag. They may have several nests, called eyries, using one each year and adding more twigs each time.

Earth

The Earth is a huge, rocky ball spinning around in space. It is more than 4,600 million years old. Its surface is covered with large areas of land surrounded by sea. The layers of air around the Earth make up its atmosphere. In the atmosphere are the gases that all living things need to stay alive.

South America

▲ Earth from space

This view was taken from a spacecraft high up above the Earth's surface. You can clearly see the shape of the continent of South America, surrounded by dark-blue water. The wispy white areas are patches of swirling clouds.

▼ Moving Earth

About 220 million years ago, all the continents were joined as one super continent, called Pangea. Very slowly, this continent began to break up.

Pangea

200 million years ago, Pangea had split into two huge continents called Laurasia and Gondwanaland

even today the continents are still moving – North America is moving very slowly away from Europe

◄ Hot rocks and metals

The outer layer of the Earth is called the crust. It is about 32 kilometres thick below the land but only 8 kilometres thick below the oceans and seas. The very centre of the Earth lies about 6,400 kilometres below the surface – that's about the same distance as crossing North America from one side of the continent to the other.

in places the temperature is so hot that the rocks and metals have melted and become liquid

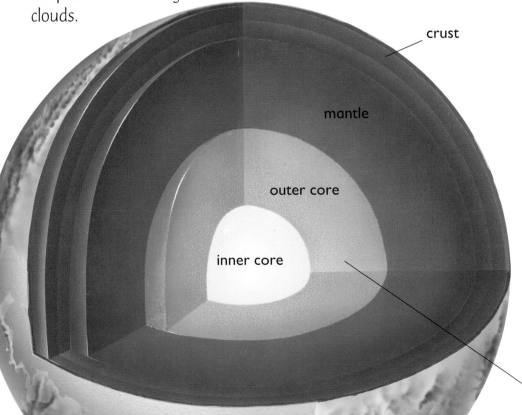

crust

mantle

outer core

inner core

Earth features

Find out more:
Deserts ◄ Mountains ► Oceans and seas ►
Rocks and minerals ► Volcanoes ►

There are many wonderful sights on the surface of our amazing planet. They include thundering waterfalls, steep cliffs by the seashore and huge caves deep underground. Some of these features took millions of years to form.

▼ On the surface

Lots of different features cover the Earth's surface, such as snowy mountains, deep valleys, rocky deserts and enormous ice sheets.

▼ Natural disaster

An earthquake is a natural disaster. It can cause serious damage in just a few seconds. It is the violent shaking of the rocks inside the Earth.

sliding plates

centre of earthquake

huge cracks can appear in the Earth's surface and can cause damage to buildings and roads.

▼ Deep down

Far below the surface of the oceans lies another landscape — on the floor of the ocean. Here there are mountains, wide plains and slopes and deep sea trenches.

continental shelf

material left by river currents

continental slope

ocean ridge

deep sea trench

Egg-laying mammals

Most mammal females give birth to babies.
But there are five kinds of mammals that are egg-layers
– these are called monotremes. One of these is the
duck-billed platypus from eastern Australia. The other
four are echidnas (spiny anteaters) from Australia
and New Guinea. Echidnas have sharp spines as
well as fur. They have huge claws to dig for
ants, termites, grubs and worms, which they
lick up with their spiny tongues.

egg in pouch

▼ How the platypus lives

The platypus lives along rivers and
billabongs. At night it noses in the
mud for worms, shellfish and other
small animals. The male has
a spur on his rear
ankle, which he
uses to jab poison
into enemies.

Wow!

The young platypus has a long
journey as it leaves its nursery
burrow to see daylight for the first
time – the burrow may be more
than 30 metres long.

▲ Echidna and egg

The short-beaked echidna rests
in her burrow, holding her egg
warm and safe in a slitlike pouch.
This develops on her belly only at
breeding time. The egg grows in
her body for 23 days, then develops
in her pouch for 10 days. After
hatching, the baby stays in the
pouch for another seven weeks, then
in a nest burrow for six months.

Word box

billabong
Australian native word meaning
'dead water', used for a natural
pool or small lake

spur
sharp claw or clawlike part on
the foot or ankle of some animals,
especially birds

Eggs

Find out more:
Amphibians ◄ Baby animals ◄ Birds ◄
Egg-laying mammals ◄ Insects ► Reptiles ►

Most female animals lay tough-shelled eggs. This includes all birds, nearly all reptiles, fish, insects, spiders and other creatures. Each egg contains a tiny young animal, called an embryo, which grows and develops into a baby. When ready, it bites or tears its way out of the shell – and then often faces the world alone.

ostrich egg

bee hummingbird egg

shell membrane (lining)

embryo

yolk

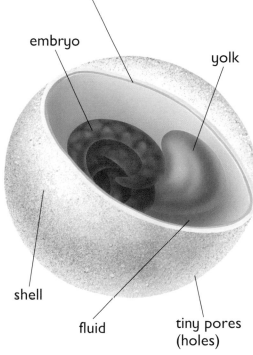

shell

fluid

tiny pores (holes)

▲ Inside an egg

A typical egg has a tough outer case or shell for protection. Inside is a store of yolk to nourish the tiny developing animal, or embryo, which floats in a pool of fluid for protection. Oxygen, the substance that all animals need to breathe, passes to the embryo through tiny pores in the shell.

▲ Size and number

The ostrich lays the largest eggs – 16 centimetres long and over 3,000 times heavier than the tiny egg of the bee hummingbird. The kiwi lays a single egg, one-quarter the size of its body. The ling fish lays more than 20 million tiny eggs.

Wow!

Small creatures called fairy shrimps have hatched out of eggs that were wetted again, after being dried and preserved for more than 2,000 years.

▼ Slimy eggs

Bird eggs have hard, rigid shells. Most other eggs have slightly flexible, leathery shells. Frog and toad eggs, called spawn, are covered with slimy jelly. Frog spawn is clumped, while toad spawn is in long strings or 'necklaces'.

frog spawn

toad spawn

▼ Hidden eggs

Many reptiles, such as this African dwarf crocodile, dig a hole and then cover the eggs with old plants. The hole is often close to water. As the plants rot they create heat. This incubates the eggs (keeps them warm) and helps them develop.

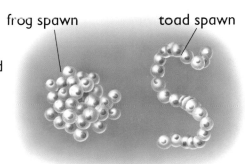

Electricity

Find out more:
Atoms and molecules ◀ Electricity in action ▶
Energy ▶ Energy sources ▶ Machines ▶

Many machines are powered by electricity, because it is clean and cheap. Electricity is produced in power stations, sometimes by burning coal, oil or gas, and sometimes by nuclear power or by the use of water to turn huge turbines. It is sent along a network of cables supported by metal towers called pylons.

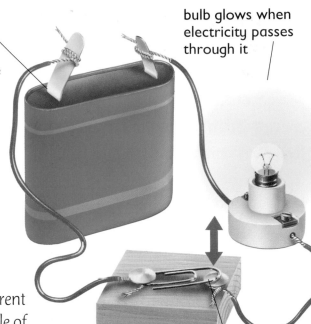

a battery contains chemicals that make electricity when the switch is turned on

bulb glows when electricity passes through it

a switch turns electricity off and on by breaking the circuit and joining it again

▶ Plus to minus

In a simple electric circuit, current flows from the positive (+) pole of a battery to the negative (-) pole. If the current flows through a light bulb, the 'resistance' of the thin metal filament (thread) inside the bulb produces heat and light.

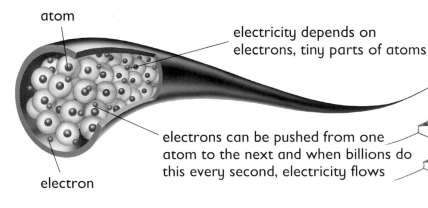

▲ Solar panels

The light or heat energy from the Sun can be turned directly into electricity by devices called solar panels. A panel does not produce much power, so many are usually joined into banks of panels. They need strong sunlight to work well, and are mostly used in hot and sunny climates.

atom

electricity depends on electrons, tiny parts of atoms

electrons can be pushed from one atom to the next and when billions do this every second, electricity flows

electron

power station

transformer

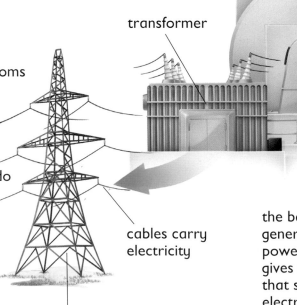

cables carry electricity

the battery or generator at a power station gives the 'push' that starts the electrons on their journey

▲ From station to home

From the generator, electricity passes to 'transformers', which produce high voltages (how the strength of electricity is measured). This electricity is then carried by cables into homes and factories.

pylon holds cables safe, far above the ground

Electricity in action

Electricity is constantly at work around you.
You switch lights on and off or watch the television. Cars need electricity to start their engines, and most trains are powered by electricity. Electricity is also produced by natural things, such as lightning, and is even present inside our own bodies.

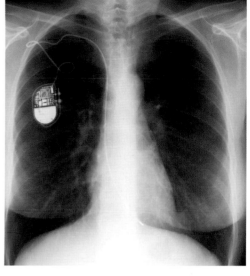

◀ Hair-raiser

Static electricity is the same as flowing electricity except that it does not move. It can make a push or pull effect like a magnet – which can be very hair-raising!

▲ Beating heart

In some heart problems, the impulses of electricity that control the heart's beating are not produced properly. So an artificial pacemaker may be put under the skin to generate electrical signals for the heart.

▼ Electric fun

Electricity can be used for decoration and for fun. Fairgrounds rely on plenty of coloured lights and rides powered by electricity.

▶ Charge!

A mobile phone's battery is rechargeable. This means that when the battery runs down, the chemicals inside can be recharged by sending electricity through them.

Make a circuit

You will need: a lightbulb, some wire, a 3-volt battery, a plastic ruler, a metal spoon, some dry card

Ask an adult to help. Join the lightbulb to the battery with pieces of wire, as shown below. Electricity flows round the circuit and lights the bulb. Make a gap in the circuit and put various objects there instead, such as the ruler. See if they allow electricity to flow again.

Elephants

No other animal looks like the elephant, with its long trunk, large tusks and huge ears.
Asian elephants and African forest elephants live mainly in woods, while African savanna elephants live on grasslands. All are under threat, shot for their ivory tusks or because they destroy farm crops. Some Asian elephants are tame and carry logs for people or let them ride on their backs.

► Asian elephant

This elephant is slightly smaller than the African types and has smaller-sized ears. An elephant's trunk is its nose and top lip joined together. It uses it to grasp food, suck up water to squirt in its mouth, sniff the air and stroke babies and friends in the herd.

▲ African elephant

Most African savanna elephants have tusks. Tusks are huge incisor teeth, made of ivory. They are used to dig for food, push down trees for their leaves, fruits and bark, for defence against enemies and to fight rival males at breeding time.

rock hyraxes

◄ Small cousins

The closest relations to elephants are the hyraxes of Africa and the Middle East. Rock hyraxes are found in dry, rocky places. Tree hyraxes are found in branches. They all live in groups and eat plants.

▼ Living in herds

A herd contains mothers and calves (young). 'Aunts' without young help with calf-care. An older female, the matriarch, leads the herd to traditional feeding places and waterholes.

Word scramble

Unscramble these words to find the names of five types of elephant food:

a. SAGRS
b. KARB
c. SEVLEA
d. STURIF
e. STORO

c. leaves d. fruits e. roots
a. grass b. bark
answers

Empires and colonies

Find out more:
Britain and Ireland ◄
Victorian Britain ►

In the 1500s and 1600s, the Europeans discovered new lands in Africa, Asia and the Americas. They wanted to take away the riches of these countries and rule the people who lived there. By the 1800s and early 1900s, Britain, France, Germany, the Netherlands, Belgium, Portugal and Spain controlled vast empires.

▲ Queen and Empress

During the reign of Queen Victoria, from 1837 to 1901, Britain ruled the world's largest ever empire. It stretched from Canada to India and from Africa to Australia and the South Pacific.

▼ Cruelty in the Caribbean

Spain, Britain and France ruled the Caribbean islands. They grew sugar cane there, using slaves from Africa. The slaves were treated with great cruelty. Slavery continued in the Caribbean until the 1830s.

▲ Bolívar of Bolivia

Spain ruled much of South America. By the 1800s, many colonists (settlers) wanted to break away from the old country. In 1811, a soldier called Simón Bolívar began to fight for the freedom of Venezuela, Colombia, Ecuador, Peru and Bolivia.

► Freedom for India

By the 1900s, nations were demanding their freedom. Sometimes they went to war against their colonial rulers. The great Indian leader, Mohandas K. Gandhi, believed in peaceful protests. The British left India in 1947.

Energy

Find out more:
Cars ◄ Electricity ◄ Energy sources ► Light at work ►
Oil and gas ► Sun ►

The engine inside a motor car needs energy to work. It gets this energy by burning a fuel such as petrol or diesel. Something that has energy is able to do work. Your body also needs energy – to run, skip, think and even to sleep. Your energy comes from the food you eat – it's your body's fuel.

▼ Heat and light

Energy from the Sun reaches the Earth as heat and light. Some of that energy is stored inside fuels such as coal, oil and gas.

oil

coal   gas

Word box

active
busy, full of energy

coiled
wound up into rings or spirals

► How much energy?

A young, active person whose body is still growing needs lots of energy. So does an athlete, or a builder doing heavy work. Older people and office workers need less energy because they are not so active.

▼ Stored energy

What has a coiled spring to do with energy? The answer is that energy is stored inside the coiled spring, ready to do work. Some watches have a spring inside. When you wind up the watch you are storing energy inside the spring. As the spring unwinds, it turns the hands of the watch.

the spring is wound and energy is slowly released

the spring is hidden beneath this wheel

bread and cereals

fish and meat

cheese, butter and oil

► Energy foods

All the energy we get from food starts out as green plants. Humans eat plants (vegetables and fruit) and animals (meat and fish). The animals we eat have received their energy from eating green plants. Here are some of the foods we get our energy from.

fruit, vegetables and dairy products

Wow!

A 100-gram serving of peanut butter contains 2,600 times more energy than 100 grams of lettuce.

Energy sources

Most of the energy in our world comes from the Sun. Without it, the plants that provide us with food could not grow. Fuels such as coal and oil are made from the remains of plants and animals that lived along ago. These living things used the Sun's energy to grow.

▲ Harmful air

When we burn oil it produces harmful waste gases and dirt that enter the air. The air in many cities is filled with these waste gases from motor cars and factories.

▼ Nuclear energy

Some of our electricity comes from nuclear power stations. Instead of using the heat from burning oil or coal, a nuclear power station uses the heat energy released when atoms of nuclear fuel are split. The splitting process is carefully controlled in order to be safe.

▲ Water power

A hydroelectric power station uses the energy in water from a fast-flowing river or a dam to produce electricity. Flowing water is a source of energy that will never run out. We call it a renewable source – one that can be used again and again.

▼ Important fuel

Oil is one of the world's most important fuels. We take oil from deep under the sea or the ground, where it lies trapped between layers of rock. Oil drilling machinery is kept on special platforms out at sea, like the one shown here.

Word box

atom
a very tiny part of something

dam
a barrier specially built to hold back water

▶ Wind power

The energy in wind has been used for many thousands of years to turn the sails of windmills. We now use this wind energy to produce electricity. A large group of wind turbines is called a wind farm.

Engines

The invention of engines allowed us to control and change the world around us. Engines let us travel. They let us transport very heavy materials around the world. Engines also power the machinery we need to mine coal and important minerals.

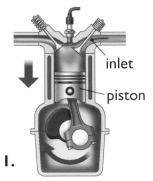

1.

▲ piston moves down to suck in fuel and air

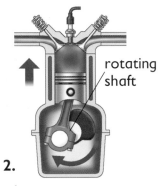

2.

▲ the piston moves up to squeeze the fuel and air

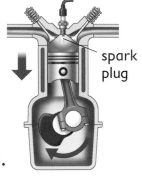

3.

▲ spark sets mixture alight pushing piston down

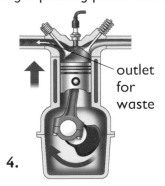

4.

▲ the piston moves up to push out waste gases

Labels: inlet, piston, rotating shaft, spark plug, outlet for waste

◀ How petrol engines work

Air and fuel is pushed into a cylinder. Tiny explosions caused by 'spark plugs' keep the piston moving up and down. This makes the shaft rotate, which connects to gears so that the wheels go round. Most cars have petrol engines.

Labels: smokestack, boiler, firebox

▲ The power of steam

Steam engines helped to develop our modern civilization. Early locomotives were steam-driven, powered by coal or wood. They have mostly been replaced by diesel or electric trains. However, steam trains are still used in some poorer countries.

Word box

cylinder
tube in which fuel is burned

diesel
an engine fuelled by diesel oil instead of petrol, that has no spark plugs

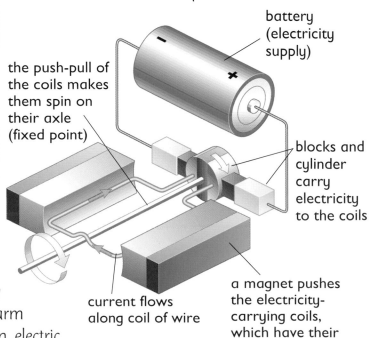

Labels: battery (electricity supply); the push-pull of the coils makes them spin on their axle (fixed point); blocks and cylinder carry electricity to the coils; current flows along coil of wire; a magnet pushes the electricity-carrying coils, which have their own magnetism

▶ Electric motors

Some of the fumes given out by petrol and diesel engines can harm the environment. For this reason, electric motors are now becoming more common in vehicles. They are powered by batteries and are cleaner, quieter and more reliable.

Europe

Europe is the smallest of the seven continents.
It is a land of pine forests, grassy plains, snow-topped mountains and hot, sunny coastlines. The northern part of Europe has cold winters and warm summers while the countries around the Mediterranean Sea have hot, dry summers and mild winters.

▲ The far north

The far north of Europe is dotted with thousands of small islands and deep sea-filled valleys called fjords, like the one above. Places in the far north have long, cold winters where it stays dark for much of each day.

▲ Flat lands

Land beside the North Sea coast is extremely flat – some of it is even below sea level. Because of this, Belgium and the Netherlands are called the 'Low Countries'.

▲ Busy river

The Danube river crosses central Europe, from its source in Germany to its mouth on the shores of the Black Sea. Ships and barges carry agricultural products, steel and chemicals on the busy waters.

▼ Snowy mountains

The Alps stretch in a curve from southeast France across northern Italy, Switzerland and into Austria. In winter, thousands of tourists come to ski on the snowy slopes.

▲ Hot and dry

In the dry, sunny climate of southern Europe, groves of olive trees and orange and lemon trees are a common sight. Vineyards produce grapes for the wine industry. Tourists spend holidays along the Mediterranean coast.

Explorers at sea

Find out more:
Australia ◄ Explorers on land ►
New Zealand and the Pacific ► Vikings ►

In the days of sailing ships, sea voyages could last many years. Sailors had to find their way across the oceans, battle with storms and survive shipwrecks. When they did land on unknown shores, they risked being attacked by the local people.

▲ Leif the Lucky

The Vikings were great seafarers. Their ships, called longships, reached Iceland and Greenland. In 1000, a sailor called Leif 'the Lucky' Eriksson reached North America.

▲ A vast fleet

Between 1405 and 1433, the Chinese admiral Zheng He made seven voyages, exploring the Indian Ocean. On his first voyage there were 62 big boats called junks, 225 small boats and 27,000 men!

► Captain Cook

James Cook was an English sea captain who was a brilliant navigator (explorer). In the 1760s and 1770s, he explored the Pacific Ocean and the coasts of New Zealand and Australia.

► Great voyages

This map shows some of the great voyages of exploration. Look at the map key to find out which explorer sailed which route.

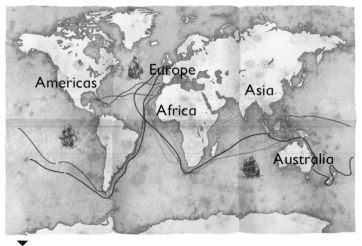

Americas
Europe
Asia
Africa
Australia

Map key

Red: Christopher Columbus, 1492
Yellow: Vasco da Gama, 1497–98
Green: Magellan, 1519–22
Purple: James Cook, 1768–71

Explorers on land

Find out more:
Explorers at sea ◄

Today, every place on Earth has been mapped. Only 200 years ago, many maps included blank areas, showing unknown lands. Travel was slow and often dangerous, but many brave men and women set out to explore the world.

▼ Tireless traveller

Ibn Batutah came from Tangiers in North Africa. He travelled from 1325 to 1354, reaching the Middle East, India, China and Southeast Asia. He also journeyed south across the Sahara Desert to the city of Timbuktu.

▼ Africa explored

From the 1850s, a Scottish explorer called David Livingstone made many journeys across Africa. By 1869 he was believed lost, so another British explorer, Henry Morton Stanley, set out to look for him. He found Livingstone in 1871.

Word scramble

Can you unscramble these words to find destinations for explorers?

a. ELOP THRON
b. EVIRR NOAMAZ
c. AHARAS DETRES
d. WEN AGUINE

answers
a. North Pole b. river Amazon c. Sahara Desert d. New Guinea

▼ To the South Pole

Howling winds and bitter cold failed to stop explorer Roald Amundsen, a Norwegian, from crossing icy Antarctica to reach the South Pole in 1911.

Roald Amundsen

◄ Jungle journeys

From 1799 to 1804, Alexander von Humboldt, from Germany, and Aimé Bonpland, from France, survived in the steamy rainforests of South America. They came across electric eels and alligators and brought back 12,000 samples of plants.

Alexander von Humboldt

Farming through the ages

Find out more:
China: beginnings ◄
Middle Ages ►

Long ago, people gathered wild plants and ate roots, leaves and seeds. They found that if they planted some of the seeds each year, they could grow crops for food. They also learned to tame wild animals, such as goats and sheep. Farming began in the Middle East, about 10,000 years ago.

▲ The first farmers

By choosing only the best seed each year, farmers turned wild grasses into useful grain crops such as wheat or barley. They harvested them with tools made of stone, wood and bone.

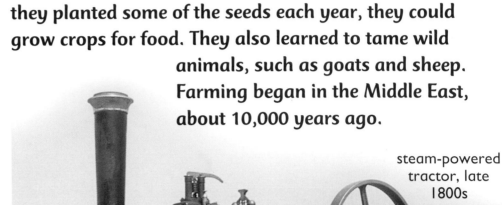

steam-powered tractor, late 1800s

▲ Nice rice!

Farming started in different parts of the world at different times. Rice was grown in China 7,000 years ago. It was often sown in flooded fields like these ones. Rice became the most important crop in Asia.

▼ Sowing seed

In Europe during the Middle Ages, horses or oxen were used to plough the soil and prepare it for sowing. Seed was scattered by hand.

▲ Soil-buster

Steam power began to be used to drive farm machinery in the 1800s. In the 1900s, the first petrol-driven tractors were made.

Word box

crops
plants that can be grown for food, such as rice or wheat, or for making cloth, such as cotton

tame
make a wild animal used to living and working with people

Farming today

Find out more:
Food through the ages ▶

Farmers across the world grow crops and rear animals to provide food for people to eat.
In poorer countries, farmers usually work on small plots of land using simple tools and traditional methods. In countries such as the United States, farming is carried out on a large scale and huge machines do much of the work.

Wow!

A cotton-picking machine harvests the same amount of cotton as 80 people picking the cotton by hand.

◄ Plains of wheat

The Prairies are the wide, grassy plains of North America. They are one of the world's largest wheat-producing areas. Large herds of cattle are reared here, too.

▲ Sheep-rearing

Farming differs from place to place, depending on the soil, climate and the shape of the land. The mild, wet climate of New Zealand is well suited to rearing sheep, because there is plenty of good grazing land. More sheep than people live in New Zealand!

▶ Giant combine harvesters

In richer countries, giant machines called combine harvesters gather in the ripe crops at harvest time. In poorer countries the harvest is cut by hand.

◄ Ploughing land

This Asian farmer is ploughing land with a plough pulled by oxen. He will use this land to grow crops such as rice, millet and wheat.

Word box

millet
a plant crop producing tiny seeds that are crushed to make flour

terrace
a flat, steplike area cut out of a piece of land

Fish

Fish can live anywhere there is water – icy oceans, freshwater lakes, fast-flowing rivers and tropical seas. Some fish, such as the walking catfish, can even survive for a few days on land. Fish come in many different sizes, from the tiny pygmy goby, which is smaller than your fingernail, to the 12-metre-long whale shark.

Word box

freshwater
non-salty water in lakes and rivers

tropical
with warm water in hot parts of the world

▶ Fishy parts

A fish has special parts called gills to let it breathe underwater. It uses its gills to take in oxygen from the water. Fish use their fins to help them swim.

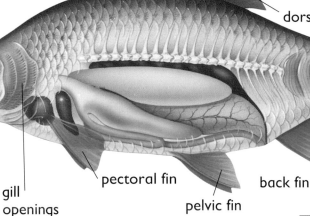

dorsal (back) fin   scales

tail fin

pectoral fin   back fin

gill openings   pelvic fin

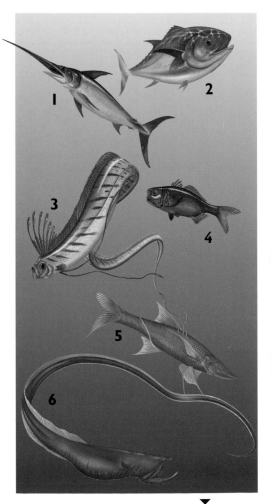

1

2

3

4

5

6

◀ Surface to floor

More than 13,000 kinds of fish live in the oceans and seas. Most swim at the surface, like the tuna (1) and the blue marlin (2). Others, such as the oar fish (3) and the lantern fish (4), live deeper down. A few, such as the tripod fish (5) and the gulper eel (6), live close to the ocean floor.

Word scramble

Unscramble these words to find the names of four saltwater fish.

a. grenhir
b. dakcodh
c. utan
d. tiblahu

d. halibut
a. herring b. haddock c. tuna
answers

▼ In freshwater

Freshwater fish such as perch and trout live in rivers, streams and lakes. Some fish live in streams that flow deep under the ground. Most freshwater fish cannot survive in the salty oceans and seas.

perch

▲ Fishy killers

Many sharks are fierce hunters. They have strong teeth and jaws and can attack fish and dolphins with great speed. This blue shark can grow up to 3.8 metres in length.

Flowers

Flowers are the brightly coloured, sweet-smelling parts of plants such as roses, tulips, orchids and lilies. Yet not all flowers are colourful and fragrant. Some plants, such as grasses, produce small flowers with no smell at all. All flowers produce seeds that are needed for new flowering plants.

◄ Busy bees

This bee is collecting pollen in tiny 'baskets' on its back legs. It will carry the pollen to another flower.

▶ Flowery parts

Each flower has male parts called stamens and female parts called carpels. Stamens produce tiny grains of pollen. Usually, pollen from one flower has to reach the female parts of another flower before seeds can start to grow.

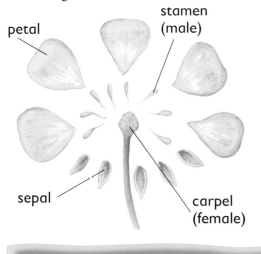

petal

stamen (male)

sepal

carpel (female)

Word box

bloom
to produce flowers

fragrant
sweet-smelling

sprout
to begin to grow

flower

leaf

stem

roots

▼ Flower gardens

You can see displays of flowers in parks and gardens everywhere. People have enjoyed growing and arranging flowers since the time of the ancient Egyptians.

▼ In the desert

Desert flowers usually bloom after a burst of rain. The seeds lie in the ground when it is dry, and then start to sprout as soon as the rain arrives.

A wildflower garden

It's really easy to grow flowers. Why don't you try planting your own wildflower garden in a spare patch of land (don't forget to ask an adult first)? Your wildflower garden will attract insects such as butterflies and bees. You could dry and press the flowers and use them to decorate your own stationery.

Food

Food gives us energy to move and keep warm.
Without it, we could not survive. People used to gather or
farm their own food. Today, big businesses and complex
scientific processes are needed to provide enough food for
lots of people and to send it long distances.

Look inside food

Look at the labels on some food packages. They tell you how much carbohydrate, protein, fats and sugar the foods contain. Some also tell you how many vitamins and minerals there are in the food.

◄ Totally tropical!

Tropical fruits grow mainly in the tropics where it is warm, as they cannot survive frost. The best known are bananas, pineapples and melons. Large quantities of these are exported (shipped to other countries). Other tropical fruits include guavas, breadfruit, mangoes and papayas.

◄ Italian favourite

Pizza was invented by the Italians. The word 'pizza' is Italian for pie. It is thought to have first been made by a baker at the royal court in Naples, southern Italy, during the 1700s. Pizza is now a favourite food around the world.

► What's in food?

Food contains special substances called nutrients. There are six main kinds of nutrients — carbohydrates, fats, proteins, fibre, vitamins and minerals. You need the right amounts of all these nutrients to stay healthy.

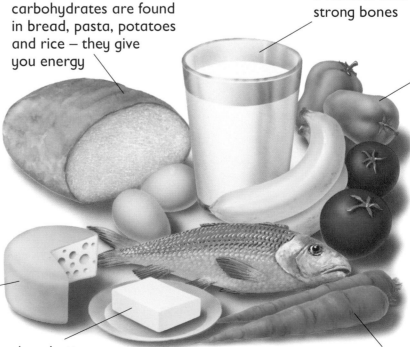

carbohydrates are found in bread, pasta, potatoes and rice — they give you energy

milk contains calcium, a mineral that gives you strong bones

fresh fruits and vegetables contain lots of vitamins and minerals. They help you fight disease, keeping you fit and healthy

proteins in cheese, meat, eggs, nuts and fish help you grow and keep your body strong

fats from foods such as butter, oil and cheese give you energy and healthy nerves

fibre is important for helping the digestive system to work properly. Fruit and vegetables are fibre-rich

Food through the ages

Find out more:
Ancient Roman life ◄ Farming through the ages ◄ Middle Ages ►

Until explorers reached the Americas in the 1500s, no Europeans had ever seen potatoes or tomatoes. For thousands of years, people only ate food that was grown locally. By the 1800s, foods were traded right around the world. Australians were drinking tea from China and Europeans were eating beef from Argentina.

tomatoes   chillies

▲▼ American foods

Foods first eaten in ancient Central and South America include tomatoes, avocado pears, chillies, squashes, potatoes and cocoa. Today they are enjoyed everywhere in the world.

avocado pear

Wow!

When Vesuvius blew its top in AD79, it buried the whole town of Herculaneum in boiling mud. It preserved the food laid out for lunch for hundreds of years.

▼ Keeping it sweet

In ancient Egypt, Greece and Rome there was no sugar made from cane. Instead, cakes and puddings were sweetened with honey. Honey bees were kept on farms.

► A castle banquet

During the Middle Ages in Europe, poor people went hungry while splendid banquets were held by lords and ladies. They dined off boar's head or swan meat, ate the finest white bread and drank wine.

▲ Roman take-away

Street stalls and bars sold food and snacks in Roman towns and cities. People ate pies and sausages on their way to the Colosseum, the circular theatre where they watched fights between gladiators.

Forces

Forces are the natural properties of the world around us. Engines produce forces that make machines work. Without the force of gravity, we would fly off the world's surface, as the Earth spins. Friction is a force that stops us from slipping over. Inertia stops us from being pushed over by a gust of wind.

◄ Wind force

Wind provides the force that pushes a sailing boat along. As the wind flows over the sail, it creates high pressure on the inner curved surface. This pushes against the lower pressure on the other outer side of the sail. The difference in pressure makes a force that moves the boat.

Slip and slide!

Place a stone on a sheet of wood, then tilt the wood until the stone begins to slide. Now spread washing-up liquid on the wood and try again. See how the stone slides much more easily. Like oil, the washing-up liquid is a lubricant, reducing friction.

▲ Pulling power

Gravity pulls a heavy object down. However, the object can be lifted by using a stronger force, pulling on a rope passing over a pulley.

◄ Under pressure

The force of gravity on our bodies produces pressure where we stand on the ground. This is why footprints show up on snow or mud.

▼ Keep moving!

There is a natural law (rule) which says that, once something is set in motion, it will carry on in the same direction and at the same speed until some other forces act on it. Air resistance or friction will slow this ball down. Gravity will pull it towards the ground.

path of the ball without gravity or air resistance

air resistance

path of ball when gravity and air resistance are at work

air resistance

the ball is kicked

gravity pushes down on the ball

gravity pushes down on the ball

Fossils

Find out more:
Dinosaurs ◄

A fossil is the remains of a plant or animal that lived a very long time ago. It can be the shell, the skeleton or just the outline shape of a dead animal. It can also be the marks left by an animal as it moved across the land. By studying fossils, scientists have learned much about the plants and animals that lived on the Earth thousands and millions of years ago.

▲ Trapped!

The whole body of this insect has turned into a fossil. Millions of years ago, it was trapped inside the sticky substance that oozed from pine trees. The sticky stuff hardened to form amber, which we make into jewellery and ornaments.

▼ Making fossils

Fossils are usually found inside rocks that were once covered by seawater.

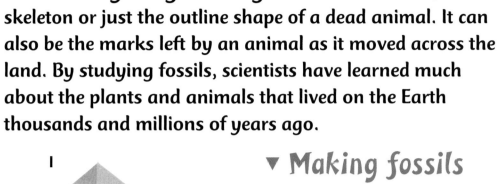

1

2

3

4

1. when a sea creature died, its body fell to the sea-bed

2. it was then covered by mud and sand

3. seawater dissolved the bones, and the mud and sand slowly turned into rock

4. the hollow shape of the animal was left in the rock

Solve the riddle

Solve this riddle to find a five-letter word.
My first is in RAIN but not in REIGN.
My second is in MOLE but not in POLES.
My third is in ABLE but not in TALE.
My fourth is in TEA but not in TAR.
My last is in ROSE but not in TOES.

answer: AMBER

► Discovered!

In far northern parts of the world, scientists have found the bodies of woolly mammoths which lived thousands of years ago. The skin, hair and body parts of the mammoths, such as those shown here, had been preserved in the frozen ground.

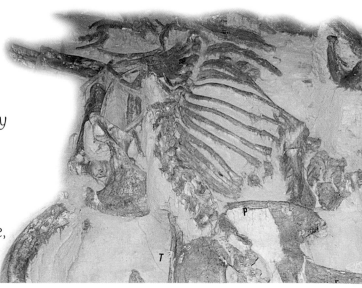

After the Romans left Gaul (France), it was invaded by the Franks, who came from Germany. So the country became known as France. During the Middle Ages, France became one of the most powerful countries in Europe, famous for its arts and learning and the fine manners of its knights and ladies.

▲ Charlemagne

This great king of the Franks lived from AD747 to AD814. He ruled over an empire that stretched all the way from the borders of Spain to central Europe. Charlemagne means 'Charles the Great'.

▲ The Sun King

Louis XIV (Louis the Fourteenth) was king of France from 1643 to 1715. He ruled over a glittering court and was very powerful. He was nicknamed the 'Sun King'.

◄ Notre Dame

In 1163, workers began to build an impressive cathedral beside the river Seine, in Paris. It was called Notre Dame, which means 'Our Lady'.

▲ Joan of Arc

During the Middle Ages, France was forever at war with England. In the 1420s, a girl called Joan of Arc claimed that she heard voices from God, saying that the English soldiers must be thrown out of France. She fought with the French army until she was captured and burnt alive by the English.

Word box

cathedral
an important church building, headed by a bishop or an archbishop

court
the lords, ladies and officials at a royal palace

French Revolution and after

Find out more:
France ◄

In 1789, the whole of Europe was shocked by what was going on in France. The French kings had become more and more powerful and unpopular. They made people pay unfair taxes, so the French people seized control of their country in a violent revolution. In 1793, they even beheaded the king and queen, Louis XVI (Louis the Sixteenth) and Marie-Antoinette.

◄ 'Long live the emperor!'

Napoleon Bonaparte lived from 1761 to 1821. He was a brilliant soldier who fought in the Revolution, and later made himself emperor of France. He won great battles all over Europe and made new laws.

▲ Days of terror

This dreadful machine was called the guillotine. It was designed for cutting off people's heads. During the Revolution, rich lords and ladies were sent to the guillotine. Then the rebels began to quarrel amongst themselves and sent each other to be killed instead.

Word scramble

In the 1800s, Napoleon's armies fought against the following countries. Can you unscramble their names?

a. ISURATA
b. ASSURI
c. PASSIRU
d. REGAT NIBITAR

answers
a. Austria b. Russia c. Prussia d. Great Britain

▲ Waterloo

The cannons crash, soldiers yell and horses neigh. In 1815, the French and their emperor, Napoleon, were finally defeated at Waterloo, in Belgium, by the British and Prussian armies.

◄ Naughty nineties

In the 1890s, Paris was famous for the wild lives led by its artists, poets, dancers and performers. A high-kicking dance called the cancan was all the rage.

Germany

Find out more:
Holy Roman Empire ▶

GERMANY UNITES
1815–1871

SWEDEN
DENMARK
UNITED KINGDOM
GERMANY
RUSSIA
AUSTRIA
FRANCE
HUNGARY
ITALY

■ German Confederation 1815
■ Prussia 1866
■ German Empire 1871

For centuries, Germany was made up of hundreds of different states and nations. Some of them were part of the Holy Roman Empire. During the 1800s, they began to group together and, by 1871, a united German Empire had been formed.

▼ Music-makers

In the 1700s and 1800s, Germany became a centre of the arts. Some of the world's greatest musicians lived here at this time, including Ludwig van Beethoven. Amongst his many masterpieces, he wrote nine symphonies, an opera, *Fidelio,* and a religious work called a Mass.

▲ Prussian power

The German kingdom of Prussia was founded in 1701. In 1756, it fought against Austria, starting the Seven Years War. By the 1800s, Prussia was the most powerful German nation.

◀ Fairy-tale palace

This fantastic castle was built for King Ludwig II. He ruled the southern kingdom of Bavaria from 1864 until 1886, when he was declared mad.

Wow!
The world's tallest cathedral spire is to be seen in Ulm, Germany. It soars to a height of over 160 metres.

▼ One country

King Wilhelm I of Prussia was made emperor of all Germany in 1871. Berlin became the capital city of the united country. At this time many new factories, steelworks and mines were being built in Germany.

Grasslands

Find out more:
Africa ◄ Farming today ◄

Wide, flat areas of grassland are found in most of the world's continents. Grasslands have different names in different places of the world. The hot, dry grasslands of East Africa are savannahs, while those in South America are known as pampas. The grassy plains in central Asia are called steppes.

◄ From place to place

Mongolian nomads live on the grassland steppes of central Asia, where they raise herds of goats, cattle and yaks. These nomads live in tents called yurts, which are traditionally covered with felt.

Word box

felt
cloth made from pieces of wool that are pressed together

hide
the skin of an animal

nomad
someone who moves from place to place in search of grazing land

▼ The prairies

The grasslands of North America are called prairies. The soil here is fertile, and most of the grasslands have been ploughed up and turned into farmland for growing crops and rearing beef cattle.

Animal antics

Which of these animals lives on the grasslands of Africa?

a. lion
b. crocodile
c. gorilla
d. ostrich

a. lion d. ostrich
answers

▲ Buffaloes

Millions of American bison, or buffalo, used to graze on the North American Prairies. Between 1850 and 1890, European settlers killed around 20 million of them, for their meat and hides. By 1889, only 551 bison were left alive.

► In Africa

Large herds of zebra, antelope, wildebeest and other grazing animals wander across the savannah of East Africa. The animals are always on the look-out for danger from hunters such as lions and leopards.

Gravity

Gravity is a natural force that tries to press us down towards the centre of the Earth. It is gravity that stops you from jumping very high. Astronauts need immense rockets to break away from the Earth's gravity when they travel into space.

◀ Floating in space

The further away an object is from the centre of the Earth, the less the pull of gravity on it. In space, astronauts are so far from the Earth's centre that gravity has little effect on them. They become weightless, so that when they move around, they appear to be floating.

▲ Weightless

The only easy way for you to feel weightless is by floating or swimming. The water supports your weight so you do not feel gravity pulling you down.

Wow!

When astronauts go to sleep in space, they have to strap themselves to their beds so that they don't float around!

▼ Using friction

On a rollercoaster ride, the force of gravity moves the car. Gravity pulls the car faster downhill but also slows the car down as it climbs the uphill parts of the ride. Air friction slows the car, too, until it coasts gently to a halt once all of its stored energy has been used.

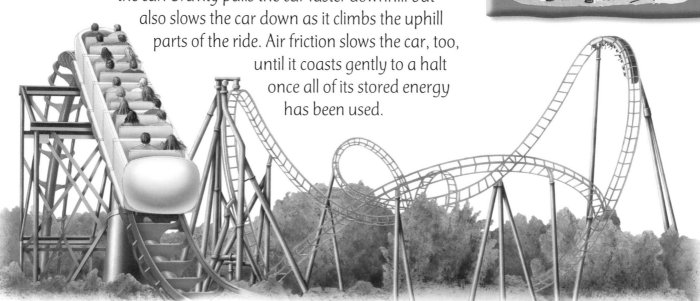

Health

Good health is the result of eating the right foods, taking exercise and getting enough rest and sleep. These all help to keep your body working properly. Looking after your health in this way makes it less likely that you will become ill.

◀ Sleeping soundly

We know that too little sleep can affect our health. Young babies sleep for most of the time. Many elderly people need less sleep than when they were younger because they are less active.

▼ Keeping fit

Exercise such as running, cycling or walking is vital for developing strong muscles, and keeping your heart healthy. It is just as important for adults, to prevent diseases as the body gets older.

▲ Long life

Some of the oldest people in the world live in countries like Japan. There, the diet is very different from a Western one. In areas where people are long-lived, they usually eat simple diets, such as raw fish. This is full of vitamins and protein, but low in fat.

▼ Health checks

Even when you feel perfectly healthy, you should have regular check-ups at the doctor's. Many health problems can be spotted early on and treated before they get worse. Checks on the teeth and eyes are very important.

▲ Healthy food

Many of us eat too much ready-prepared, processed food. Eating fresh food is very important. For example, we should all eat plenty of fresh fruit and vegetables. However, if we store them for too long or over-cook them, we destroy their goodness.

Heat

Heat is an important form of energy. It is produced in our own bodies as we break down and use the food we eat. We can release stored heat energy by burning fuels such as wood or coal. Heat can move from one substance to another in three different ways: by convection, by radiation and by conduction.

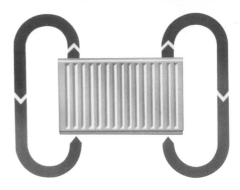

▲ Heat: convection

Above a radiator, warmed air gets lighter and rises. Cold air moves in to replace it, and is heated up. This is called 'convection'.

▲ Heat: radiation

Radiation is rays of energy. The Sun's rays travel through space and reach us as heat and light energy.

▲ Releasing energy

When we burn wood or coal on a fire, we start a chemical reaction that releases energy stored in the fuel. Flames are the area where substances in the fuel combine with oxygen in the air to release energy as heat and light.

Heat-carriers

Ask an adult to help. Take a metal spoon, a wooden ruler and a plastic spatula. Fix a frozen pea to one end of each with butter. Put the other ends in a jug of hot water. Heat is conducted from the water up each object, melting the butter. One of the objects is the best conductor – which one is it?

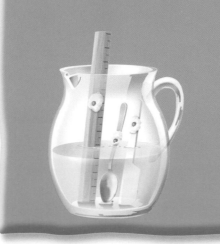

▲ Heat: conduction

Conduction is the way heat spreads through a solid or liquid object. Metal is a faster conductor than glass.

Word box

conductor
a substance that heat or electricity passes through easily

insulator
a substance that does not conduct heat or electricity well

While heat is a form of energy, temperature is a measure of heat. Temperature tells us how hot or cold something is, or how much heat it contains. It is measured in degrees Celsius (°C) or Fahrenheit (°F) or the absolute temperature scale, measured in kelvins (K).

solar panel

pipes of hot water

15,000,000°C	Centre of Sun
30,000°C	Inside lightning bolt
5,000°C	Centre of Earth
1,000°C	Lava from volcano
200 °C	Oil in frying pan
100°C	Boiling water
37°C	Body temperature
0°C	Water freezes
−78.5°C	Solid carbon dioxide ('dry ice')
Absolute zero −273.16°C	

▲ Using the Sun

In some countries, houses are centrally heated using solar (sun) energy. A solar panel filled with liquid is placed on the roof of the house. The Sun's warmth heats up the liquid, which passes into the house to heat up radiators and hot water.

▼ How warm are you?

A thermometer is used for measuring heat. Digital thermometers contain an electronic part that is sensitive to heat. Your normal body temperature is about 37 degrees Celsius (°C), or 98.6 degrees Fahrenheit (°F).

◀ Heat extremes

There is no limit to how hot things can become. The hottest ever temperature achieved in a laboratory is 400,000,000°C! But cold things do have a limit — scientists have come close to reaching absolute zero, at −273.16°C (−459.69°F), or 0 K on the absolute temperature scale.

Holland and Belgium

Find out more:
Art ◄ Farming through the ages ◄
Middle Ages ►

Belgium and the Netherlands (meaning 'lowlands') border the North Sea. Part of the Netherlands is called Holland, and many people use the word 'Netherlands' instead of Holland. The people of this region fought many European wars, but their greatest enemy has always been the sea, which has flooded this coast for thousands of years.

◄ Tulip madness!

In the 1600s, Holland became a rich nation that traded around the world. At this time, there was a huge craze amongst merchants for buying and selling tulip bulbs. Tulips and other flowers are still traded today.

◄ Why windmills?

The countryside in Holland is dotted with old windmills. For hundreds of years, wind power was used to pump water out of the soggy farmland.

▲ Old Antwerp

Antwerp is an old Belgian port on the river Scheldt. In the Middle Ages it was an important centre for the cloth trade. This statue is of the painter Peter Paul Rubens, who made the city his home in 1608.

What did they do?

Can you find out? Match these famous Lowlanders with the part they played in history:

1. Jan van Eyck
2. Abel Janszoon Tasman
3. Erasmus of Rotterdam
4. Leopold I
5. William of Orange

a. The first king of independent Belgium
b. A great scholar
c. A Dutch ruler who became king of England
d. A famous painter of the Middle Ages
e. An explorer of the 1600s

1d 2e 3b 4a 5c
answers

Wow!

More than 40 percent of Dutch land used to be under the waves! Over the years it has been sealed off by sea walls and then drained.

▲ The lacemaker

Many great Dutch painters lived in the 1600s. This picture by Jan Vermeer shows a lacemaker. Holland and Belgium were famous for their fine lace.

The Holy Roman Empire was an alliance of many small European states and nations. It followed on from the empire of Charlemagne. The states had their own rulers, but they recognized the Holy Roman emperor as their leader. The Empire lasted from AD962 to 1806 and was at its height during the Middle Ages.

LAND OF THE EMPERORS IN THE MIDDLE AGES

Lowlands   Saxony
GERMANY
Franconia   BOHEMIA
Austria
BURGUNDY   Bavaria
LOMBARDY
SICILY

► The Empire

The Holy Roman Empire was a group of lands that at various times included the Netherlands, Austria, much of Germany, central Europe and Italy.

▲ Red Beard

Frederick I, who became emperor in 1152, belonged to a powerful German family called Hohenstaufen. He was nicknamed Barbarossa, which means 'red beard'. He was drowned while on a Crusade in 1190.

► A two-headed eagle

The badge of the Holy Roman Empire was a two-headed eagle. After 1452, the Empire was ruled by an Austrian family called the Habsburgs. They also became rulers of Spain.

◄ Castle of wonders

Castel del Monte was built in about 1240 in southern Italy. It was one of the many strong castles built for the emperor Frederick II, who was Barbarossa's grandson. He was nicknamed 'Wonder of the World'.

Homes around the world

Find out more:
Buildings and bridges ◀

Your home protects you from the heat and the cold, and from rain and snow. It is the place where you usually sleep, eat your meals and relax with family and friends. Around the world people build many different styles of home to suit their way of life, the local climate and the building materials that are available.

▶ Tall homes

A multi-storey block of apartments is one way of saving space in a crowded city centre. Large numbers of families can make their home inside a single building.

▲ Keeping cool

These houses in Africa are made from wood and thick straw. The thick roofs help to keep the inside of the house cool when temperatures outside are very hot.

▼ Up on stilts

These homes in southeast Asia are built on stilts to protect the occupants from swampy ground around their village. The land sometimes floods, so the stilts keep the houses above the water level.

▲ Houses in rows

A row of homes joined together like this is typical of many European cities and towns. These houses are built from baked clay bricks.

▲ A tented home

Bedouins live in large tents in the hot deserts of the Middle East and North Africa. Bedouins raise herds of sheep, goats and camels. They move their tents from place to place in search of water and fresh grazing for their animals.

Horses and zebras

The horse's cousins include three kinds of zebras in Africa and two kinds of wild asses in Africa and Asia. Over 100 years ago, before cars and trucks were invented, horses were widely used for pulling loads and carrying people.

▶ Asses and donkeys

A few wild asses still roam dry areas in northeast Africa, the Middle East and central Asia. They survive great heat. Donkeys are domesticated versions of asses. They were tamed by people more than 5,000 years ago in the Middle East to be strong and carry heavy loads.

donkey

Wow!

The wild horse no longer lives wild. It is rare and kept mainly in parks and nature reserves.

▼ Species of horses

All domesticated horses belong to the same group or species — from massive and powerful heavy horses such as shires to agile polo ponies, often used for playing polo, a ball game. Horses have been bred by people for different jobs for more than 4,000 years.

Word scramble

Unscramble these words to find the names of five breeds or types of horses:

a. HOCARERSE
b. SHRIE EROHS
c. RETHUN
d. STUMNAG
e. NIMOLOPA

answers
a. racehorse b. Shire horse c. hunter d. mustang e. palomino

heavy horse

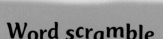
polo pony

◀ Zebras

Like all horses and their relatives, zebras eat mainly grass. They have long legs, each with one large toe, capped by a hard hoof. Their keen senses detect distant danger and they can race away at more than 60 kilometres an hour. Each group or herd consists of mares (females) and foals (young), led by a stallion (adult male).

Housing through the ages

Find out more:
Cities of ancient times ◄
Cities of modern times ◄

Human beings have always needed shelter and shade. They have learned to make homes from whatever materials are available. Tents could be sewn from animal skins or cloth. Huts could be made from turf, branches, leaves or bamboo canes. Houses have been built from timber, clay or stone. Over the ages, people learned how to make bricks, concrete, steel girders and glass windows.

◄ Cave-dwellers

During the Stone Age, caves offered families shelter and protection from wild animals. However, they were often damp, dark and draughty.

▲ Brick and slate

Big cities were built in Britain in the 1800s, with inexpensive housing for factory workers. Bricks and slates for the roofs could be carried from far away by canals or railways.

▼ Timber frame

In the Middle Ages, most houses were built with timber frames. These made criss-cross patterns on the walls, as seen on this German house.

heated swimming pool

courtyard

dining room

walled garden

kitchen

▲ A Roman home

Roman villas were built with tiled roofs and central courtyards. Many had beautiful gardens decorated with statues.

Human body

Your body is like a busy, complicated machine.
Every machine needs fuel and regular use, and it's
the same for your body. Your body has many
different parts that work together to keep you
alive. The brain is your body's control centre and it
tells your body what to do. How you breathe,
move, think and feel are controlled by your brain.

▼ Pumping blood

blood with oxygen is taken to the body

Your heart beats about 100,000 times a day to pump blood around your body. Fresh blood travels from your heart to every part of your body. Stale blood goes back to your heart and then to your lungs to collect supplies of oxygen.

stale blood enters the heart

fresh blood is pumped around your body

► From head to toe

Skin covers your body from the top of your head to the soles of your feet. Your skin is tough and stretchy – and it's waterproof, too. It keeps out harmful germs and stops you from getting too hot or too cold.

pore   hair

nerve endings   sweat gland

◄ Your senses

You have five senses that tell you what is happening around you. They let you see, hear, smell, touch and taste. Your brain sends messages to your sense organs. These are your eyes, ears, nose, skin and mouth.

▼

messages from your brain travel to every part of your body

you use your lungs to breathe

your heart pumps blood around your body

your kidneys get rid of waste material from your blood

broken-down pieces of food pass from your intestines into your blood

Count your heartbeat

Place two fingers on the inside of your wrist. If you press gently you will feel a throbbing. This is your pulse. Each throb is one heartbeat, as your heart pumps blood around your body. How many times does your heart beat in one minute?

Ice ages

Between about a million and ten thousand years ago, the Earth went through several periods when it was bitterly cold. Huge sheets of ice spread out from the Poles. During these ice ages, lands that now have a mild climate were deep in snow and their rivers were frozen solid.

Word box

climate
the kind of weather experienced in one place over a long period of time

Poles
the most northerly and southerly points on Earth

upright man, about 1.6 million years ago

Neanderthal man, about 200,000 to 30,000 years ago

modern man, about 40,000 years ago to present day

▲ Ice age people

Various types of human being lived through the ice ages and learned how to survive the cold. By the end of the ice ages, only modern man, our direct ancestor (relative from a long time ago), lived on Earth.

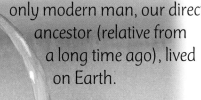

▲ Mammoth hunters

Big hairy elephants called woolly mammoths and woolly rhinoceroses roamed the land during the ice ages. People hunted them with weapons made of wood and stone.

Incas

When Spanish explorers reached South America in the 1500s they heard rumours of a fabulous land rich in gold. In fact, there had been splendid civilizations in the Andes Mountains and along the Pacific coast for thousands of years. The latest great empire was that of the Incas. It lasted from about 1100 to 1532, when it was conquered by the Spanish.

Wow!

The Temple of the Sun in Cuzco had a garden in which everything, including model plants and animals, was made of solid silver and gold.

▲ Nazca puzzles

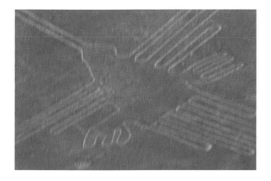

The Nazca civilization was one of many before the Incas. It lasted from about 200BC to AD750. Its people scraped patterns on the desert floor. These may have shown routes for religious processions. Some, like this hummingbird, were animal shaped.

▲ Road-runner

Messengers like this one carried the emperor's orders through the Inca Empire. He carries a *quipu*, or bunch of cords. These were knotted as a way of remembering numbers or other information.

▼ The Inca Empire

The Inca Empire was called Tawantisuyu, which means 'the Four Quarters'. It was centred on Peru and also took in large areas of Ecuador, Chile and Bolivia. It stretched 3,600 kilometres from north to south.

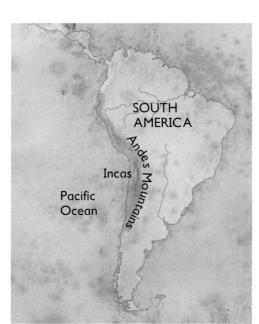

SOUTH AMERICA

Andes Mountains

Incas

Pacific Ocean

◄ Machu Picchu

The remains of this Inca town can be found high in the mountain peaks of Peru. The Incas were great builders, farmers and craftworkers.

India

Rich cloth, beautiful stone carvings, paintings and wonderful poetry were produced in ancient India. Several great empires grew up there. The Maurya Empire was at its height around 250BC and Gupta rule in about AD350. Hinduism and Buddhism also grew and spread during this period.

◄ Mughal Empire

Northern India was under Muslim rule from 1211. In 1526, the Mughal Empire was founded. This is Emperor Shah Jahan, who lived from 1592 to 1666.

▼ Taj Mahal

Shah Jahan had this marble monument built by the river Yamuna in honour of his wife, Mumtaz Mahal, who died in 1631. It was decorated with precious stones.

▲ Holy caves

There is a cave temple on Elephanta Island near Mumbai (Bombay) that is more than 1,200 years old. The temple has wonderful carvings of Hindu gods, such as Shiva.

◄ Indian dance

Indian dance has a history dating back thousands of years. It is said that the Hindu god, Shiva, set the world spinning by his dancing.

Indus Valley

Cities of ancient times ◀

Find out more:
Farming through the ages ◀
▶ Money and trade

The Indus River flows through Pakistan to the Arabian Sea. Between about 2500BC and 1750BC, a great civilization grew up in the Indus Valley. The people living there grew cotton and grain. They worked in metal and produced pottery, cloth and jewellery, trading with the peoples of western Asia.

◀ Mystery man

This stone head was made in Mohenjo-daro in about 2100BC. Whose face is it? Nobody really knows for certain. It might belong to a god, a king or a priest.

▼ How they lived

Pottery models, such as this one showing a two-wheeled cart drawn by bullocks, show us how people used to live in Harappa.

▲ Mohenjo-daro

The two greatest cities of the Indus Valley were Harappa and Mohenjo-daro. They had streets and proper drains, and houses built of bricks.

▲ Trade marks

Stone seals were used by the merchants of Mohenjo-daro to mark bundles of trade goods. Many show animals or a name.

◀ The great river

Flooding from the Indus river left behind rich soil for farming. The civilization that grew up along the riverbanks stretched into India.

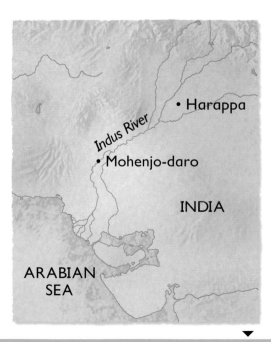

Harappa
Indus River
Mohenjo-daro
INDIA
ARABIAN SEA

Make a stone seal

1. Ask an adult to help you. Take a block of modelling clay. Using a knife, cut a design based on your favourite animal.
2. Write your name along the top, and allow clay to harden.
3. Press the top into a saucer of paint or ink, then press onto a piece of paper or card.

Industrial Revolution

The age of factories and machines began in Europe and North America in the 1700s and 1800s. It is called the Industrial Revolution, a term used to describe the changes brought about when people used steam to make goods. At first, the people who worked in the new factories had to work long hours for little pay.

▼ Cities and smoke

During the Industrial Revolution, cities grew and spread across Europe. This is a typical British city scene. It had street after street of small red-brick houses and tall chimneys belching out smoke.

Word box

factory
a building where machines are used to make goods on a large scale

steam engine
any machine whose movement is powered by the force of steam (which is made when water boils)

▼ Steam power

The factory age was possible because of the invention of the steam engine. This engine was made in the 1700s, by an inventor called Thomas Newcomen.

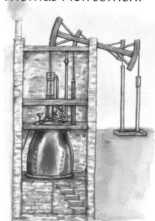

Insects

Butterflies and bees, moths and mosquitoes, cockroaches and crickets are all types of insect. Altogether there are almost one million different kinds of insect – and scientists think there are millions more that have not yet been named. Most insects are very small creatures, less than one centimetre long. There are some large ones, however, such as the giant Hercules moth from Australia, whose open wings measure 30 centimetres from tip to tip.

leg

abdomen

thorax

head

antenna

stag beetle

Word box

hatch
to come out of an egg

pupa
protective covering around a developing butterfly

thorax
the part of an insect that bears its legs and wings

◀ Body parts

All insects have six legs arranged in pairs. An insect's body is divided into three main parts: the head, the thorax and the abdomen. Most insects have wings and antennae, too.

▼ All colours

Some insects, such as dragon flies, are very colourful but others are a dull brown or black colour. Some look like leaves, sticks or tree bark to hide themselves from enemies. Others have bold spots or stripes to scare enemies away.

dragon fly

▶ Butterfly life

All insects begin life as an egg. Caterpillars hatch from the eggs of a butterfly. A young caterpillar looks nothing like the adult butterfly. When a caterpillar stops growing, it turns into a pupa. Finally, an adult butterfly crawls out of the pupa.

1. the female butterfly lays her eggs and dies

5. the butterfly is ready to fly after about an hour

4. finally the adult butterfly pushes its way out of the pupa

2. the caterpillar hatches from the egg. It spends most of its time eating

3. when the caterpillar is fully grown, it is ready to turn into a pupa. A hard shell begins to form around it, protecting the butterfly developing inside

Insects at work

Most insects have a very busy life. They have to build a home, look for a partner, hunt and collect food, fight enemies, lay eggs and look after their young. Some insects bite, spread disease and damage crops. However, insects are very important for life because they pollinate plants which form food for humans and animals.

bees carry pollen grains from plant to plant

▼ Huge nests

Termites live in big family groups called colonies. Some build tall nests that are home to thousands of termites. All the termites in a colony are the children of one female termite, the queen.

'chimney' can be 6 metres tall

wall made of earth

► Hungry insects

Locusts are a kind of grasshopper. They can travel long distances in huge crowds called swarms. One swarm may contain millions and millions of locusts. They swoop down to eat crops and other plants, destroying huge areas of plant life in a very short time.

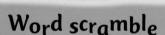
locust

▼ Insect lights

Some insects even use special effects to help them find a mate. This firefly is able to flash a yellowish light on and off to attract other flies.

Word scramble

Unscramble these words to find the names of four insects:

a. AGRIWE
b. EBLETE
c. BLIYDRAD
d. GRANDLYOF

a. earwig b. beetle c. ladybird d. dragonfly
answers

chamber

air passage

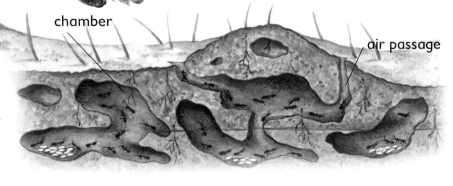

► Going underground

These tall termite nests continue for some distance underground. Inside is a maze of chambers (rooms) where young are looked after by 'worker' termites and food is stored. Air passages keep the nest cool.

Across the world, millions of computers are able to 'talk' to one another. This system is called the Internet. Information is mostly passed from computer to computer by telephone wires. The Internet lets people get hold of all kinds of information, in just a few seconds.

Word box

modem
device which lets computers send or receive information using phone lines

server
computer that holds information used by other computers

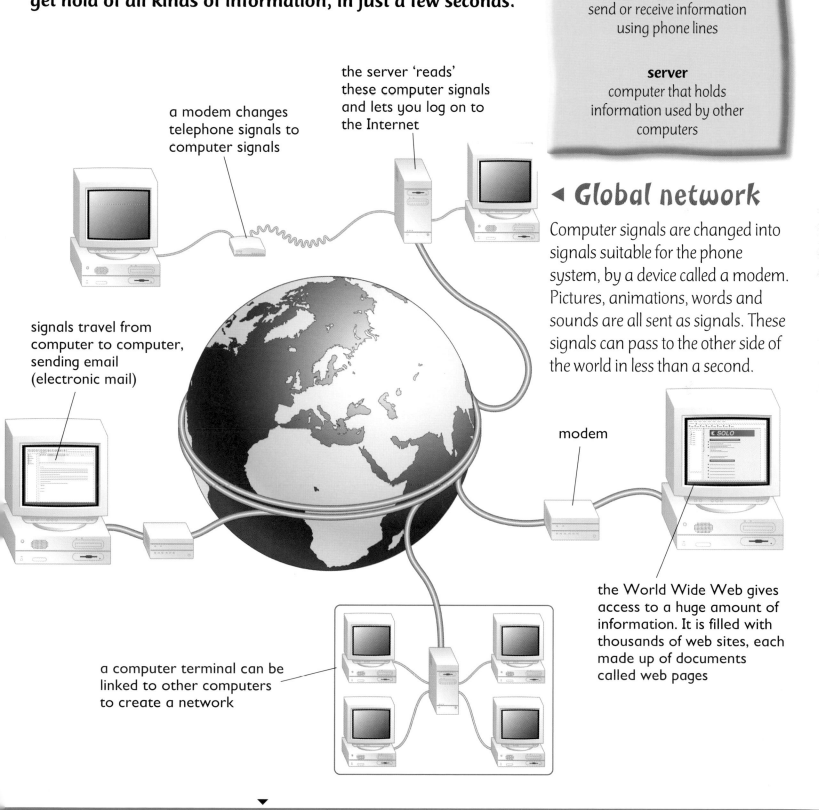

the server 'reads' these computer signals and lets you log on to the Internet

a modem changes telephone signals to computer signals

signals travel from computer to computer, sending email (electronic mail)

◄ Global network

Computer signals are changed into signals suitable for the phone system, by a device called a modem. Pictures, animations, words and sounds are all sent as signals. These signals can pass to the other side of the world in less than a second.

modem

the World Wide Web gives access to a huge amount of information. It is filled with thousands of web sites, each made up of documents called web pages

a computer terminal can be linked to other computers to create a network

Inventions

Can you imagine a world without wheels, without petrol engines, without medicines? For thousands of years clever people have invented machines and gadgets. Many of these have made our lives easier, safer or more healthy.

Word scramble

Can you unscramble these useful inventions? When you have found what they are, see if you can find out when they were first used:

**a. SLCEPCATSE
b. SCHETAM
c. PERAP
d. POSELECET
e. ADIRO**

answers
a. spectacles b. matches
c. paper d. telescope e. radio

▲ The wheel

The wheel is one of the most important things ever invented. Flat wheels were probably first used by potters, to turn their clay into round pots. By about 3500BC, upright wheels were being used for transport on chariots or wagons in the Middle East.

Hooke's microscope

◀ Magnification

Microscopes make even the tiniest objects look big. The first ones were made in the Netherlands in about 1590. This one was made in England in 1665, by a scientist called Robert Hooke. It was the first one to look like a modern microscope. Hooke used it to study the structure of chemicals and plants.

▼ North, south, east, west

Compasses use magnetism to show which direction to travel in — north, south, east or west. The first compasses were made in China over 2,300 years ago. At first, they looked like metal spoons with handles that pointed south. Later, steel needles were floated in bowls of water.

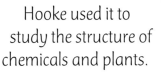

▶ Thomas Edison

An American called Thomas Edison invented the electric light bulb in 1879. He had already invented the phonograph, which recorded sound and played it back again.

Iron Age

Learning how to work iron was one of the most important discoveries ever made by human beings. Iron could now be used to make much stronger weapons and tools than had been possible before. It was being smelted by west Asian peoples, such as the Hittites, about 4,000 years ago. Iron-working skills soon spread to Europe, North Africa and other parts of Asia.

Word box

bellows
machines designed to puff air at glowing coals in a furnace, to make them hotter

ploughshare
the blade on a plough that turns over the soil

smelting
heating rock so that the metal it contains is melted and taken out

◄ Chinese plough

The ancient Chinese were very skilled iron workers. They made the first iron ploughshares in the world, over 2,500 years ago, to a design still in use today. They also invented cast iron, over 2,300 years ago.

◄ Iron swords

Iron was a deadly metal when used for making weapons. This short Roman sword was called a *gladius*. It was used by Roman armies to cut down their enemies.

bellows forced air through the clay pipes to make the fire hotter

firewood for burning

furnace

the fire in the furnace needed to be extremely hot to melt the metal

bellows

clay pipes

◄ Iron in Africa

These men are using bellows to fan an iron-smelting furnace in Africa. Iron was being used south of the Sahara Desert by about 500BC, and had reached southern Africa by 200BC.

Italy

During the Middle Ages, Italy was split up into small states. Some of them were ruled by other nations, others were independent republics. The great city of Rome was the centre of the Catholic Church and the home of its leader, the Pope. It was not until the 1800s that the different regions of Italy began to join together as a single nation.

▲ Leaning tower

This bell tower in the city of Pisa was built in 1170. Standing on sandy soil it soon started to tilt – and is still leaning over at an angle today.

▼ Popes of Rome

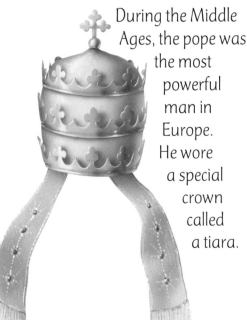

During the Middle Ages, the pope was the most powerful man in Europe. He wore a special crown called a tiara.

▲ The Red Shirts

In the 1860s, Giuseppe Garibaldi and his followers, the 'Red Shirts', fought for a united Italy. By 1871, Italy had become one nation again.

Make your own carnival mask

1. Ask an adult to help you. Cut a card mask to fit your face.

2. Paint it in gold or silver paint and decorate it with felt-tip pens.

3. Pierce two holes level with your ears. Tie string through the holes to attach the mask to your face.

▲ Venetian Carnival

The winter festival of Carnival has been held in Venice since the Middle Ages. People still wear masks and fancy costumes to the Carnival today.

Japan and Korea

Farmers have been growing rice on the lands around the Sea of Japan for over 2,000 years. Over the centuries, the islands of Japan were ruled by emperors and warriors, while powerful kings ruled over Korea. Beautiful buildings, pottery, paintings, prints, poetry and plays were all produced in this part of Asia.

◀ Knights of the East

The samurai were Japanese knights. They held great power between the 1100s and 1600s. The samurai fought for local lords, armed with sharp swords, bows and arrows, and later with guns.

▲ Fine writing

In Korea, as in China, calligraphy (fine handwriting) is very much admired. Chinese, Western and Korean forms of writing may be seen in Korea. The Korean script is called *hangeul* and it dates back as far as the 1400s.

▼ Tea time

In the 1400s, Buddhist monks in Japan made tea according to a long and complicated ritual. This became known as *chanoyu*, a tea-drinking ceremony which still takes place in Japan today. It aims to show off polite manners, friendship and beauty and takes several hours.

▲ Japanese castles

During the 1500s, Japanese lords built towering castles. They were very strong, being made of timber, earth and stone.

Wow!

Japan's royal family is the oldest in the world. It has ruled the country for over 2,000 years.

Jobs

Teacher, truck driver, dentist, sales assistant, builder and banker are kinds of job. A job is the work you do to earn money. Some people do outdoor jobs working on the land or at sea. Other jobs involve making things in factories and workshops, such as cars and computers. Some jobs provide help and information for others, for example in shops, hospitals, offices and banks.

Word box

assemble
to put together

natural resource
something useful from the land or the sea

▲ By hand

This potter is working with his hands. He uses machines as well in his job, such as a special oven called a kiln to bake the pots hard.

▲ Helping others

Jobs in offices, banks, hotels and shops are called service jobs. These jobs involve organizing and helping instead of working with natural resources or making goods.

◄ Healing power

People who work in the medical profession such as nurses, doctors and surgeons, have important jobs. Surgeons carry out complicated operations on their patients using the latest technology. This patient is having laser treatment to help correct his eyesight.

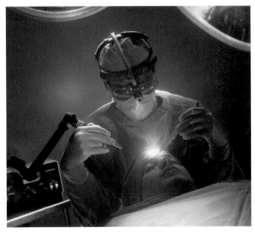

◄ Dangerous jobs

Fire-fighting can be a dangerous job. Fire-fighters have to be fit and strong and ready to risk their lives for other people. They also have to know about preventing fires, rescuing people and giving first aid in an emergency.

Job search

The names of five jobs are hidden in this grid. Can you find them?

C	R	O	L	I	T	D	V
H	S	D	A	R	M	O	E
E	K	A	R	T	I	S	T
F	Z	G	I	O	N	H	R
P	L	W	Y	E	R	U
U	W	S	A	L	R	E	N

answers: vet lawyer miner chef artist

Kangaroos and wallabies

Find out more:
Mammals ▶

One of the world's speediest animals bounds along on its huge back feet at more than 50 kilometres an hour – the red kangaroo. At almost 2 metres tall, it is the largest of about 50 kinds of kangaroos and smaller wallabies. These marsupial mammals live in Australia, with a few in Papua New Guinea.

▲ Wallaby

There are many kinds of wallabies, with names such as wallaroos, pademelons, bettongs and prettyfaces. Some live in forests, while others prefer rocky scrub or grassy plains. Like kangaroos, they use their tail for balance when bounding and to lean on at rest.

Wow!

Some kangaroos live in trees! Tree kangaroos dwell in forests in Papua New Guinea and northeast Australia and have grasping hands and padded feet.

◀ Boomers and fliers

A big male red kangaroo, or 'boomer', can clear a fence 3 metres tall. Many red kangaroos vary in colour from cream to rusty brown. They live in groups in the outback and gather at waterholes during drought.

▼ Boxing kangaroos

Male kangaroos push, pull and wrestle with their arms, and may kick out with their great feet, using the strong tail for support. They are battling for females at breeding time.

▲ Mother and joey

A newborn kangaroo is smaller than your thumb. It stays in its mother's pouch for up to six months, feeding on milk and growing fast. Then the youngster, or joey, hops out for a short while, dashing back if frightened. It finally leaves at one year old.

Word box

drought
a long, dry period with little or no rain

marsupial
pouched mammal

Kings and queens

Find out more:
Castles ◄ Empires and colonies ◄
Kings and queens of ancient times ►

Most countries used to be ruled by kings and queens, who were often very powerful.
Elizabeth I ruled England for 45 years. She beat off an invasion by a fleet of ships from Spain, and kept control over her country. Today, some countries are still ruled by kings and queens, but they have less power than in the Middle Ages.

Queen Elizabeth I

► Crown jewels

Kings and queens have always owned crowns with sparkling jewels, as an emblem (badge) of their royal power. Other emblems were held in the ruler's hands. They included big swords, rods called sceptres and globes called orbs.

▲ Women in power

In certain countries, only men were allowed to rule. But some of the world's strongest rulers have been women. Queen Elizabeth I ruled England from 1558 to 1603. Nobody dared to argue with her!

◄ Rulers no more

In 1917, many Russians decided that they did not want to be ruled by their tsar (emperor) any longer. In the revolution that followed, Nicholas II and his whole family were killed.

► Beheaded!

Throughout history, people have sometimes turned against their king and tried to get rid of him. Charles I was king of England and Scotland in the 1600s. Although he lost a civil war in Britain, Charles still refused to give up his powers. He was finally beheaded in London on January 31, 1649.

Kings and queens of ancient times

Many kings and queens have ruled over people and kingdoms for hundreds of years. Sometimes, they claimed to rule by the will of God. When they died, their children often ruled the country after them.

◄ Poisoned queen

Cleopatra was the queen of ancient Egypt, in North Africa, when the country was under the control of the Romans. According to legend, she killed herself by allowing a poisonous snake to bite her arm.

Word box

legend
a traditional story that has come to be known as true, but is not confirmed as true

▲ King Solomon

Solomon ruled over Israel about 1,000 years before the birth of Jesus Christ. He was a wise king and also a great builder. He ordered the building of the Temple in the city of Jerusalem.

► Warrior queen

About 950 years ago a queen called Boudicca ruled the Iceni tribe in Britain. She led her army against the Romans. Boudicca and her soldiers destroyed Roman towns and killed many soldiers. She poisoned herself to avoid being captured.

Wow!

Louis XIV's palace at Versailles, outside Paris, is almost half a kilometre long and has around 1,300 rooms.

Knights

In Europe, between about 1000 and 1500, horseback fighters that were heavily armed became the most important soldiers on the battlefield. They were called knights. Many knights were well rewarded with land and money. They went on to become powerful lords.

chain mail

plate armour

▲ Shining armour

In the 1000s, knights wore armour made of small iron rings, called chain mail. Later, they wore plates of metal joined together to cover the whole body. This was plate armour.

◄ Take that!

Knights liked to take part in mock battles called tournaments, or jousts, to show off their fighting skills. They wore fancy armour and helmets.

sword

◄ Heavy weapons

Knights fought with long spears called lances, and with axes, swords and clubs called maces.

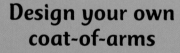
mace

▲ Code of honour

Knights were expected to behave in an honourable way and to respect ladies. People loved to hear stories about chivalry, the noble manners of knights. In reality, many knights were brutal and selfish.

Design your own coat-of-arms

1. Ask an adult to help you. Cut out the shape of a shield from cardboard.
2. Design and colour in your own coat-of-arms. You might want to show things you are interested in, or base the design on your name – a loaf for Baker, say, or a pot for Potter. If your name is Green or Brown, you might want to use that when choosing colours.

▼ Coats-of-arms

It was often hard to tell which knight was which when they were dressed in full armour. So the knights decorated their shields with their family badges, called coats-of-arms.

Lasers

Light from a torch spreads out quickly and does not travel very far. Light from a piece of equipment called a laser, however, is very powerful. It can travel as far as the Moon, in a narrow beam. Lasers have many uses. They can be found in everyday household things such as CD and DVD players, or in factories, hospitals and even concerts.

▶ DVD lasers

A DVD (digital versatile disc) uses a tiny laser. This produces a very strong light beam. The beam scans (passes over) the DVDs surface. It 'reads' data (information) such as pictures, music and movies.

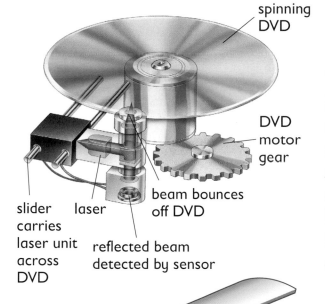

spinning DVD

DVD motor gear

slider carries laser unit across DVD

laser

beam bounces off DVD

reflected beam detected by sensor

▲ Lasers in industry

Laser light can contain enough energy to melt and cut through metal or almost any other substance. Factories that make clothes use computer-controlled lasers. They can cut out one shape in many thicknesses of fabric very quickly and accurately.

rays bounce off the mirrors at both ends, building up energy

mirror

half-mirror

laser light bursts from one end of the crystal

▼ Laser surgery

Lasers can be used to perform very delicate surgery, such as eye operations. Laser light does not spread out as normal light does. This means the beam can be very accurately directed and controlled.

particles bounce around in ruby crystal

▲ How a laser works

Laser light is made by feeding energy, such as ordinary light or electricity, into a substance called the active medium. A rod of ruby crystal is the active medium in this laser. A powerful lamp causes the tiny particles inside the crystal to vibrate. The light builds up and is bounced between mirrors. The energy becomes so strong that it escapes from the laser as an intense beam.

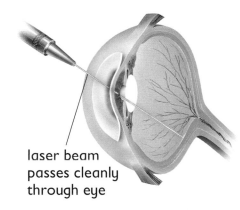

laser beam passes cleanly through eye

Light is a type of energy that you can see. It is usually produced by a very hot object such as a light bulb or a fire, and heat is released. But there are also 'cold' types of light – for example, the light produced by deep-sea fish or by glow-worms.

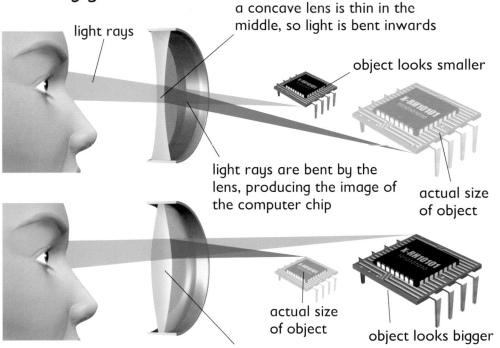

light rays

a concave lens is thin in the middle, so light is bent inwards

object looks smaller

light rays are bent by the lens, producing the image of the computer chip

actual size of object

actual size of object

object looks bigger

a convex lens is thicker in the middle, so light is bent outwards

▲ Bending light

When a straw is placed in water, it looks as though it is slightly bent. This is because light rays bend when they pass through water. This bending of rays is called refraction.

▲ Using lenses

Lenses are found in many optical (seeing) instruments, such as glasses, cameras and microscopes. The lenses are curved, so when light hits them, the rays bend. This makes an object look bigger or smaller than it really is.

▼ Mirror images

When light hits a very smooth surface such as a mirror, it reflects (bounces) off the surface. If it hits a mirror at an angle, it is reflected off at exactly the same angle.

Mirror fun

Take a shiny metal spoon, and look at your reflection in its bowl. Notice how your reflection gets larger and smaller, and even turns upside down! This is because light is working in a similar way to the diagram above, bouncing off the curved surface into your eyes.

actual object

light rays bounce off mirror

the eye receives a reflection of the image

Light at work

Find out more:
Electricity ◀ Energy ◀ Lasers ◀ Light ◀

Light is essential for all kinds of things.
Plants need the Sun's light for energy. We need
light to grow food to eat and to be able to see
around us. We make our own light
with electricity or gas. In earlier
times, people used fires,
candles or oil for lighting.

◀ Cold light

Some animals produce an unusual kind
of light that gives off no heat. Fireflies and
glow-worms are insects that can make parts
of their bodies glow with light. They do this to
attract a mate. Some plants and
moulds also glow in the dark.

Wow!
Light travels through space at
300,000 kilometres a second. It is
the fastest thing in the Universe!

▲ Stop or go?

Train drivers obey signal lights, just
as drivers on the road obey traffic
lights. Train signals show just two
colours – red for stop and green for
go. Road traffic lights have one
extra colour – amber (yellow).

▼ Light shows

Light can be used to create exciting
displays. Laser light shows are often
used at pop concerts. The beam
from the laser is controlled by a
computer, allowing it to make
patterns in the air.

◀ Watch out!

For at least 2,000 years,
lighthouses have used their
flashing light to warn ships
of danger. Lighthouses are
tall, so that they can be seen
from far away. Each
lighthouse has its own
pattern of light flashes, so
that it can be easily
identified. People used to
work in lighthouses, but
modern ones are automatic.

Machines

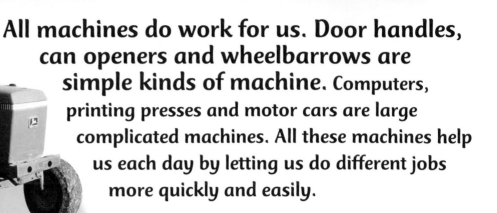

All machines do work for us. Door handles, can openers and wheelbarrows are simple kinds of machine. Computers, printing presses and motor cars are large complicated machines. All these machines help us each day by letting us do different jobs more quickly and easily.

▼ Heavy loads

We use a wheelbarrow to move a load that is too heavy to lift by hand. It is really a simple machine called a lever. Levers help you to lift heavy weights without using a lot of effort. You move one end of a lever in order to lift a heavy load at the other end.

▶ In the home

Everyday machines such as vacuum cleaners, electric kettles, food processors and dishwashers help us to clean, cook and wash up more quickly.

vacuum cleaner

▶ Cranes

You can see cranes on building sites, in factories and in docks. We use cranes to lift and move heavy loads. A crane is a type of pulley, which is a simple machine made up of a wheel with a rope over it. You pull on one end of the rope to lift a heavy load attached to the other end.

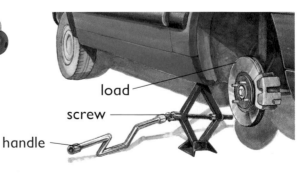

load
screw
handle

▼ Jet power

A jet engine is a very powerful machine. Large passenger aircraft have three or four jet engines. A stream of gases shoots out of the back of the engine and pushes the aircraft forwards through the air.

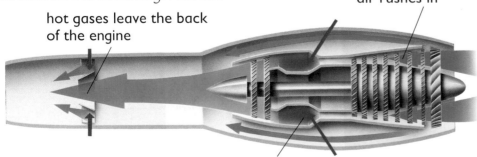

hot gases leave the back of the engine

air rushes in

a mixture of air and fuel burn

▲ Simple jack

A jack is made up of two kinds of simple machine: a lever and a screw. By moving the jack's handle, or lever, you turn the screw and lift up a heavy load such as a car. We use a jack when taking off an old car tyre or putting on a new one.

Machines in history

the *Gutenberg* Press

▲ Printing machine

This printing press was made in Germany about 550 years ago. The printer used it to make many copies of the same page of a book.

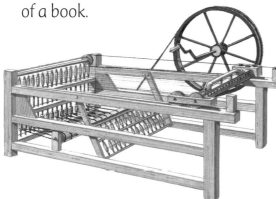

▲ Spinning jenny

This machine is called a spinning jenny. It is a kind of spinning wheel that spins lots of cotton threads at the same time. Before this machine was invented in 1764, each spinning wheel could only spin one thread at a time. In the cotton factories, spinning jennies allowed the spinners to produce enough cotton thread to keep the cotton weavers busy at work.

From the 1700s onwards, people started to use machines more and more to do their work. The first steam engine was made to pump water out of a tin mine in Cornwall, England. Later, steam engines were used to provide the power for hundreds of different machines, from weaving looms and spinning wheels to cars and ships.

► Archimedes' screw

This 'Archimedean screw' is named after the ancient Greek inventor, Archimedes. For thousands of years, it has been used to lift water from rivers to irrigate (bring water to) fields where crops grow. It is still used today in some Middle Eastern countries.

▼ Motor cars

The motor car is one of the world's most popular machines. One of the first proper motor cars was this three-wheeled vehicle. It was built in 1886 by a German named Karl Benz. Its engine was powered by gas.

Wow!

The pyramids in Egypt were built about 4,500 years ago from huge blocks of stone. But no one really knows what machines were used to haul them into place.

Motorwagen, built by Karl Benz

Mammals

Bats and bears, monkeys and moles, wallabies and whales – all these animals are mammals. Human beings are mammals, so are many of the animals we see around us – our pet cats and dogs, and farm animals such as sheep, cows and goats. Altogether there are about 4,500 different kinds of mammal.

dolphin

▲ Odd mammals

The giant anteater of South America is a very strange-looking mammal. It eats only ants or termites, and its sharp claws are ideal for breaking into insect nests. The anteater's tongue extends to a length of 60 centimetres!

◄ Keeping warm

Whales, dolphins and porpoises are mammals that live in the water. Unlike most mammals, they do not have fur or hair. Instead, they have a layer of fat under the skin to keep their bodies warm.

▼ The smallest

One of the smallest mammals is a bat. It is called Kitti's hog-nosed bat and is less than 2 centimetres long – about the same size as a bumble bee.

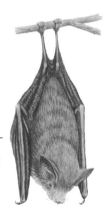

◄ Brainy!

Mammals have better developed brains than any other animal group. The most intelligent mammals, after humans, are monkeys and apes. Some chimpanzees use sticks as tools to catch termites!

▼ Comparing size

There are about 4,500 different types of mammal. The biggest, the blue whale, is shown to scale here with some other mammals. Even the biggest land mammal, the elephant, looks tiny next to the blue whale.

blue whale
33.5 metres long

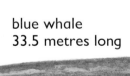

giraffe 5.5 metres tall

human
1.7 metres tall

brown bear
2.4 metres tall

African elephant
3.3 metres tall

Mammals and their babies

Find out more:
Animal kingdom ◄
Babies ◄ Mammals ◄

Mammals are the only animals that feed their young on milk. Many young mammals are born with hair or fur and they are cared for by their parents afterwards. A chimpanzee baby, for example, stays with its mother until it is about six years old.

▼ Living in a pouch

Kangaroos and koalas belong to a group of mammals called marsupials. They give birth to tiny, undeveloped babies. The babies crawl to a pouch on their mother's stomach. They stay there for about eight months, drinking their mother's milk until they are fully developed.

pouch entrance

1. newborn kangaroo crawls to its mother's pouch

2. in the pouch, the baby drinks its mother's milk

duck-billed platypus

▲ Laying eggs

A few mammals lay eggs from which their young hatch. These mammals live in Australia and New Guinea. The duck-billed platypus is one of them. Its baby licks milk off its mother's belly.

the young kangaroo (joey) stays in the pouch until quite large, and covered in fur

▲ Biggest baby

The biggest mammal of all, the blue whale, also gives birth to the biggest baby. When it is born, the blue whale calf is already six to eight metres long. Its mother's milk is rich, which helps the baby to grow quickly.

▼ Caring for young

Most mammals care for their young for some time after they are born. Many young, like these cheetah cubs, rely on their mother for food and protection. They also learn how to hunt and look after themselves in the wild.

Word box

pouch
a pocket of skin

undeveloped
not fully-grown

Materials

Wool, paper, copper, steel, concrete and plastic – all of these are materials. We use materials to make things. We choose the right material for the right thing. For example, a ball is not made out of glass or paper because they are not suitable materials. Instead we choose a material, such as rubber, because it is stretchy and bouncy.

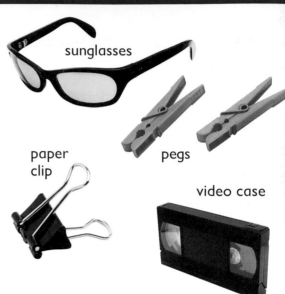

sunglasses

paper clip

pegs

video case

▲ Useful steel

Stainless steel is a very useful material because it does not rust easily. At a steelworks, the metal is heated to a high temperature and then welded into different shapes.

▼ Plants and animals

Many of the materials that we use every day come from plants or animals.

wood, paper and rubber come from trees

the wool for a warm sweater comes from sheep or goats

the cotton to make a t-shirt comes from cotton plants

▲ Useful plastic

Look around and count how many plastic things you can see. The answer is probably 'lots'. Plastic is one of our most useful materials because we can make it into many different shapes. Plastic can be clear or coloured; it can bend and stretch and be hard or soft. Most plastic is made from petroleum.

Wow!

A strong but lightweight metal called magnesium is found in seawater – we use it to make parts for cars and planes.

Word box

petroleum
a thick oil found under the ground or under the sea-bed

space shuttle
a spacecraft that can be used again and again

▶ Protective materials

The space shuttle becomes very, very hot when it returns to the Earth from space. The underneath part is covered with special tiles made from ceramic, a mixture of baked clay and other materials. The tiles protect the shuttle from the extreme heat.

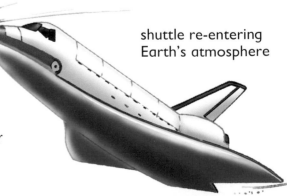

shuttle re-entering Earth's atmosphere

Measuring

Measuring helps you find the answer to questions such as 'How tall am I? How much do I weigh?' We use measurements all the time – in the kitchen, in shops, in the classroom, on a building site. We use many different tools to help us measure, such as scales and tape measures, clocks and thermometers, rulers and metre sticks.

▼ Hot and cold

A thermometer tells you how hot or cold something is – it measures temperature. A scale is marked along the side of the thermometer. Temperature is measured in degrees Celsius (°C) or Fahrenheit (°F).

▼ Telling the time

A clock tells you what time it is. We measure time in hours, minutes and seconds. The time of day is split into morning and afternoon – a.m. stands for morning and p.m. for afternoon.

▼ How long?

We use rulers or tape measures to find out how long something is. Every measurement consists of a number and a unit. If the side of a box measures 10 centimetres in length, then 10 is the number and centimetres (cm for short) is the unit of measurement.

ruler

▼ How heavy?

Balances and scales help us to find out how heavy something is. The needle on the dial points to the correct weight.

Length and weight

This table explains units of length and weight. The units are sometimes shortened, or abbreviated, to save time and space. For example, mm is short for millimetre, and kg is short for kilogram.

Units of length
10 millimetres (mm) = 1 centimetre (cm)
100 cm = 1 metre (m)
1000 m = 1 kilometre (km)

Units of weight
1000 milligrams (mg) = 1 gram (g)
1000 g = 1 kilogram (kg)
1000 kg = 1 tonne (t)

Word box

scale
a row of steps or marks that are used for measuring something

Medicine

Our body can usually look after itself very well, but sometimes things go wrong. Some of the thousands of chemicals in the body may get out of balance. Perhaps a part wears out. Germs may attack and cause disease. Medicines are designed to put these things right and to make us feel better.

▲ Pills and capsules

Most medicines are swallowed as tablets or capsules. These are specially designed to dissolve properly in the stomach so they will be absorbed, or taken into your body. They are made in all kinds of colours, so people do not mix them up.

Word box

anaesthetic
a drug that takes away any feeling, so that no pain is felt during an operation

antibiotics
medicines used to treat illnesses caused by bacteria

vaccination
medicine given to a person to stop them getting a harmful disease

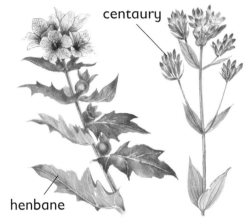

centaury

henbane

▲ Nature's cures

Plants have been used as medicines for thousands of years. Some, like henbane, can be very poisonous unless they are used in tiny amounts. Bitter-tasting centaury is still used as a tonic and to reduce fevers.

▼ Self-protection

People are vaccinated by being given doses of a dead or harmless germ. The body thinks that these are dangerous, so it produces lots of substances called antibodies. These prevent you from getting the real disease later on.

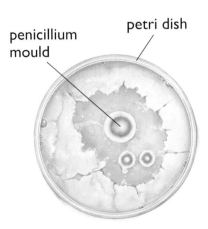

petri dish

penicillium mould

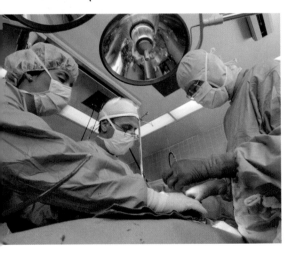

▲ Body repair

Doctors called surgeons repair damage and remove diseased parts during operations. The invention of substances called anaesthetics meant that people could have operations without pain. Heart and liver transplants are among the most complicated types of surgery.

▲ Bacteria-killer

Penicillin is an antibiotic that has saved the lives of millions of people. It first came from a mould – like the blue mould seen on stale bread. This was accidentally found to be able to kill bacteria.

Medicine in history

Doctors have been treating ill people for thousands of years, but with much less knowledge than doctors today. Some of them discovered useful plants for medicines, but many of the potions they mixed up did not help their patients at all. Great advances in medical knowledge came in the 1600s, and by the 1800s and 1900s many lives were saved.

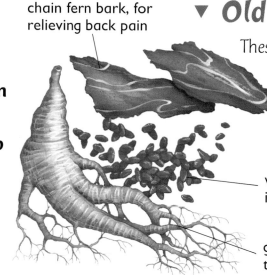

▼ Old remedies

These Chinese medicines have been used for hundreds of years, and are still in use today.

chain fern bark, for relieving back pain

wolfberry, for improving eyesight

ginseng, a root used to stimulate the body

▲ Florence Nightingale

In the 1850s, Florence Nightingale became famous for her care of wounded British soldiers. Horrified by poor standards in hospitals, she devoted her life to improving them and set up nurse training schools.

Lister's antiseptic spray

◄ Safe operations

In 1867, an English surgeon called Joseph Lister worked out how to kill germs during operations. He used a chemical spray such as this one and saved many lives.

▲ Understanding germs

A French scientist called Louis Pasteur, who lived from 1822 to 1895, helped us to understand how diseases are spread by germs or bacteria.

Metals are mostly shiny, strong materials that are solid at room temperature. They can be hammered into different shapes. They can also be shaped by being melted and poured into a mould. Metals have been used since earliest times and have allowed modern civilization to develop.

▲ Save and reuse

It is mostly cheaper and less wasteful to reuse metal than to dig up more ore and process it. Metals such as old drinks cans, cars and other waste can be recycled (reused). They are crushed into blocks and sent off to be melted down again.

Word box

alloy
a mixture of metals, or a metal and a non-metal

ore
a mixture of different substances, of which metal is one

▲ Metal money

Coins are stamped out of strips of metal such as copper, silver or mixtures of metals called alloys. Coins are heavy and difficult to handle, so paper notes are used for large amounts of money.

▼ Old iron bridge

The world's first cast-iron bridge was built in 1779. It spans the Severn Gorge at Ironbridge, Shropshire, England. Cast-iron is a hard and brittle form of iron.It is made by putting molten (melted) metal into moulds and allowing it to harden.

Word scramble

Unscramble these words to find the names of different kinds of metal or alloy:

a. NIRO

b. ZENORB

c. POPERC

d. NIT

answers
a. iron b. bronze c. copper d. tin

▶ The age of bronze

Bronze is an alloy (mix) of copper and tin. Copper is a very soft metal, but adding tin makes it much harder and stronger. This was discovered thousands of years ago, during the Bronze Age, when people made bronze axes that still survive today.

Mice and rats

Mice are smaller than rats – otherwise there is little difference between them. All are rodents, with long incisor teeth for nibbling and nipping. Most eat plant foods such as seeds, fruits and roots. They have big eyes and ears, long whiskers and a long tail. They move quickly to escape enemies and breed quickly to keep up their numbers.

mouse

▲ Friendly or harmful?

Mice and rats can be bred and raised as friendly pets. Others are used in scientific research. Wild rats and mice can cause damage to buildings and spread diseases.

Word box

scientific research
experiments that are carried out to find out more about something

sewage
human waste that is carried away in drains

Make some whiskers!

Mice and rats use whiskers to feel in the dark – you can too!

1. Ask an adult to help. Cut a straight line from the edge of a paper plate to its centre. Roll the plate into a cone shape.

2. Stick a few straws onto either side of the cone.

3. Thread some elastic through two tiny holes at the wide end of your cone, to hold the whiskers on your nose.
Now you have your very own mouse whiskers!

▶ Desert-dweller

Like a tiny kangaroo, the jerboa hops at great speed across the sand of the Sahara Desert, using its long tail for balance. Like most rats and mice it hides by day in a burrow and comes out at night to feed.

▲ Country house

The tiny harvest mouse lives in the countryside. Its nest is the size and shape of a tennis ball. The female gives birth to more than ten babies.

Wow!

The house mouse is found in more places around the world than any other animal.

▶ Water-rats

Many rats can swim well. A water-rat is often just a brown rat searching for fish or crabs (or gobbling up sewage). The Australian water rat is a large rat, with a head and body 35 centimetres long. It dives well and eats frogs, fish, lizards, snakes, other rats and mice, waterbirds and even fish-catching bats.

Australian water rat

Microscopes

A microscope lets us see tiny things that we cannot see with our own eyes, such as bacteria. It works by using groups of lenses. Lenses are made from see-through materials and are shaped to make things larger or clearer for us. Electron microscopes allow us to see even smaller things, such as viruses. Studying their structure helps us produce treatments for the diseases they cause.

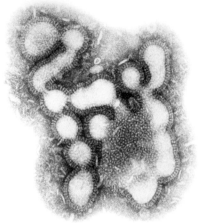

▲ The flu virus

This is the flu virus, viewed under an electron microscope. Chemicals, called fixatives, preserve the viruses so that they are not smashed by the microscope's electron beam. This allows the virus to be examined.

Word box

virus
the simplest form of life; viruses live inside a cell, so the body finds it hard to attack them

▼ 3D pictures

This piece of hair is being viewed under a binocular microscope. A binocular microscope has two eyepieces and two objective lenses. It gives a 3D view with depth.

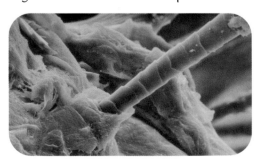

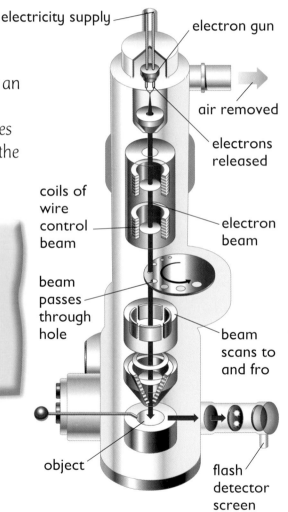

electricity supply
electron gun
air removed
electrons released
coils of wire control beam
electron beam
beam passes through hole
beam scans to and fro
object
flash detector screen

▲ Particle power

An electron microscope is very powerful. It can magnify an object (make it look larger) by millions of times. It works by firing special particles called electrons at the object. The electrons bounce off the object onto a viewing screen.

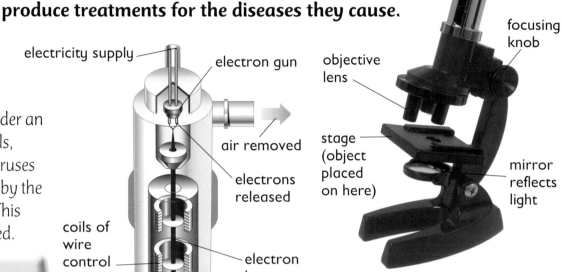

eyepiece
focusing knob
objective lens
stage (object placed on here)
mirror reflects light

▲ Using lenses

'Compound optical' microscopes use two or more lenses to make images up to 2,000 times bigger. An objective lens bends light rays to enlarge the object. An eyepiece lens then lets you see the final image.

Make a microscope

Use a magnifying glass to look at something small. Note how big the glass makes it look. Now use another magnifying glass, held under the first. The image looks even bigger. As you move the lenses up and down the size of the image changes. It will become sharp or blurred. This is what happens inside a microscope as the views are focused.

Microscopic creatures

There are millions of creatures all around us that we cannot see – they are too small. We need a microscope to view this tiny world. Some of these micro-living things are true animals, but very small. Others are made of just one living unit or 'cell' each, and they often have both animal and plant features. These are not true animals. They are known as protists.

▲ Water-bears

Big tardigrades or water-bears are just about large enough for us to see, with their tubby bodies and stubby limbs. They live in water and damp places like moss. These animals can survive being dried out, frozen or almost boiled.

► Amoeba

Like most protists, the amoeba lives in water. It is a single cell, flexible and baglike, and oozes along in pond mud. It catches even smaller living things, such as bacteria, by extending bloblike 'arms' around them or simply flowing over them.

▼ Round animals

The rotifer has a circle of micro-hairs around its mouth end, like a crown. The hairs wave and filter any edible bits from the water and pass them into its vase-shaped body. This tiny creature is also called the 'wheel-animacule'.

Word box

cell
a self-contained unit of life –
a protist is just one cell

silica
a natural substance or mineral that forms sand, glass, and the shells of some living things

tentacle
a long, slim, bendy body part

▲ Shrimp cousins

Copepods are tiny cousins of shrimps and crabs. They swim by waving their very long antennae (feelers), and swarm in their billions. Their bristly front limbs filter food particles from sea water. Copepods are food for bigger ocean animals such as baby fish.

▼ Swarming seas

A drop of sea water contains thousands of tiny living things. Heliozoans are protists with a central shell-like chamber made of silica. Their long, thin, starlike 'arms' catch even smaller prey. Foraminiferan protists look like micro-snails and also have a hard-shelled central part with flexible tentacles.

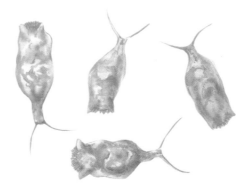

Middle Ages

Find out more:
Farming through the ages ◀ Religious buildings ▶
Writing and printing ▶

The period known in Europe as the Middle Ages lasted about 1,000 years. It was given that name because it lay in-between the ancient world and the modern age. The ancient world ended with the fall of the Roman Empire in AD476. The modern world began with the great voyages of exploration and scientific discoveries of the late 1400s and 1500s.

▲ A life of toil

In the 1100s, farm workers, called serfs, were forced to work for the local lord in exchange for some of the food they grew. They were not free to move away from their village.

▶ Holy journeys

Christians who went on journeys to holy places were called pilgrims Places of pilgrimage included Jerusalem, Rome and Canterbury in England. The pilgrims wore special badges to show which sites they had visited.

▲ In praise of God

By the 1100s, most Europeans were Christians. Many cathedrals were built at this time, including this one at Chartres in France, built between 1195 and 1220.

Make a quill

During the Middle Ages, people used feathers called quills as pens. Next time you find a big feather, cut the end like a nib, dip it in some ink and use it to write your name.

▶ Fine words

Europeans did not learn how to print until the end of the Middle Ages. Before that, books had to be carefully copied out by hand. The words were beautifully written and decorated with pictures and patterns.

Migrating animals

Find out more:
Antarctica ◄ Butterflies and moths ◄
Whales ►

Every spring in Europe, swallows and swifts appear like magic, and in North America, monarch butterflies do the same. These are migrants. They make long journeys, usually to the same place and back again each year. They go to the best place for finding food or raising their young, usually somewhere warmer.

grey whale migration route

► Birds

Birds migrate further than any other animal. Many kinds, from geese to buntings, leave Europe, central Asia and North America in spring for the Arctic summer, then return south in autumn. Swallows spend the winter in Africa and come to Europe for the summer.

Wow!

The Arctic tern travels further than any other bird. It has two summers each year, in the Arctic and Antarctic — a return trip of 30,000 kilometres.

▼ Reptiles

Sea turtles, such as green turtles, are wandering migrants that roam the oceans. Every two or three years they may swim about 1,000 kilometres to the beaches where they hatched, to lay their own eggs.

▲ Mammals

Many great whales, such as greys, swim from warm tropical waters to the far north or south, for the brief summer when food is plentiful.

◄ Insects

Monarch butterflies spend the winter crowded in roosts in south-west North America. In spring they head north to Canada, breeding as they go. Their 'grandchild' butterflies come back in autumn.

Word box

roost
a resting or sleeping place, usually for flying animals such as birds, bats and insects

tundra
treeless land around the Arctic Ocean, with low bushes and mossy bogs, covered in winter snow

Money and trade

We use money to buy things – from chocolate bars to computers, from toys to train tickets. Money can be in the form of paper notes or metal coins. We can also pay for something by writing a cheque or using a credit card.

▶ The first coins

The world's first coins were made about 2,500 years ago in a country called Lydia (part of modern Turkey). The coins, which were a mixture of gold and silver, had a design stamped on the front and back.

◀ Cash machines

You can collect money from a cashpoint machine. You insert a special card into the machine and key in your personal number. The machine, which is connected to your bank, gives you an amount of cash. The same amount is then taken out of your bank account.

▼ Making money

Money is made in a special factory called a mint. In the past, coins were made from gold, silver and other expensive metals. Modern coins are made from a mixture of metals such as zinc, nickel and copper.

▶ Long distance trade

In the ancient world, people traded over long distances. Egyptian ships carried goods from Crete, Arabia and East Africa to towns up and down the river Nile. The Romans brought spices from distant India and silk from China. The ships were propelled by sail and oar power.

Egyptian trading ship

Mongol Empire

The rolling grasslands of eastern Europe and Asia are called steppes. In ancient times and during the Middle Ages, most of the people living there were nomads. They moved across the land with their herds and flocks, living in tents rather than towns. Some of the fiercest warriors came from the steppes of Mongolia.

▶ Riders of the steppes

Wild horses were first tamed on the grasslands. The peoples of the steppes were all expert riders.

▲ Into China

In 1211, the Mongols crossed the Great Wall and invaded northern China. Kublai Khan, grandson of Temujin, became the Chinese emperor in 1271.

▼ Genghis Khan

Temujin lived from about 1162 to 1227. He became the ruler of the Mongols when he was just 13 and was soon leading his warriors into battle across Asia and eastern Europe. He became known as Genghis Khan, or 'mighty ruler'.

▼ Samarkand

Timur the Lame, or Tamberlaine, ruled over Samarkand, a city in Uzbekistan. He lived from 1336 to 1405 and conquered lands stretching from Russia to India.

Word box

nomad
somebody who does not live in the same place all the time, but travels from one place to another

Monkeys

Find out more:
Apes ◄ Mammals ◄

Most monkeys are bright-eyed, long-tailed, clever, day-active tree-dwellers with grasping hands and feet. They live in troops, communicate with noisy whoops and chattering, and eat plant foods such as flowers, fruits, berries and shoots. There are 240 different kinds of monkey.

▼ White-cheeked

Over 20 kinds of small monkeys live in Central and South America. Many have long, silky fur, and claws rather than fingernails and toenails. Manabeys sleep and spend nearly all their time in the trees. Troops of about 10 to 30 live together and are extremely noisy, constantly chattering across the treetops.

white-cheeked mangabey

Word scramble

Unscramble these words to find the names of five types of monkeys:

a. EQUACAM
b. LIRDNALM
c. RELSQURI YEKNOM
d. REDISP YEKNOM
e. BUSCOLO

answers
a. macaque b. mandrill c. squirrel monkey d. spider monkey e. colobus

▲ Strong bond

In the Amazon rainforest, the female and male dusky titi monkey stay together, not just during courtship, but all year. Each dawn they sit side by side on a branch, wrap their tails together and sing loudly.

▶ Vervets

Vervets range widely across Africa. They climb well, run fast and swim rapidly. They live in grassland, scrub and forest. Vervets eat plants, small animals and insects.

▶ Ring-tailed lemurs

Monkeys are in the primate group of mammals, along with apes and prosimians – 80 kinds of lemurs, bushbabies, pottos, lorises and tarsiers. These are mostly small tree-dwellers. Lemurs, such as this ring-tailed lemur, are found only on Madagascar, an island east of Africa.

Moon

The Moon is our closest neighbour — it is nearer to the Earth than any other object in space. The Moon travels around the Earth and takes about one month to make a complete journey. The Moon seems to be shining because it reflects light from the Sun.

◀ Close up

This is a close-up view of the Moon taken from space. The darker patches are plains, called maria. The word 'maria' means seas, but there is no water on the Moon. The lighter areas are highlands. There are also lots of craters on the surface of the Moon.

Wow!

An Italian scientist called Galileo Galilei used his telescope to make the first real study of the Moon almost 400 years ago.

▲ In the shadows

When the Moon passes into the Earth's shadow, it is called a lunar (Moon) eclipse. The Moon grows darker and redder. A solar (Sun) eclipse is when the Moon passes between the Earth and the Sun, blocking the Sun's light (above).

▼ Changing shape

The Moon seems to change shape from day to day. It takes 28.73 days to pass through all these changes, which we call phases. Sometimes we see just a tiny slice of the Moon — this is because the rest of the Moon is in darkness.

new Moon

crescent Moon

first quarter

gibbous Moon

full Moon

Word box

crater
a dent in the ground

plain
a wide, flat area

▶ Moon walk

The Apollo missions began in 1961. Out of the 11 crewed missions, only six managed to land on the Moon itself.

Mountain animals

Mountains are harsh, dangerous places, as snowstorms howl across icy cliffs. Yet some animals are specialized to survive here. Mountain creatures need warm coverings of thick fur or feathers, and feet with strong grips for slippery rocks. Many larger animals migrate or journey higher in summer, as the ice melts and plants grow in alpine meadows. They travel back down to the sheltered lower forests for winter.

▼ Lammergeier

Great birds of prey seek old, sick or injured animals to eat. The lammergeier, a vulture of Europe, Africa and Asia, takes an animal bone up high. It drops it onto a rock, to break open and reveal the soft marrow inside.

▲ Mountain lion

The mountain lion, also called the puma or cougar, is not a real lion — but is a similar colour. It once thrived in many habitats throughout the Americas. But hunting by people drove it to remote mountains. This cat eats a variety of prey, from rabbits to mountain goats, sheep and deer.

▼ Chilly chinchilla

Many mountain animals have become rare, killed for the thick fur that keeps them warm on the cold heights. The chinchilla, a plant-eating rodent of the Andes Mountains, in South America, is still rare in the wild. But it is also bred for its fur, and as a soft, cuddly pet.

▲ Apollo butterfly

The apollo of Europe and Asia can flap strongly in the wind to fly at over 3,000 metres — higher than almost any butterfly. It feeds on nectar from alpine flowers. Most mountain insects survive winter as eggs, or hide in cracks in rocks.

Word box

alpine
to do with mountains — Alpine with a capital 'A' is to do with the Alps range of mountains in Europe

marrow
soft, jelly-like substance inside many types of bones

remote
distant

Mountains

Find out more:
North America ▶ Rocks ▶
Rocks and minerals ▶

Sharp peaks covered with ice and snow, long steep slopes, rivers that flow quickly, rocky valleys – these are just some of the sights you might see in the mountains. A mountain is usually much higher than the land around it. When several mountains are grouped together they form a mountain range. The Alps in Europe are an example of this.

▼ Mountain forms

There are three main ways in which mountains are formed.

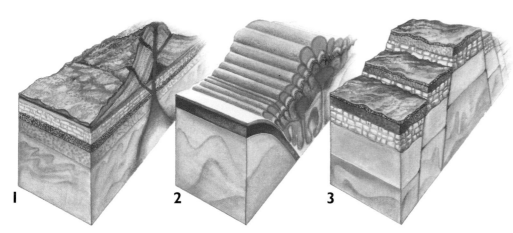

1. volcanoes form mountains when lava inside the Earth cools and hardens

2. layers of rocks are forced up into 'folds'

3. rocks may crack, causing faults, allowing large areas of rock to be pushed up

Word scramble

Unscramble these words to find the names of five large mountain ranges:

a. SPAL
b. SKICORE
c. NASED
d. ASLAMYAIH
e. SALTA

answers
a. ALPS b. ROCKIES c. ANDES d. HIMALAYAS e. ATLAS

▲ Mountain range

A group of mountain ranges called the Alps stretches across parts of France, Italy, Switzerland and Austria. The Alps are very popular for winter sports, such as skiing.

▼ Mountain life

This mountain goat has a thick coat to keep it warm, and feet that are good for climbing in rocky places.

▼ The Rockies

The Rocky Mountains run for about 3,000 kilometres down the west coast of North America. There are several national parks and ski resorts in the spectacular scenery.

▼ Top of the world

For hundreds of years people have enjoyed climbing mountains. In 1953 two climbers reached the top of the world's highest mountain, Mount Everest, in Asia. They were Edmund Hillary from New Zealand, and Tenzing Norgay, his guide.

Music and dance

Find out more:
Music and dance in history ▶ Sound ▶

You can hear the sounds of music almost everywhere you go. Music can be a pop song on the radio, a choir singing in church or an orchestra performing. We listen to music to enjoy ourselves and to relax. People dance, usually to music, all over the world. It may be as part of a ceremony or celebration, to express themselves, to entertain others – or simply to have fun.

Wow!

The Austrian composer Wolfgang Amadeus Mozart composed his first piece of music at the age of five.

▼ Playing music

Music is played on instruments such as the piano, recorder or clarinet. Many children learn to play a musical instrument at school. Can you play any of these instruments?

trumpet

guitar

violin

flute

◀ Traditional dances

In African villages, dances are usually performed to celebrate important events such as births and weddings. These people from Gambia sing and clap as they dance in time to the beat of the drums.

▲ Electronic sounds

Many modern musicians use electronic instruments to create sounds in recording studios. These instruments, called synthesizers, can copy perfectly the sound of, say, a drum or a guitar.

Word box

float
a vehicle decorated to be in a street parade

orchestra
large group of musicians playing different instruments

▶ Carnival dances

In Brazil, people dance in the street during carnival time. They wear brightly coloured costumes and perform a dance called the samba. They compete for prizes in a parade of magnificent floats.

Music and dance in history

Find out more:
Art ◄
Theatre ►

Stone Age people used to make pipes and whistles from bones and reeds. Drums too have been used for many thousands of years. People danced in honour of the gods or as a thanksgiving for spring or the harvest. Different kinds of music developed across the world at the same time.

▼ Flamenco!

Flamenco music is played in Spain. It includes strummed guitars, singing, shouting and clapping. Dancers strut, whirl and stamp. Flamenco probably began in the 1400s, when the Roma people (gypsies) first arrived in Europe. Over the years it has blended with Arab, Jewish and Spanish musical styles.

▲ Ancient Egypt

Ancient Egyptian musicians played harps, rattles and bells while dancers performed in temples and at royal feasts.

Wolfgang Amadeus Mozart

Johann Sebastian Bach

►▲ Great composers

In Europe, a great tradition of music developed. Two of the greatest composers were the German Johann Sebastian Bach, who lived from 1685 to 1750, and the Austrian Wolfgang Amadeus Mozart, who lived from 1756 to 1791.

◄ That's jazz!

From the early 1900s, African American bands played a new kind of music called jazz. Players made up some of it as they went along. Louis Armstrong (1901–71) was one of the greatest jazz stars.

Native Americans

Find out more:
New World ▶ United States of America ▶
Wild West ▶

Perhaps as much as 30,000 years ago, hunters from Asia crossed into North America. They were the ancestors (distant relatives) of the Native Americans, the first people to live in what is now the United States. Native American peoples lived by hunting and fishing, and many also became farmers.

birch bark canoe

▲ Travelling light

Around the Great Lakes and rivers of the Midwest, canoes made of birch bark were the best way of travelling.

▼ Plains hunters

Peoples of the Great Plains hunted buffalos which roamed the prairies. Buffalos provided meat and skins for making clothes. People lived in tents called tipis that were also sewn together from buffalo skins.

▲ Troubled times

In the 1800s, more and more settlers of European descent moved into the United States. They called the Native Americans 'Indians'. They stole their land and killed the buffalo. From the 1860s to the 1890s, the Native Americans were defeated in a series of brutal wars.

▲ Ancient ones

A farming people who lived in the canyons of the southwest between about AD500 and 1200 are known as the Anasazi, or 'ancient ones'. By the 1100s, they were living in cliff dwellings, like these ones at Mesa Verde.

Nests

Our homes are, in a way, our nests. A nest is a place where a creature can safely rest and raise its young. It is usually comfortable, lined with grass, moss, hairs, leaves or feathers. Birds are well-known nesters. Some build nests from twigs. Others peck a hole in a tree or steal another animal's burrow. Many other animals make nests too, from ants to alligators.

bubbles

cichlids

► Bubble-nesting fish

Some fish make nests of mud, twigs, pebbles – or bubbles. Certain gouramis and cichlids 'blow' long-lasting bubbles with a foamy liquid. The bubbles collect under a leaf or among stems. The female lays her eggs there and the male protects them until the baby fish develop.

▲ Wasp nest

Insects that make nests include bees, wasps, ants and termites. Wasps make a papery substance by chewing wood with their saliva (spit), and build their nest with it.

Wow!

The biggest mammal nests, made in bushes by wild pigs and hogs, are 3 metres across, with bent-over branches forming a roof.

▲ Food delivery

Many birds use natural holes rather than building a nest. The colourful hoopoe of Europe, Africa and Asia nests in a hole or opening in a bank, wall, tree or even a building. The female sits on her eggs to keep them warm and safe for about 18 days, and the male brings her food.

New World

In 1492, a European explorer called Christopher Columbus landed in the Americas. He was the first of many. Soon the Spanish and Portuguese were greedily claiming large areas of Central and South America, while the English, Dutch and French were settling in North America. They had discovered a 'New World' of land and natural riches.

▲ Conquistadors

Spanish soldiers called *conquistadors* invaded Mexico in 1519. Their leader was called Hernán Cortés. His forces defeated the Aztec people who lived there.

▲ Pocahontas

Pocahontas lived from 1595 to 1617. She was the daughter of a Native American chief called Powhatan. She tried to make peace between her people and the English, who were settling in Virginia. She married John Rolfe, one of the settlers, but died during a visit to England.

◄ African slaves

In the 1500s, the Europeans started a cruel trade in slaves. People were taken by force from West Africa and shipped to the Americas. There, rich landowners made them work for no money on plantations of sugar or cotton.

► The Pilgrims

These English people left Europe because of their strict religious beliefs and so became known as 'pilgrims'. In 1620, they sailed to North America in a ship called *The Mayflower*. They built a new settlement called Plymouth.

Word box

plantation
a piece of land given over to the growing of a particular crop for money

slave
someone whose freedom is taken away and who is forced to work for no money

Little islands and coral reefs are scattered over a vast area of the South Pacific Ocean. Over thousands of years they were settled by seafarers. We call these peoples Melanesians, Micronesians and Polynesians. They grew coconuts and sweet potatoes, fished and raised pigs. In the 1800s, many of the islands were settled by Europeans.

▲ The voyagers

The Polynesians originally came from Southeast Asia, sailing in canoes. Between about 1500BC and AD1000 they settled an area of ocean twice the size of the USA.

▲ Big heads

In about AD400, the Polynesians sailed from Tahiti to Easter Island. Between 1000 and 1600 they created these huge heads of carved stone on the island.

▲ The Maoris

A Polynesian people called the Maoris reached New Zealand over a thousand years ago. They hunted the big birds that lived there and farmed the land. Maoris continue to live in New Zealand, keeping their traditions and ceremonies alive.

◄ Wool wagons in New Zealand

In the 1800s, British settlers came to New Zealand for sheep-farming. Here they are using ox-carts to carry bales of wool to market.

Normans

In the AD900s, the Vikings made many attacks on northern France. The French king decided to buy some peace by giving them land. Their leader, Hrolf, married a French princess called Giselle. This region became known as Normandy ('land of the Northmen') and their descendants were known as Normans.

▼ William the Conqueror

Duke William of Normandy was crowned King of England in London, on Christmas Day 1066. Within two years, most of the country was under Norman rule.

▲ Battle of Hastings

In the summer of 1066, a big Norman fleet arrived on the south coast of England. Their knights attacked the English near Hastings, and killed King Harold II. The Bayeux Tapestry (above) tells the story of the battle.

▲ Domesday Book

The Normans wanted to make the English pay taxes. To do this, they wrote down details of nearly all the land in England. In the 1080s, this information was put together in the Domesday Book.

Wow!

Hrolf, the first Duke of Normandy, was said to be so tall that he could not ride a horse. He was nicknamed 'the ganger', which means 'walker'.

▼ Normans ashore

In 1060, the Normans invaded the island of Sicily, in Italy. They conquered England in 1066, and went on to seize land in Wales and Ireland and to settle in parts of Scotland.

North America

Find out more:
World ▶

North America is made up of the three large countries of Canada, the United States of America and Mexico, as well as a number of smaller countries. These smaller nations include the island of Greenland, the small countries of Central America and the islands dotted around the Caribbean Sea.

▼ Tallest trees

Thick forests of huge redwoods, cedars, firs and spruces can be found in California and Oregon.

These huge trees thrive on mountain side slopes which face the Pacific Ocean. Redwoods are the tallest living things and can grow to heights of 80 metres.

▶ From north to south

In the far north of the continent of North America are the frozen lands of Alaska, which border the Arctic Ocean. Mountains run down both the east and west sides of the continent, with wide plains, long rivers and large lakes in the centre. In the far south are the sandy beaches of the Caribbean islands and the hot, wet jungles of Central America.

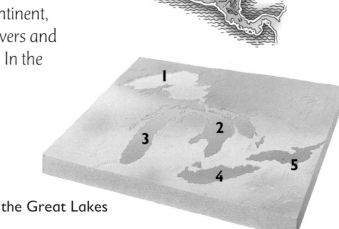

the Great Lakes

◀ Very deep

In the southwest of the continent is the amazing Grand Canyon, the deepest canyon in the world. This steep-sided valley was carved out by the Colorado river over millions of years.

▲ Great Lakes

On the border between Canada and the United States are the five Great Lakes: **1** Superior, **2** Huron, **3** Erie, **4** Ontario, **5** Michigan. Together these lakes make up the largest body of fresh water to be found anywhere in the world. Lake Superior is the biggest of all fresh water lakes.

Numbers

Numbers are how we store information about amounts. They also let us calculate (do sums). In the simplest type of calculation, we use our fingers to help us count. Modern computers can make trillions of calculations in just one second.

▲ Fun with numbers

Numbers can be fun! Many games use numbers to count scores and to have fun with your skill and luck. Card and dice games are major number-users. They have been played for hundreds of years and are still popular.

▲ Computer bits

Computers use a code called the binary code to make calculations. This code uses only two numbers: 0 and 1. Each 0 or 1 is called a 'bit', short for binary digit. The 'bits' combine in different ways to make letters, symbols and numbers. Each combination of 'bits' is called a 'byte'.

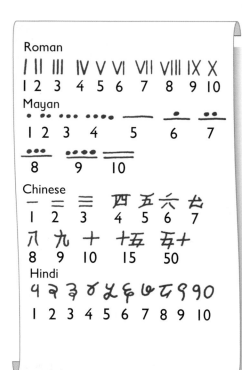

Roman									
I	II	III	IV	V	VI	VII	VIII	IX	X
1	2	3	4	5	6	7	8	9	10

Mayan
1 2 3 4 5 6 7
8 9 10

Chinese
一 二 三 四 五 六 七
1 2 3 4 5 6 7
八 九 十 十五 五十
8 9 10 15 50

Hindi
१ २ ३ ४ ५ ६ ७ ८ ९ १०
1 2 3 4 5 6 7 8 9 10

▲ Round the world

Many civilizations invented systems of numbers. Most ancient systems did not use the number zero. This made counting hard. Arabic numbers are now the main system, because they are easy to use.

Wow!
Any number between 10 and 99, when written three times, can be divided by seven to give a whole number as a result. For example, 121212 divided by 7 = 17316

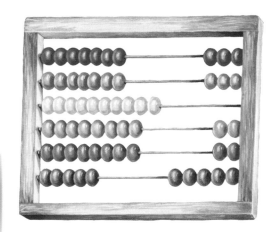

▲ Ancient adding

The abacus is a very ancient adding machine. It uses a series of sliding beads to count, and it is still used today in some countries. It looks very simple, but with practice people can add large sums really quickly.

Oceania

Australia is by far the largest country in the continent of Oceania. The two other sizeable countries are New Zealand and Papua New Guinea. The rest of Oceania is made up of hundreds of islands in the Pacific Ocean.

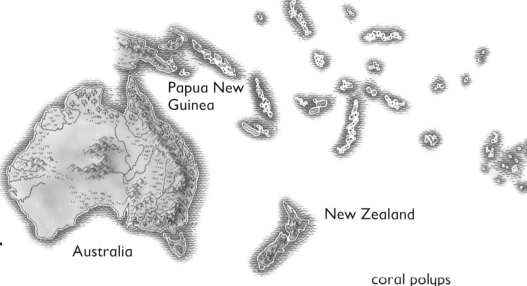

Papua New Guinea

New Zealand

Australia

▲ Traditional craft workers

Wood carving is a traditional craft of the Maoris of New Zealand. They decorate their meeting house with carvings.

▲ Island continent

The land of Australia is mostly flat. In the east, mountains separate the dry inland areas from a narrow strip of fertile land along the coast. New Zealand is made up of two islands: North Island and South Island. High mountain peaks, active volcanoes, hot, bubbling springs and green lowlands are to be found on the islands. Mountains and thick forests cover much of Papua New Guinea, Oceania's third largest country.

coral polyps

▲ The largest reef

The Great Barrier Reef lies off the northeastern coast of Australia. It is the world's largest coral reef and stretches for 2,000 kilometres. Coral is made up of the skeletons of tiny sea animals called polyps.

▶ Koalas

The koala is one of Australia's most famous animals. It eats only one kind of food – the young leaves and shoots of eucalyptus trees. Like a kangaroo, a koala mother keeps her baby in a pouch on her stomach.

▶ Active volcanoes

On the small islands around New Zealand can be found active volcanoes. This means there is a chance they could erupt. This volcano is on White Island and it often gives off smoke.

Oceans and life

Find out more:
Animal kingdom ◄ Fish ◄
Oceans and seas ► Water ►

The oceans are filled with living things. These range from the tiny shrimp-like creatures that float on the surface to strange-looking fish that crawl across the sea-bed. Most ocean creatures live in the warmer, sunlit waters near the surface, where most of their food supply is found.

▼ Floating life

Tiny plants and animals called plankton drift across the surface of the water in huge numbers. They become food for larger ocean creatures.

▼ Ocean creatures

Sharks, dolphins and turtles live near the water's surface. Large mammals such as the sei whale dive to lower levels. The waters at the bottom of the ocean receive almost no sunlight. Only a few kinds of sea creatures can survive in this cold, dark world.

1 dusky dolphin	8 sunfish	14 banded sea snake
2 kittiwake	9 turtle	15 tuna
3 right whale	10 cuttlefish	16 squid
4 jellyfish	11 tiger shark	17 mako shark
5 great skuas	12 yellow-bellied	18 nautilus
6 common dolphin	sea snake	19 white-sided dolphin
7 broad-billed prion	13 tarpon	20 sei whale

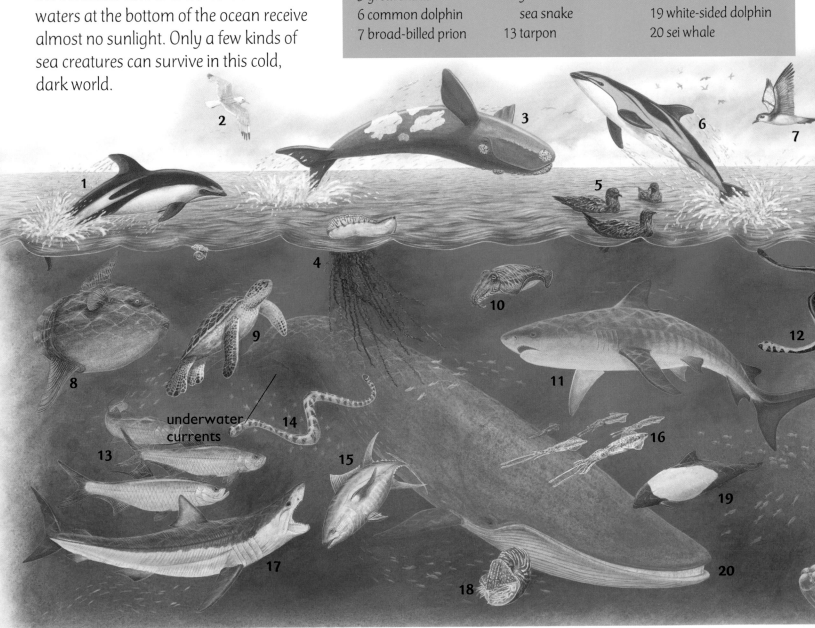

underwater currents

Oceans and seas

Oceans and seas cover more than two-thirds of the Earth's surface. Amazingly, they contain 97 percent of all the water in the world. The oceans are about four kilometres deep on average, but in some places the ocean floor plunges down even deeper. The deepest place in the world is at the bottom of the Pacific Ocean – the Marianas Trench is more than 11 kilometres below the water's surface.

Wow!

In May 1985, a tsunami struck the shores of Bangladesh, killing more than 10,000 people.

► Ocean waters

There are five great oceans, which are joined together by smaller seas and other stretches of water. From largest to smallest, the oceans are: the Pacific, the Atlantic, the Indian, the Arctic and the Southern.

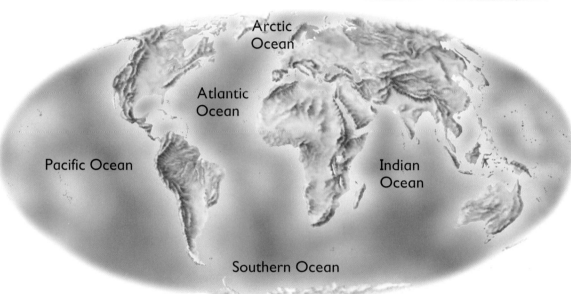

Arctic Ocean

Atlantic Ocean

Pacific Ocean

Indian Ocean

Southern Ocean

► Moving water

The water in our oceans and seas is always moving. As wind blows across the water's surface, it creates waves. Waves move around the world in swirling, circular patterns called currents.

surface currents

wave movement

▼ Giant waves

Earthquakes under the sea-bed can produce giant waves that race towards land at speeds as fast as 970 kilometres an hour. These waves may be 30 metres high near the shore. They are called *tsunamis*.

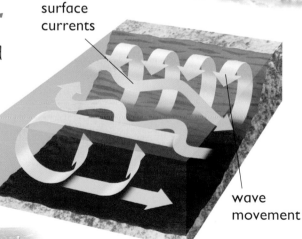

◄ Seaweed harvest

Some farmers grow seaweed. In shallow, tropical waters, people grow their own on plots on the seabed. The harvested seaweed is a useful ingredient in products such as plant fertilizer and ice cream.

Oil and gas

We use oil and gas to power our cars, planes and trains, to heat our homes, and to make electricity. Oil supplies about half of all the energy we use in the world. We find oil and gas in rocks deep under the ground or below the sea-bed.

▲ Out at sea

This oil rig is floating in the middle of the sea off the coast of Scotland. Special anchor ropes hold the rig in place. Oil workers sleep, eat and work on the rig or on a separate rig nearby. They travel to and from the rig by helicopter.

► Transporting oil

The oil taken from under the ground or under the sea is called crude oil. It is transported along a pipeline or by a tanker. The tanker may be a ship, lorry or part of a train. The oil is taken to a refinery where it is turned into petrol for cars, diesel fuel for lorries and buses, and lots of other useful substances.

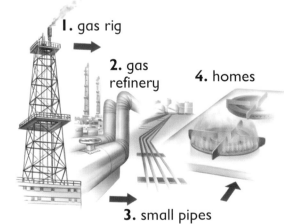

▼ Burning gas

We burn gas to heat our homes and for cooking. Gas comes into our homes through pipes under the ground. Many factories use gas to heat and cut metals.

► Useful products

Plastic items, lipstick, soap powder, fertilizer, nylon and paint – these are just some of the many things we make from oil.

paint

soap powder

plastic cutlery set

lipstick

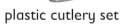

1. gas rig

2. gas refinery

4. homes

3. small pipes

◄ Running out

Almost half of the world's crude oil is used to make fuel for cars and small planes. But one day this oil will run out. Scientists think that there is possibly only enough oil to last for another 50 or 60 years.

Wow!

The Trans-Alaska Pipeline in North America crosses three mountain ranges, hundreds of kilometres of frozen ground and 300 rivers and streams.

Owls

No other bird looks quite like an owl.
There are about 200 kinds. These birds hunt prey in darkness using their huge eyes and amazingly good hearing. They catch it with their large, strong toes tipped with sharp talons. By day, most owls rest on a branch or in a hollow tree, cave or quiet building.

◄ Tawny owl

Most medium-sized owls, such as the tawny, hunt mice, rats, baby rabbits, insects such as large beetles and grasshoppers, and perhaps small birds and bats. As it rests on a tree branch by day, its patterned brown plumage makes it very difficult to see.

◄ Spotted eagle owl

Eagle owls are among the biggest owls, with wings spanning 150 centimetres. They mainly catch other birds as they sleep, including pigeons, blackbirds and thrushes. Bats and other owls, such as tawnies, are also their prey, and they even snatch baby eagles or hawks from their nests.

Wow!

The barn owl lives almost everywhere except icy Antarctica – no other land bird is so widespread.

Word scramble

Unscramble these words to find the names of five types of owls:

a. NOWYS
b. NYWAT
c. NOGL-REDEA
d. SHROT-RAEDE
e. RINGOWRUB

answers
a. snowy b. tawny
c. long-eared d. short-eared
e. burrowing

► Barn owl

The ghostly-white barn owl once roosted and nested in hollow trees or caves, but barns, churches and outbuildings do just as well. Like other owls it has a wide, round, bowl-shaped face. Its feathers have very soft edges so they make almost no sound as the owl flies and swoops.

Pets

Some of our best friends are animals – dogs, cats, gerbils, hamsters and budgies. Pets are animals we look after, and they provide interest and fun. Some people keep unusual pets such as snakes or lizards, or even tarantulas! Various kinds of pets are popular in different parts of the world, such as monkeys in Asia, parrots in South America, possums in Australia, raccoons in North America and mongooses in Africa.

Word scramble

Unscramble these words to find the names of five types of dogs and cats:

a. PANSILE
b. BATYB
c. BOLARRAD
d. SEEMAIS
e. REXBO

answers
a. spaniel b. tabby c. labrador d. siamese e. boxer

◄ Lots of space

A pony needs lots of space, time, food and care. It can give rides or pull a cart. Like many pets, it can be taken to shows and maybe win prizes!

zebra fish

◄ Fish

Fish in an aquarium or tank depend completely on their owner. They need to be fed daily. The tank must be regularly topped up with water – and cleaned out.

◄ Best friend

Dogs can be marvellous pets, but sometimes they have a hard time. They may not be taken for enough walks. They try to behave well, but their owners may teach them badly, and then shout at them. With time and thought from a caring owner, a dog's life can be very happy.

▼ Suitable pet

Hamsters are small, quiet, and happy in a large cage with plenty of toys, tunnels and rooms. They suit people who have little space.

► Pet needs

Cats can look after themselves and be left alone more than dogs. But like any pet, they have needs – fresh water, healthy food and cleaning out when necessary. Cats need a quiet place to rest and sleep, and, like other cuddly pets, a friendly stroke.

bulldog

Photography

Photography is the process of making pictures by using light. Photographs are made using cameras. Like the human eye, some cameras take in light from an object, and record this image on film. Images can also be produced in digital cameras, which, instead of using film, are processed in computers.

▲ Digital photos

Ordinary cameras record pictures on film, but the modern digital camera records them in electronic form. The pictures can be loaded into a computer, printed or viewed on screen. The digital image can be changed in any way you want.

Wow!

Some cameras can see in the dark. They make a black and white picture by picking up the faintest traces of light from the stars or the Moon.

▼ Old times

The first photographs were made in the 1840s. Early photography used a different method for printing. Instead of being printed in black and white, the pictures came out in a brownish colour called sepia.

▼ Get snappy!

Modern automatic cameras do most of the work for you! They control the amount of light falling onto the film, the size of the image, and how long the light falls on the film (the shutter speed). With the older manual camera, you would have to make all these calculations and adjustments yourself.

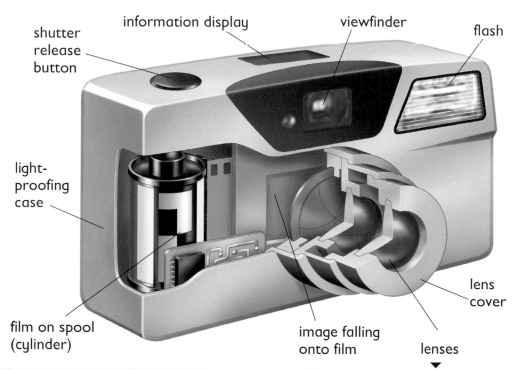

shutter release button

information display

viewfinder

flash

light-proofing case

film on spool (cylinder)

image falling onto film

lenses

lens cover

▶ Watch out!

Digital cameras are now made so small that they can be fitted into a watch. Wrist camera watches record images which can then be transferred to a computer and viewed in full colour.

Pirates

The sight every sailor feared was a pirate ship on the horizon.
For thousands of years, pirates robbed ships and attacked or killed their crews. Some pirates were adventurers seeking treasure and thrills. Others were murderers and madmen.

▲ Buccaneers

All sorts of outlaws and criminals settled on the Caribbean islands in the 1600s. These 'buccaneers' lived by hunting wild pigs and by attacking Spanish ships that were laden with treasure from the New World.

▲ Women pirates

Mary Read and Anne Bonny dressed as men and sailed with pirate crews in the Bahamas. The whole crew was captured in 1720 but the women were not executed.

▶ Blackbeard

Edward Teach, or 'Blackbeard', terrorized the North American coast, in his ship the *Queen Anne's Revenge*. He was killed in 1718 and his head was cut off. People believe he buried treasure somewhere before he died. They have been searching for it ever since!

Wow!

When Blackbeard went into battle, he lit the fuses used to fire guns and tied them in his hair. They smoked and fizzled and made him look like the devil!

▶ Scary flags

Pirate captains flew their own flags, called blackjacks, to strike terror into the enemy.

Planets

Planets are large bodies of rock, metal and gas that travel round a star. Nine planets, including Earth, orbit our own star, the Sun. The Earth is a small planet, while planets such as Jupiter and Saturn are far bigger. Earth is the only planet that is the right distance from the Sun for any life to exist here.

Word box

orbit
travel round

star
a ball of very hot gas

► Saturn's rings

Saturn is often called the Ringed Planet. It is the second largest planet in our Solar System, almost ten times the size of Earth. It is surrounded by flat rings that can be clearly seen through a telescope. They are only one kilometre thick – the planet's width is 60,000 kilometres. Although the rings look smooth, they are made up of millions of pieces of ice and rock. These orbit the planet and stretch thousands of kilometres out into space.

▼ Our Solar System

Together with the Sun, various moons and lumps of rock, the planets make up the Solar System. Mercury, Venus, Earth and Mars are known as the 'inner planets' because they are closest to the Sun. Jupiter, Saturn, Uranus, Neptune and Pluto lie farther away, so are known as the 'outer planets'. Outer planets take much longer for each orbit – Pluto takes 248 of our years.

Sun
Venus Mercury
Moon Earth
Jupiter Mars
Saturn
Uranus
Neptune
Pluto

Plant kingdom

Find out more:
Energy ◀ Plant life ▶

Like the animal kingdom, the plant kingdom includes a huge range of living things. Unlike animals, plants can make their own food, from water and air. Using photosynthesis, they change sunlight into sugar. This gives them energy for life and growth.

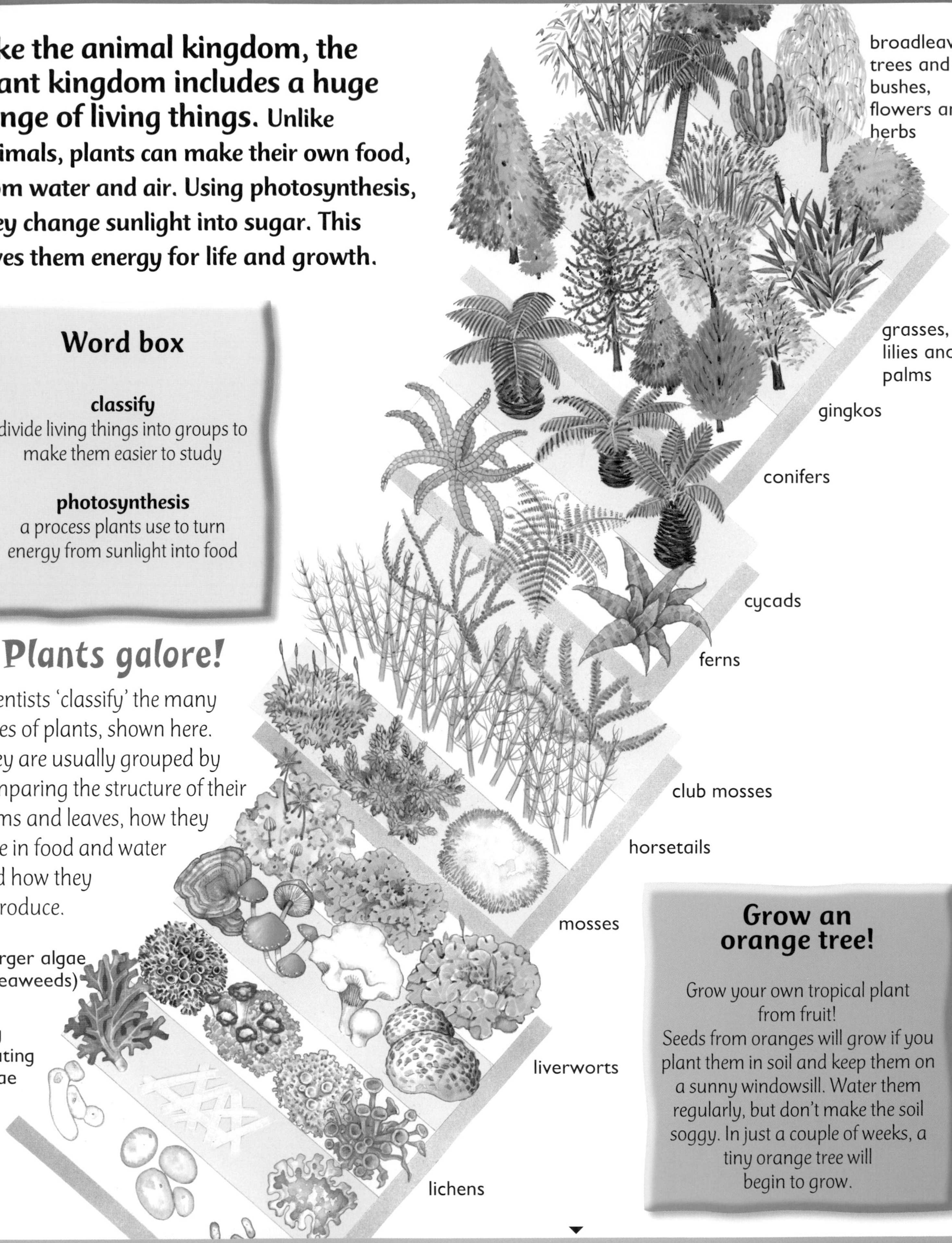
broadleaved trees and bushes, flowers and herbs
grasses, lilies and palms
gingkos
conifers
cycads
ferns
club mosses
horsetails
mosses
liverworts
lichens
larger algae (seaweeds)
tiny floating algae

Word box

classify
divide living things into groups to make them easier to study

photosynthesis
a process plants use to turn energy from sunlight into food

▶ Plants galore!

Scientists 'classify' the many types of plants, shown here. They are usually grouped by comparing the structure of their stems and leaves, how they take in food and water and how they reproduce.

Grow an orange tree!

Grow your own tropical plant from fruit!
Seeds from oranges will grow if you plant them in soil and keep them on a sunny windowsill. Water them regularly, but don't make the soil soggy. In just a couple of weeks, a tiny orange tree will begin to grow.

Plant life

The way a plant lives depends on many things, such as climate and soil. The simplest plants, such as algae ('*algee*'), do not even need soil. They grow in ponds, lakes and oceans. Other plants, such as cacti ('*cacteye*'), grow in dry deserts. They can live without water for long periods of time.

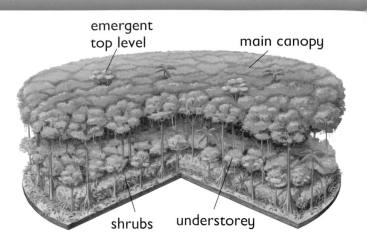

emergent top level • main canopy • shrubs • understorey

◀ Desert plants

Cacti are specially adapted to stop them from losing too much water in the hot sun. They are often covered with spikes, to prevent animals from eating them.

▲ Layers and layers

In tropical rainforests, different plants grow at different heights, depending on the amount of light available. Sunlight passes through the highest trees to a more even layer — the main canopy. This thick layer blocks out most of the light, so that only a few plants, creepers or bushes, can grow underneath.

Word box

canopy
layer of plants in the rainforest 'roof'

understorey
layer of plants in the rainforest found below the main canopy

▲ Going up...

Weather conditions get colder and windier high up in the mountains. On lower slopes, conifer trees such as pines and firs grow. Higher up, above what is called the tree-line, it is too cold for trees. Instead, shrubs, grasses and tiny flowers grow.

▶ Living together

Scientists are always trying to find out more about how plants and humans live together. *Biosphere 2* was an enclosed living space where people stayed for a while. They experimented with growing many types of plants in different conditions.

Pollution

Find out more:
Conservation ◄

Humans do all kinds of things that produce waste materials, and these pollute our world. Smoke from factories damages the air. Waste from factories, homes and similar places pours into rivers and is carried out to sea. Cars and other vehicles produce huge amounts of pollution in many of the world's cities, even making it hard to breathe.

▼ Self-destruction

We are beginning to see the damage we are doing to the world around us. New filters and chemicals called catalysts can reduce dangerous fumes. Many organizations are now working to stop us doing further harm. But we still have a long way to go.

Wow!

If pollution continues at the current rate, 30 to 50 per cent of all living species may be extinct by the middle of the 21st century.

▲ Water pollution

Factory and human waste are the usual causes of river pollution. These waste materials take oxygen from the water. This kills fish and other water life.

factories pump out chemicals that escape into the atmosphere, making rainwater acidic. This can kill trees and damage soil

cutting down trees destroys forests and wildlife

factories make huge piles of waste

rubbish is dumped in rivers or landfill sites

exhaust fumes from traffic can make it hard to breathe

Prehistoric life

Find out more:
Art ◄ Dinosaur ages ◄ Dinosaurs ◄

The first human beings lived on Earth a long time ago – around two million years ago.
At this time most of the world was cold and icy, but Africa, South America and parts of Asia were warmer. These early people learned how to make fire, hunted animals and made simple tools from wood, stone and animal bones.

Word box

bison
huge prehistoric cattle

prehistoric
the time before history was written down

woolly mammoth

▼ A long time ago

The word 'prehistoric' means the time before people could write. It is the time before about 5,000 years ago. This period of prehistory is called the Stone Age. People made their own tools and weapons out of stone.

this stone tool was used for scraping flesh from the skin of wild animals

▲ Making fire

The earliest use of fire-making was for warmth. But people eventually discovered the uses of fire – for cooking, to shape weapons and tools, and to give light.

▲ Mammoth hunts

Early people hunted birds, small reptiles and larger animals such as deer, bison, bears and huge elephant-like animals called woolly mammoths.

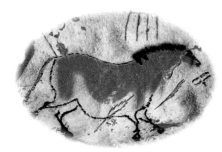

▲ Cave art

Prehistoric people painted pictures of animals and everyday life on cave walls. The first person to find any of these pictures was a 12-year-old Spanish girl, more than 100 years ago.

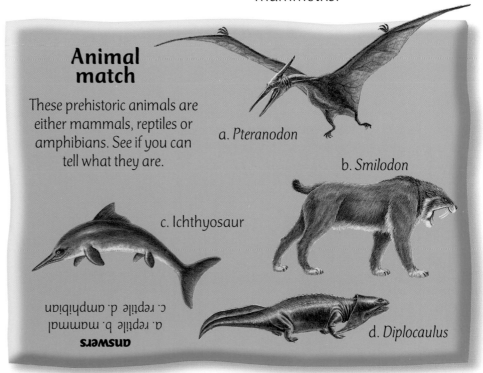

Animal match

These prehistoric animals are either mammals, reptiles or amphibians. See if you can tell what they are.

a. *Pteranodon*

b. *Smilodon*

c. Ichthyosaur

d. *Diplocaulus*

answers
a. reptile b. mammal c. reptile d. amphibian

Rainforests

Rainforests are thick forests of tall trees that grow in hot, rainy parts of the world. These forests stay green all year round. The largest rainforest of all, the Amazon, takes up one-third of the continent of South America. Many thousands of different kinds of animals and plants live in rainforests.

▼ Top to bottom

A rainforest is packed with life. The treetops form a covering, called the canopy. Eagles (1), monkeys (2), butterflies (3) and macaws (4) live in the canopy. Sloths (5) hang from the middle branches, and jaguars (6) climb into lower branches. On the forest floor, millipedes (7) and beetles (8) move through the leaves.

► Bright colours

Many rainforest animals are very colourful, like this orange bird wing butterfly. Its colours warn other animals that it is not good to eat.

Wow!

Every second, humans cut down an area of tropical rainforest that measures the same size as a football pitch.

▼ Destruction

Farmers clear land in rainforests by cutting down trees and burning them. The soil in many rainforests is poor, and after a few years the farmers' crops no longer grow well. This means they have to clear another patch of rainforest. In this way people are destroying large areas of the world's rainforests.

◄ Rainy forest

In a tropical rainforest, you need your umbrella every day! Rainforests have rainy weather all year round – but there is still a wet and a dry season. It is just that the wet season is even wetter!

Recycling

Pollution is less of a problem when waste materials are reused instead of being thrown away. Glass is easily melted down for recycling. Paper can also be recycled, saving millions of trees. Today there are all kinds of schemes that help people to recycle things.

▼ How we recycle

Waste material from homes and factories is taken to recycling centres. In the recycling process, useful materials are picked out and stored, ready to be changed back into many of the things we use every day.

Recycle it!

Keep an eye on the things that your family throws away each day – but don't start sorting through yucky rubbish! Try to think of things that could be taken to your local recycling centre, such as paper, plastic, cans and bottles. As much as half of your family's waste can be recycled.

▲ Farming trees

Instead of destroying forest trees for wood and paper, it is better to grow trees specially, on big plantations like this one. Fast-growing trees are used. They are cut down as soon as they reach a useful size and are quickly replaced with new trees.

1. used glass or plastic bottles, aluminium cans and newspapers are collected from recycling centres

2. the objects are recycled to make raw materials

3. the raw materials are reused to make new bottles, cans and paper

▲ Sorting it out

Useful rubbish from ordinary homes needs to be sorted out first by hand, before it goes to the recycling centre.

Religion

As people tried to make sense of the world around them, they came to believe in spirits and gods, in good and in evil. Many of today's world faiths have their origins in Asia. They share some of the same values and ideas.

▲ The Buddha

Siddhartha was a prince who lived from about 563BC to 483BC. He gave up his wealth, declaring that it is worldly desire that makes people unhappy. He became known as the Buddha, which means 'the enlightened one'. Buddhism spread through India, Sri Lanka, China, Japan and Southeast Asia.

Word box

enlightened
seeing the light, or understanding the truth

prophet
someone who speaks the words of God

▼ Prayer for all

Muslims believe that there is only one God, Allah, and that Muhammad is his prophet. Muslims pray five times a day, facing Mecca – in the morning, afternoon, mid-afternoon, after sunset and at bedtime.

▶ Hindu beliefs

Hinduism grew up in India over 5,000 years ago. Hindus believe that we are reborn many times. Some believe in many different gods and goddesses, others in one god that appears in various forms.

◀ Jesus

Christians believe that a Jew called Jesus, who lived 2,000 years ago, was the Son of God. They believe he was killed by the Romans, but came back to life and then went to heaven. This picture of Christ was made in Roman Britain, when Christianity was beginning to spread across Europe.

◀ The Torah

The holy book of the Jews is the Torah, or Law. Jews believe that God gave it to a prophet called Moses over 2,100 years ago.

Religion and people

Find out more:
Religion ◄

Each religion has its own group of followers – Christians, Hindus, Buddhists, Muslims and Jews are some of the best-known ones. Many believers follow the rules of their religion very strictly. For example Muslims, who follow the religion of Islam, must pray five times each day: at sunrise, at midday, in the afternoon, in the evening and at sunset.

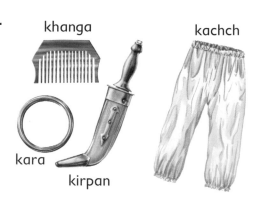

khanga

kachch

kara

kirpan

► Holy waters

The ancient religion of Hinduism is at least 4,000 years old. More than three-quarters of the people in India are Hindus. The Ganges river in India is a very holy place for them. Pilgrims come from all over India to bathe in its waters. By doing this they wash away their sins, and become pure.

▲ Religious symbols

The Sikh religion was founded in the Punjab area of India in the 1500s. Spiritual teachers set guide lines on how people should lead their lives. Followers of the religion wear the five 'Ks'— kesh (uncut hair), khanga (comb), kirpan (sword), kara (steel bangle) and kachch (knee-length trousers).

▲ Muslims at Mecca

The holiest place for Muslims is the city of Mecca in Saudi Arabia. Inside the Great Mosque is a black stone, which Muslims believe came from their God, whom they call Allah. All Muslims try to visit Mecca at least once in their life. Around one million people crowd into the city each year during the six days set aside for this visit.

▼ Let's all get together

Here, Jewish people are praying at the Western Wall in Jerusalem. This wall is the only remaining part of The Temple, a very holy place of worship founded by King Solomon almost 3,000 years ago. Jewish people travel from all over the world to pray here.

Religious buildings

Find out more:
India ◄ Japan and Korea ◄ Religion ◄

Ancient peoples often believed that parts of the landscape, such as mountains or springs, were holy. They soon began to build their own sacred places, too. These included shrines, places of worship such as temples or churches, and monasteries, where monks could live in peace.

► Lalibela

This Christian church is in the African country of Ethiopia. It was cut from solid rock nearly 800 years ago. It is in the shape of a Christian cross. In this picture, part of the rock has been cut away, to let you see the whole church.

entrance

▲ Way of the spirits

Traditional Japanese people believe that Mount Fuji is a holy mountain. It rises behind this Shinto shrine. Shinto means the 'way of the spirits' and is based on belief in the powers of nature. It is the most ancient religion in Japan.

▼ All-seeing eyes

Holy mounds called *stupas* have been built by Buddhists in Nepal for over 2,000 years. This one near Kathmandu is decorated with eyes looking north, south, east and west.

Religious symbols

Religions have used special symbols for thousands of years. Can you find out which symbol belongs to which religion?

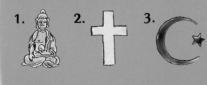

1.   2.   3.

a. Christianity **b.** Islam **c.** Buddhism

answers
1c, 2a, 3b

▼ Golden Temple

This beautiful temple, with its golden roofs and pools of water, is in Amritsar, India. It dates back to the 1500s and is the centre of the Sikh religion.

Renaissance

Find out more:
Art ◄

Between 1350 and 1600 there were many changes in Europe. This period has come to be called the Renaissance, meaning the rebirth. The Renaissance saw a growing interest in science, architecture, poetry, music and art, as well as ancient Greek and Roman culture. Students went to new universities in France, Italy and England.

a model of Leonardo da Vinci's helicopter design

▲ 'Look up!'

Michelangelo, an Italian genius, painted the ceiling of the Sistine Chapel in Rome between 1508 and 1512. Although he had to work on high scaffolding, often lying on his back, everyone agrees that these pictures are some of the best ever painted.

▲ Renaissance man

Leonardo da Vinci lived in Italy from 1452 to 1519. He was a brilliant artist, sculptor, inventor, engineer, architect and musician. This picture is based on a drawing he made of a helicopter. The first modern version, built in 1939, was inspired by his design.

◄ The city of Florence

The Renaissance began in Italy. The wealthy city of Florence became a centre of painting, architecture and sculpture. This is the Duomo, a cathedral that dates from 1296.

▲ New discoveries

The new interest in finding out how things worked led to great scientific discoveries. The Italian scientist Galileo Galilei, who lived from 1564 to 1642, studied the Sun, Moon and planets.

Reptiles

Find out more:
Animal kingdom ◀ Dinosaurs ◀
Reptiles of the world ▶

Alligators and crocodiles, lizards and snakes, tortoises and turtles are different kinds of reptile. Most reptiles have a dry skin covered with tough scales. Reptiles are cold-blooded, which means they lie in the sun to warm up before they can move around. There are about 6,000 different kinds of reptile.

Word box

flesh
the soft part of a body under the skin

snout
the nose and mouth parts of an animal

▲ Slow movers

Tortoises are very slow-moving reptiles. They live on land, whereas turtles live in water. Some live for over 150 years. The world's largest tortoise comes from the island of Aldabra off the coast of East Africa. It can reach 1.8 metres in length.

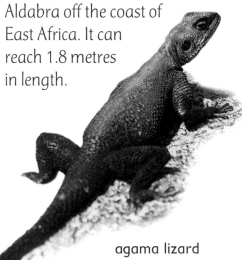

agama lizard

▲ Warming up

This lizard is warming its body in the sunshine. Unlike mammals, including humans, reptiles are cold-blooded. This means they have to bask in the sun to warm up and make themselves active. If they get too hot, they have to scuttle into some shade.

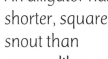
grass snake

▼ Fierce hunters

Alligators and crocodiles are fierce hunters with huge, sharp teeth. They use these teeth to hold onto prey in the water and to tear flesh. Their tails are long and powerful, helping them to swim swiftly. An alligator has a shorter, squarer snout than a crocodile.

◀ Egg layers

Most reptiles lay their eggs in a warm, dry place. The heat of the sunshine makes the eggs hatch. A mother grass snake may lay her eggs in compost or manure heaps. The heat given off by these heaps helps to speed up the development of the eggs.

Reptiles of the world

Find out more:
Animal kingdom ◄
Dinosaurs ◄ Reptiles ◄

Reptiles live in most places, except in the very cold areas in the far north and far south of the world. **Many snakes and lizards live in hot deserts. Some kinds of reptile, such as sea turtles, spend most of their life in the water.**

tree gecko

▶ On the beach

Mother sea turtles come onto land to lay their eggs. They bury the eggs in a hole in a sandy beach and then go back to sea. When the baby turtles hatch, they make their own way to the water. They have to avoid the hungry birds and crabs waiting to catch them.

▲ Sticky feet

The gecko is a lizard found in most warm countries. The biggest gecko lives in Southeast Asia and can be 30 centimetres in length. The tree gecko has hairs on its feet, which have a sticking effect. This enables it to walk on any surface, and even hang on by just one toe!

▼ Like a dinosaur

The tuatara lives on the islands of New Zealand. It belongs to a group of reptiles called 'beak heads', and first lived around the time of the dinosaurs, reptiles that roamed the Earth millions of years ago.

◄ Skin change

Many snakes, such as this grass snake, get rid of the skin on their body several times each year. The new skin grows under the old one and makes it loose. When the new skin is ready, the snake wriggles out of the old one.

▶ Dragon lizards

The Komodo dragon is the largest lizard and can grow up to three metres in length. It lives on small islands in Indonesia. These lizards are very fierce, and will eat almost anything. Perhaps that's how they got their dragon name!

Wow!

A lizard that lives in the forests of Asia can glide from tree to tree through the air — it is known as a 'flying dragon'.

We see only shadowy shapes near the surface. Yet rivers, lakes, streams, ponds and other fresh water habitats teem with animal life. In small puddles there are tiny worms and water-fleas that would easily fit into this 'o'. Then there are aquatic insects, snails, thousands of kinds of fish, frogs and snakes, waterbirds and otters. The largest water animals are giant hippos and crocodiles.

▼ Lightweight trotter

Jacanas or lilytrotters have very long toes, angled out wide to spread their weight, so they really can walk on lily pads. Like many waterbirds they swim well. They eat a mix of small animals and plants.

▲ Deadly teeth

Piranhas eat all kinds of foods, from seeds to worms. If a large animal in the water struggles or bleeds, dozens of piranhas gather in a 'feeding frenzy' and bite lumps off it. In a minute or two they strip its flesh, leaving just the bones.

Word scramble

Unscramble these words to find the names of five types of river and pond animals:

a. SHIFERGINK (bird)
b. RATEW WERSH (mammal)
c. ERGEN GROF (amphibian)
d. GIVNID ELEBET (insect)
e. SHERFRATEW SELSUM (shellfish)

answers
a. kingfisher b. water shrew c. green frog d. diving beetle e. freshwater mussel

◄ Grazing giant

Hippos wallow in African rivers and lakes by day, then graze on nearby grasslands at night. Males fight in water with their huge, tusk-like teeth to claim their territory, so they can mate with females.

Word box

freshwater
made of non-salty water

graze
to eat grasses and other low-growing plants

rodent
gnawing mammal, like a rat

► Huge gnawer

The capybara of South America is the largest rodent. It weighs 60 kilograms – as much as an adult person. It lives in family groups around swamps and lakes. To escape its main enemy on land, the jaguar, it dives into the water. But it may be snapped up by a crocodile-like caiman.

Rivers and lakes

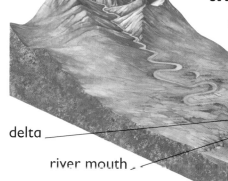

source
delta
river mouth

A river makes a long journey from its beginning, to the place where it empties into the sea, a lake or another river. Rivers give us water for drinking, washing and watering our crops. They also supply us with fish to eat. Rivers are important travel routes, and many towns and cities have grown up beside a river.

▲ Start to finish

The place where a river starts is called its source. It is often high up in the mountains, where melting snows begin to trickle downhill. Near the source, the land is often steep and the river is quite narrow, so its waters flow quickly. Lower down, the river becomes wider and flows more slowly and smoothly.

▶ Amazon

The huge Amazon river in South America carries more water than any other river in the world. It is so wide in places that if you stand on one bank you cannot see the river bank on the opposite side.

◀ Making a lake

A lake is an area of water with land all around it. Some very large lakes are actually called seas, for example the Dead Sea and the Caspian Sea. This is Lake Kariba in southern Africa. It is an artificial lake, which was made by blocking the waters of the Zambezi river.

Word box

artificial
made by people

rapids
part of a river where water moves quickly and dangerously

▼ Water sport

Fast-flowing rivers are exciting places for canoeists. Paddling through fast water is often called 'shooting the rapids'.

◀ Shopping by boat

In parts of Asia, people use waterways to buy and sell food. These Chinese people have come by boat to shop at a floating market.

Word scramble

Can you unscramble these words to find the names of five large rivers?

a. SMATHE
b. NIHER
c. ZANAMO
d. ISPISIMISPS
e. SGEGNA

answers
a. Thames b. Rhine
c. Amazon d. Mississippi
e. Ganges

Roads

Millions of motor cars, buses and lorries travel along roads each day. Fast, straight roads called motorways link cities and large towns together. In the countryside, small narrow roads run between villages. About 2,000 years ago, the Romans built paved roads across parts of Europe and North Africa.

▼ Building a road

To make a new road, huge earth-moving machines are used to cut away earth, flatten surfaces and smooth concrete.

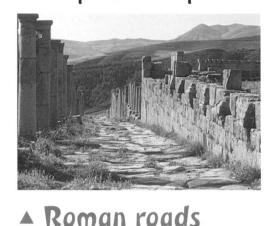

▲ Roman roads

The Romans built long, straight roads covered with flat stones, such as this one in Algeria, North Africa. They used these roads to move soldiers quickly from place to place.

1. a bulldozer pushes away earth

2. a scraper levels the ground and smooths a path

3. a dumptruck brings crushed rock

4. a grader smooths rocks to make a flat base

5. a paving machine spreads on a mixture of sand, stones and tar (asphalt), which is then rolled by a rolling machine

◀ So many roads

We are building more roads to cope with the increasing amounts of traffic. Motorways can help to take the strain of all this traffic away from smaller roads, where traffic jams may begin.

▼ Heavy loads

You see many huge lorries like this one on motorways and other fast roads. They transport large loads, often from one country to another. These very large lorries are called 'juggernauts'.

Wow!
The world's longest truck, the Arctic Snow Train, is over 170 metres long, has 54 wheels and needs a team of six drivers.

Rocks

The hard surface of the Earth is made of rock. Many of these rocks were made deep inside the Earth, where it is very hot. Other rocks formed from mud and sand, under enormous pressure (force) and heat.

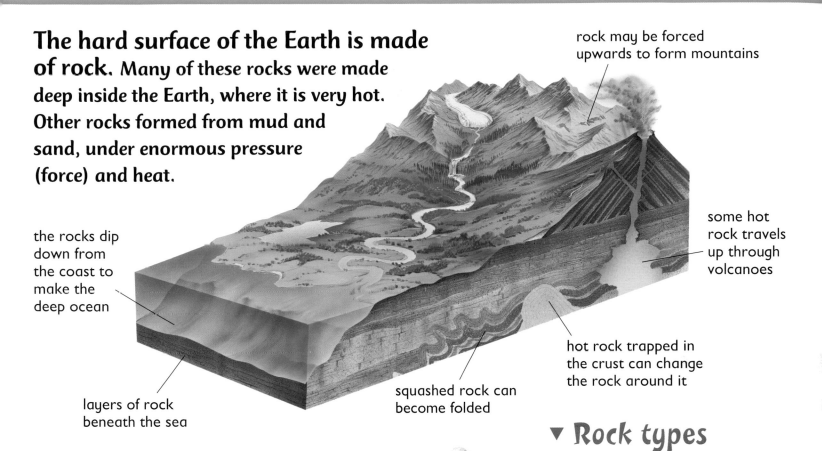

rock may be forced upwards to form mountains

some hot rock travels up through volcanoes

hot rock trapped in the crust can change the rock around it

squashed rock can become folded

the rocks dip down from the coast to make the deep ocean

layers of rock beneath the sea

▲ Above and below

Layers of rock form underground, in the Earth's crust. Some of the rock may be changed by great heat found deep inside the Earth. Rock can also be crushed and folded to form features such as mountain ranges.

chalk forms at the bottom of the seabed

limestone is made from seashells

mudstone is made from squashed mud

▼ Rock types

There are many different types of rock. Their appearance, colour and structure depend on how they were formed. Some form as a result of volcanic activity. Others are produced from material that is carried by rivers and deposited (dropped) in the sea.

► Wearing away

Strong desert winds carry grains of sand that erode (wear away) the rocks. Soft rocks may be worn into strange shapes like this arch. The sea and freezing weather can both wear away soft cliffs and rocks.

Rocks and minerals

Rocks are seen on hillsides and in mountains and river valleys. The tall cliffs at the seaside are made of rock. In other places you cannot see rocks because they are covered by soil and trees, grass and other plants. Every kind of rock is made up of smaller pieces called minerals.

► Buried treasure

Gold is a precious mineral that is found inside rocks, deep under the ground. Silver and quartz are other common minerals.

quartz

gold

silver

Word box

mineral
very small pieces of rock

monument
something built in memory of a special person or event

▼ Beautiful marble

A rock called marble comes in different colours and patterns. The ancient Greeks carved statues out of marble. Today, we use it for buildings, floor and wall tiles, as well as for monuments. The Taj Mahal in India (right) has beautiful marble detail.

▼ Diamonds

Diamond is the hardest substance in nature. This mineral is used in industry for cutting. Cut diamonds sparkle so brightly that they make valuable gemstones.

▼ Rare minerals

Some minerals are very rare and beautiful – and expensive too! We call them gemstones, or gems for short. Rubies, emeralds and sapphires are well-known gems that we make into jewellery and ornaments.

rubies

Wow!
About three-quarters of all the gold produced in the world each year comes from South Africa.

▼ Giant's rocks

The Giant's Causeway in Northern Ireland is made up of thousands of pillars of a black rock called basalt. It formed when hot, liquid rocks from deep inside the Earth gushed out onto the surface and then cooled and gradually hardened.

Match the names

Do you know the most common colour of these gemstones? Match the name of each gem with the correct colour.

1. **emerald**   a. **blue**
2. **sapphire**   b. **yellow**
3. **ruby**   c. **white**
4. **pearl**   d. **green**
5. **topaz**   e. **red**

1d 2a 3e 4c 5b
answers

Russia

Find out more:
World ▶

Russia is the biggest country in the world. Its western part was settled by a people called the Slavs after about AD400. In the Middle Ages the country was attacked by Mongols, but in the 1500s it united as a single country, with its capital at Moscow.

▼ St Basil's

In the AD800s, monks from the Byzantine Empire brought Christianity to the Slavs. This cathedral, with its colourful onion-shaped domes, is St Basil's, in the centre of Moscow. Building on it began in 1555.

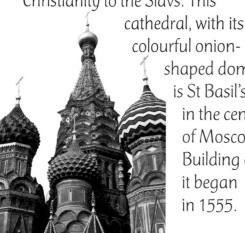

▶ Catherine the Great

Catherine the Great was empress of Russia from 1762 to 1796. Under her reign, Russia gained many new lands in Europe and Asia.

▲ Revolution, 1917

The tsar (emperor) and nobles in Russia had great power and wealth, while ordinary people had little freedom. Many of them starved. During the 1800s more and more Russians tried to change the way in which their country was ruled. After revolutions in 1917, the communists seized power. They wanted to give power to working people.

▶ Soviet Union

In 1922, the leader of the Russian Revolution, Lenin (left), founded a new country called the Soviet Union. In 1924, Stalin (right) became leader. Communist rule lasted until 1990, when the Soviet Union started to break up.

Lenin   Stalin

Wow!

When Peter the Great came to the throne in 1682, he hated the long, bushy beards worn by the nobles, so he ordered them all to shave. He even cut some of their beards off himself!

Scandinavia

Find out more:
Vikings ▶

The far north of Europe is called Scandinavia. It is a snowy land of forests and farmlands, taking in the countries of Norway, Sweden and Denmark. In about AD800, Scandinavia was home to the Vikings. In the later Middle Ages, they set up Christian kingdoms. Sometimes one ruler united the kingdoms, sometimes they were separate countries, as they are today.

▼ Sky watch

This building is an observatory for looking at the stars and planets. It was called *Uraniborg*, meaning 'Castle of the Heavens', and was built in 1576 by a Danish astronomer called Tycho Brahe.

▼ Wooden church

Wooden churches like this one were built in Norway during the Middle Ages. The Christian faith first reached Norway during the reign of King Olaf I, between AD995 and 1000.

▲ A battling king

In the 1600s, Sweden was one of the most powerful countries in Europe. It fought against the Holy Roman Empire during the Thirty Years War. The Swedes won the Battle of Lützen in 1632, but their king, Gustavus Adolphus, was killed in the fighting.

▼ The Little Mermaid

This statue in Copenhagen, Denmark, shows the Little Mermaid, from the famous story by Hans Christian Andersen. This author, who lived from 1805 to 1875, wrote many famous children's tales.

Word scramble

Can you unscramble these children's stories? They were all written by Hans Christian Andersen in the 1800s:

a. EHT YGLU GLINKCUD
b. HET WONS NEQUE
c. TEH NIT RODLIES
d. HET SROMPREE WEN SETHCOL

answers
a. *The Ugly Duckling*
b. *The Snow Queen*
c. *The Tin Soldier*
d. *The Emperor's New Clothes*

Schools

In the Stone Age, children were taught how to hunt or gather food by their parents. As people learned to write and do sums, children needed all sorts of new lessons, with teachers and proper schools. Often it was only the boys from rich families who were sent to school. Girls stayed at home and learned how to cook or sew.

▲ Class of 1898

This class was photographed in Canada in 1898. By then, education was beginning to spread and poor children, including girls, started going to school.

▲ In ancient Egypt

Egyptian boys went to school each morning. They learned to do sums and practised their writing on broken bits of pottery. They were expected to behave well and were beaten if they misbehaved.

▶ Learning to read

In the 1500s, English school children learned to read letters and standard sentences on this hand-held panel, called a 'hornbook'.

▶ Roman lessons

Roman children learned arithmetic. They learned to read and write in Greek, as well as in their own language, Latin. Older pupils were taught history, poetry and how to speak well in public.

Word box

arithmetic
a kind of mathematics that involves doing sums

education
teaching and learning

Sciences

Science is the study of everything about us, from the living world to the stars and planets. Sciences, such as astronomy and mathematics, are many centuries old. Other sciences, such as computer science, did not exist until 60 years ago. Science never stands still – new things are being discovered all the time.

► Which science?

There are many different kinds of science. Here are a few examples. All aim to examine a certain part of the world or Universe, and find an explanation. Many scientists work in more than one area, such as biochemistry (biology and chemistry).

Biology
How animals and plants live, grow, produce young and find food.
Why are leaves green?

Chemistry
What things are made from, and how they behave in different ways.
What is salt made of?

Physics
How the Universe works, how and why things happen to it.
How does an aircraft fly?

Geology
How the Earth was made, its structure, rocks and minerals.
How do mountains form?

Astronomy
The study of the Universe, its planets, stars and galaxies.
When did the Universe begin?

Archaeology
The study of ancient remains, such as skulls and bones.
How tall were the ancient Egyptians?

◄ Scientists at work

Some scientists work in laboratories. Here, they start with an idea, or theory, which asks how something will react in a certain situation. They then carry out experiments, or tests, to see what will happen. The results – what happens at the end – are written down and studied. Finally, the scientist thinks of reasons, or conclusions, for why certain things occurred during the experiment.

Scientists

Find out more:
Sciences ◂

The first true scientists were people who would not accept traditional or everyday ideas about how things worked, but wanted to find out for themselves. Their new ideas were often disliked by other people, who were used to thinking in a certain way.

1500s   **1600s**

1500   1550   1600   1650   1700

▼ **Leonardo da Vinci (1452–1519)**

An Italian artist who designed many devices, including a type of aircraft (see below). He also made detailed scientific drawings of the human anatomy.

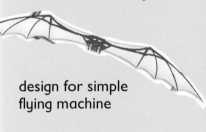

design for simple flying machine

▼ **Isaac Newton (1642–1727)**

An English mathematician who devised the laws of motion and gravity. He also built the first reflecting telescope.

▲ **Galileo Galilei (1564–1642)**

An Italian astronomer who invented the first thermometer, and proved that the planets move around the Sun.

◂▾ Great minds

This chart shows just a few of the many scientists who have made ground-breaking discoveries in the last 500 years. Of course, many brilliant thinkers existed before this time. Around 235BC, for example, a Greek mathematician called Archimedes made several important scientific discoveries. These included how levers work and why an object floats.

1700s   **1800s**   **1900s**

1700   1750   1800   1850   1900   1950   2000

▲ **Antoine Lavoisier (1743–1794)**

A French scientist who discovered water was made of oxygen and hydrogen. He began the modern system of naming chemicals.

▼ **Michael Faraday (1791–1867)**

An English scientist who invented many electrical machines, like the motor and the dynamo.

◂ **Albert Einstein (1879–1955)**

German-born physicist who made discoveries about space and time, and about nuclear energy and the atom bomb.

▸ **Alexander Fleming (1881–1955)**

A Scottish doctor who discovered penicillin, a substance important as an antibiotic (medicine used to treat illnesses).

Sea animals

Find out more:
Dolphins ◀ Fish ◀ Sharks ▶

The sea is the world's biggest habitat. It extends from rocky coasts, the shallows of coral reefs, and the icebergs of the polar regions. The vast open ocean stretches over most of the Earth and plumbs the darkest depths. Apart from insects, all kinds of animals live in the sea. Scientists are still discovering new kinds of creatures in bays, undersea caves and canyons.

▼ Snakes at sea?

Sea snakes are not just ordinary snakes out for a swim. They are fully suited to ocean life, with a flattened, paddle-like tail, for swimming. Sea snakes are cousins of cobras and just as poisonous, killing fish for food.

Word box

canyon
a deep, narrow, steep-sided valley

food chain
series of stages where a plant is eaten by an animal, and that animal is eaten by another, and so on

plankton
tiny plants and animals drifting in water

▲ Millions of fish

Small fish move around in vast shoals of many millions. They are important links in the sea food chains. They feed on tiny plants and animals in the plankton, then they become meals for bigger fish and other sea predators.

◀ 'Cow' of the sea

Manatees or dugongs live in tropical waters. They stay near the shore and eat sea-grasses and other plants, giving these animals the nickname of 'sea-cows'.

◀ Not what they seem

Sea creatures are often unfamiliar and puzzling. Jellyfish may look like floppy flowers, but they are proper animals – in fact they are deadly predators. Their trailing tentacles sting and capture prey, such as small fish.

▼

Sea birds

Sea birds depend on the sea for their food. Sea birds include huge albatrosses, smaller petrels and prions, tropic-birds, frigate-birds, gannets, boobies, gulls and auks. Most have long, slim wings for soaring, webbed feet for swimming and catch fish and squid from near the water's surface.

Wow!

The wandering albatross has the longest wings of any bird – more than 3 metres from tip to tip.

▲ Dive of death

The gannet plunge dives like an arrow from 30 metres up in the air and seizes its unsuspecting prey in its dagger-like bill.

▼ A place to breed

Most sea birds breed along cliffs and rocky shores. Puffins lay their eggs in burrows, which they build themselves or have taken over from rabbits or other birds.

Word box

incubate
to keep something warm so it develops properly, like a bird sitting on its egg

krill
small shrimplike creatures of the ocean

▲ Amazing albatross

An albatross glides for days without flapping, gaining height by heading into the wind. It swoops down to snatch food from the sea and touches land only to breed.

▲ Storm petrel

True to its name, the tiny storm petrel flies in the worst storms and gales. It skims over the sea, looking for food such as krill and baby fish. Some petrels form vast flocks of many millions of birds.

Seashore life

The seashore is the place where the water from an ocean or sea reaches the land. Some seashores are rocky places with colourful seaweeds and rockpools filled with crabs, shrimps and other sea creatures. Other seashores are covered with sand or mud, where crabs and small worms burrow beneath the soft, wet surface.

▼ Seashore life

The part of the seashore closest to the sea is wet for most of each day. Higher up the shore, it dries out when the tide goes out. The animals and plants that live on the seashore have to survive both wet and dry conditions.

oyster catcher

Word box

anchor
to stop something from moving

burrow
to dig deeply

1. many seabirds build nests on high cliffs overlooking the shore. Some, such as the guillemot, never actually build a nest. Female guillemots lay eggs on narrow ledges

2. seabirds such as curlews and oystercatchers have long, pointed beaks. They use these to stab shellfish, tear open shells or find worms that burrow in the sand

curlew

3. small sea creatures such as shrimps and crabs hide in rockpools to avoid being eaten by hungry birds

shrimp

▶ In a rockpool

Rockpool creatures such as mussels and limpets cling to the rocks so they are not washed away by waves. Their shells protect them from the sea and the Sun.

4. seaweeds grow along the seashore. They have a special part that anchors them to the rocks. This is called a holdfast

crab

limpet

mussel

Sharks

Find out more:
Fish ◄ Sea animals ◄

There are 330 kinds of shark and they are all meat-eaters. Some sharks filter prey from the water, or lie in wait for victims on the sea bed, rather than speeding through the open ocean after them. Although most fish are bony, the skeleton of a shark is made of cartilage. This is lighter and more elastic than bone.

◄ Hammerhead

Like all sharks, this 6-metre hunter has an amazing sense of smell and can detect blood in the water from many kilometres away. A shark's skin is like sandpaper, because its scales are shaped like tiny versions of the sharp teeth in its mouth. Most sharks live alone, but hammerheads will gather together in groups to breed.

▼ Stingray

Rays are close cousins of sharks. Most glide across the sea bed on their wide 'wings', searching for buried shellfish and worms, which they crush with their wide, flat-topped teeth. The stingray's poison sting is like a dagger blade halfway along its tail.

sting

Wow!

The whale shark is the world's biggest fish, 13 metres long and 15 tonnes in weight – yet it eats only tiny creatures such as krill and baby fish.

▼ Super-hunter

The great white shark is the biggest meat-eating fish, at 7 metres long. Its teeth are up to 8 centimetres – as long as a finger. This shark eats whatever it likes! Other fish, seals, sea birds, sea turtles, small dolphins and giant whales are all its victims. The smallest members of the shark group include dogfish, which are less than 60 centimetres long.

great white shark

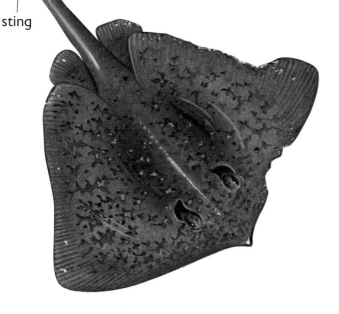

Ships and boats

Ships sail across open seas and lakes or travel along rivers and canals. They carry people and goods from place to place. Luxury ocean liners take thousands of passengers on holiday cruises. Giant oil tankers transport millions of tonnes of oil across rough seas. Cargo ships carry foods, cars and coal from one side of the world to the other.

◄ Small boats

A boat is a much smaller craft than a ship. Many boats have no engine and are propelled through the water by oars or sails. Most cannot travel across oceans or large bodies of water.

▲ Racing yachts

We sail yachts for pleasure and also for racing. Most yachts have one or more sails, but some have a motor engine only. Large racing yachts sail around the world with a crew of about 20 people on board.

► Sailing in style

The *Grand Princess*, built in 1998, is the second-largest passenger ship in service. It is second only to the *Voyager of the Seas*, launched in 2000. The *Grand Princess* is a huge, luxurious, floating hotel, weighing 109,000 tonnes. It has rooms for 2,600 passengers.

▼ Floating on air

A hovercraft is a ship that floats on a cushion of air. It can travel over land or water. Some hovercraft operate like car ferries and carry passengers and cars across water.

▼ Car ferries

Large ships called car ferries carry people and vehicles across small stretches of water. People drive their vehicles on and off through enormous doors at the bow (front) and stern (back) of the ferry.

Wow!
The largest tankers are over half a kilometre long. Sailors travel from one end of the tanker to the other by bicycle.

Ships in history

The first ships were either rafts made by tying logs together, or dugout canoes made from tree trunks. At first, boats were propelled by paddles, and then sails were added. Over 200 years ago came the invention of steam-powered boats. About this time, shipbuilders began to build iron ships instead of wooden ones.

▲ Reed boats

More than 5,000 years ago the Egyptians built lightweight river boats out of bundles of reeds. They were propelled by a long pole and, later on, by oars.

Word box

propelled
pushed forwards

propeller
a set of spinning blades that drives a ship

Greek cargo ship

◄ Strong and fast

The ancient Greeks built cargo ships which carried goods for trading. On the side of the ship were painted 'eyes'. The sailors believed these scared away evil spirits and protected them from harm.

SS Great Britain

◄ Fighting ships

Ships called galleons sailed the seas and oceans during the 1500s. They were used as fighting ships and to carry cargo. Galleons from Spain and England fought against each other in a famous sea battle off the south coast of England.

▲ Propeller power

The SS Great Britain was built in 1843. It was the first ship powered by a propeller to cross the Atlantic. The SS Great Britain was one of the first ships made of iron.

Wow!

Viking lords from northern Europe liked their warships so much that they asked to be buried inside them. They believed the ships would take them safely to the 'land of the dead'.

Snakes

Find out more:
Reptiles ◀ Sea animals ◀

It is hard to mistake a snake – it has no legs.
Because snakes are hunters they have long teeth for
grabbing prey. But these reptiles cannot chew – they must
swallow food whole. There are almost 3,000 kinds of
snakes, and apart from the icy polar regions, they live
all over the world – even in the open ocean. Less than
30 types of snakes are truly deadly to people.

Wow!
The longest snakes are royal
pythons, which grow up to 10 metres
long. They could
wrap around you
12 times!

▼ Poisonous fangs

Poisonous snakes, such as this cobra, use their venom to kill or
quieten prey, so it cannot run away or struggle while being
swallowed. Cobras, kraits, mambas and coral-snakes have their
poison-jabbing fangs near the front of the mouth. The fangs of
vipers, sidewinders, adders
and rattlesnakes are hinged to
fold back when not being used.

Word box

pits
holes

vibrations
shaking movements

▲ A big hug

Pythons and boas, like this
Madagascan tree boa, are mostly
big, heavy snakes. They can wrap
around prey so it cannot breathe.
Big pythons and boas can swallow
prey as large as wild pigs and small
antelopes – including the horns!

▶ See, hear, smell and taste

The Aruba rattlesnake shows how sensitive snakes
are. It sees quite well, especially movements. It hears well
too, and feels vibrations in the ground. The tongue flicks out
to smell and 'taste' the air. Rattlesnakes are pit-vipers and have
pits under the eyes. These detect heat, so the snake can catch
a warm-blooded victim like a mouse even in complete darkness.

Solids, liquids and gases

Find out more:
Air ◄ Atoms and molecules ◄

Most substances exist in different forms.

Temperature and pressure play a major role. For example, most metals are solid at normal temperatures. However, they become liquid if they are heated strongly. The gas carbon dioxide becomes solid, like snow, if it is cold enough. Nitrogen gas turns into liquid when very cold.

Wow!
'Dry ice' is used for keeping things cold. But it isn't real ice — it is made from a gas called carbon dioxide.

solid — atoms or molecules cannot move

gas — atoms or molecules can move fast, and also come nearer or move farther apart from each other

heated liquid, such as lava from a volcano, changes into vapour, or gas

warm air rises and cools

clouds form when air containing water vapour cools and forms droplets

liquid water cools and freezes and becomes solid ice

liquid — atoms or molecules can move or flow but they stay the same distance apart

▲ Our world

Everything around us is either a solid, liquid or gas, made up of units called atoms. Solid matter, like a volcano's rocks, is made up of tightly packed molecules that cannot move about. Liquids, such as water, contain molecules that are more widely spaced, and can move about more easily. Gases, such as air, are made up of molecules that can move about freely.

Sound

We hear sound all the time – from a ticking clock and a singing bird to a ringing doorbell or a car in the street. Every sound is made in the same way. An object shakes gently when it makes a noise. This shaking movement is called a vibration. The air around the object also starts to vibrate, and these vibrations travel through the air as waves of sound.

Concorde

▲ At top speed

Sound travels through the air at about 340 metres a second. Sound waves travel more slowly than waves of light – light travels about one million times more quickly. Some jet aircraft travel faster than the speed of sound. When they do, they make a loud, booming noise.

◄ Bouncing waves

Bats produce high-pitched sounds that cannot be heard by humans or other animals. The sound waves bounce off the food they hunt, such as insects, then back to the bat, telling the bat where their food is.

clarinet

sound wave bounces back to bat

bat

moth

sound wave from bat

► Speak up!

Our voices make sounds by vibrating our vocal cords. These are the soft flaps of skin in the voice box, at the back of the throat. When air passes over the vocal cords, they vibrate and make a sound. We then use our tongue and lips to change the sounds and form words.

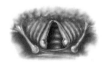

vocal cords are open and no sound is made

vocal cords close and air is forced out

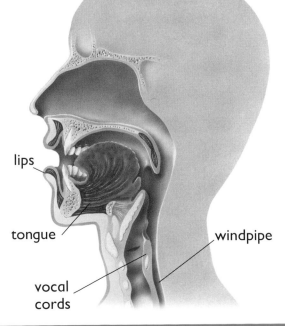

lips

tongue

windpipe

vocal cords

▲ Musical sounds

Musical sounds are made in many different ways. The sound from a guitar is made by plucking the strings, which start to vibrate. When a musician blows into an oboe or a flute, the air inside the instrument vibrates, creating sound. The skin across the top of a drum vibrates when it is hit with a drumstick or a hand.

▼

Sound and hearing

Find out more:
Human body ◄ Music and dance ◄
Music and dance in history ◄ Sound ◄

The sounds you hear have travelled through the air and into your ears. They travel as invisible sound waves. As they enter your ears, the sound waves make your eardrums vibrate. These vibrations pass to nerves in your ears, which carry messages about the sounds to the brain. Your brain helps you to understand the different sounds you hear.

Wow!

The smallest bone in your body is inside your ear — it is tinier than a grain of rice.

► Into the ear

Your ear is divided into three main parts: the outer ear, which is the part you can see and touch, the middle ear and the inner ear. Your eardrum (a piece of flexible skin) separates your outer ear from your middle ear.

▼ Levels of sound

Sound is measured in units called decibels (dB). For example, a whisper measures only 20 decibels, while an atomic explosion measures 200 decibels.

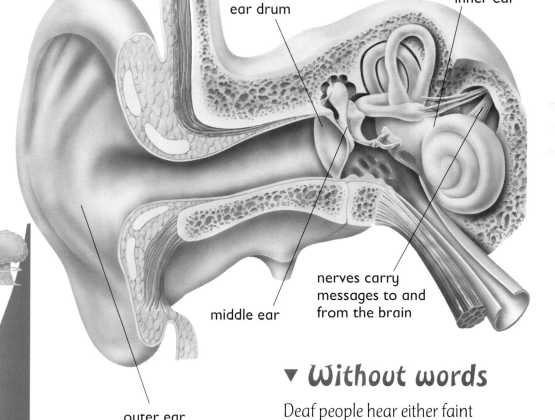

ear drum

inner ear

nerves carry messages to and from the brain

middle ear

outer ear

▼ Without words

Deaf people hear either faint sounds or no sounds at all. Many deaf people communicate with each other with the help of sign language. They use their hands, face and the top half of their body to make signs. Each sign has a different meaning.

▼ On the move

You can listen to music on the move with the help of a small personal stereo. If you listen to very loud music too often, you may damage your ears.

Word box

atomic
to do with atoms, the smallest parts of anything

nerve
a tiny thread that carries messages to the brain

South America

Find out more:
Mountains ◄ Rainforests ◄ Rivers and lakes ◄

South America is the fourth biggest continent in the world. You can find almost every kind of land feature there. South America has hot, steamy rainforests and dry deserts, towering, snow-capped mountain peaks and wide, grassy plains, active volcanoes and spectacular waterfalls. By far the biggest country in South America is Brazil, which covers almost half of the continent.

▶ Copper mines

South America has huge amounts of valuable minerals such as gold, copper and lead. Some of the world's biggest copper mines are in Chile. Miners remove the copper from mines or open pits on the surface.

▶ High and low

High up among the jagged peaks of the Andes Mountains rise the snow-covered tips of active volcanoes, such as Cotopaxi. This volcano, which is in Ecuador, has erupted over 25 times during the past 400 years.

▼ Full of life

In the basin of the Amazon river lies the Amazon rainforest, the largest in the world. It contains more kinds of plants and animals than any other forest.

parrot

jaguar

snakes

toucan

monkey

Word box

basin
the area where a river collects its water

jagged
sharp and pointed

mineral
tiny pieces of rock

Space travel

The first person to travel in space was a Russian called Yuri Gagarin. In 1961 he circled the Earth for about 90 minutes in a tiny *Vostok* spacecraft. Eight years later, the first men walked on the surface of the Moon. Since then, astronauts have walked in space, repaired telescopes in space and lived for months at a time inside space stations.

Yuri Gagarin

▼ Space dog

A dog named Laika was the first living thing to go into space. In 1957 she travelled in a Russian spacecraft called *Sputnik 2*, and stayed in space for two weeks.

Word box

astronaut
a space traveller

cosmonaut
a Russian space traveller

Wow!

A Russian cosmonaut spent 438 days in space inside the *Mir* space station.

▲ Protective suits

This astronaut is walking in space. His extra-thick suit protects him from any dangerous rays in space. A safety line attaches the astronaut to his spacecraft.

▼ To the Moon

Three American astronauts flew to the Moon in the *Apollo 11* spacecraft. While one astronaut stayed in the main spacecraft, the others landed on the Moon in a smaller vehicle.

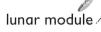

rocket

Apollo 11 command module

lunar module

◀ Visiting crews

The American *Skylab* was launched in 1973. It was the second space station to be launched, beaten by the Russian *Salyut 1* in 1971. Despite a few problems, three 3-man crews visited *Skylab* and the longest mission lasted 84 days. The 75-tonne space station eventually burned up in the atmosphere in 1979.

Spacecraft

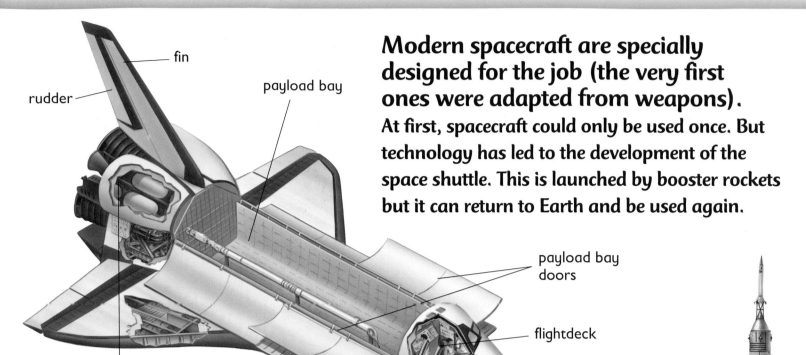

fin

rudder

payload bay

payload bay doors

flightdeck

rocket engines

Modern spacecraft are specially designed for the job (the very first ones were adapted from weapons). At first, spacecraft could only be used once. But technology has led to the development of the space shuttle. This is launched by booster rockets but it can return to Earth and be used again.

Word box

capsule
small cabin that is carried into space by rockets

manned
with people on board

satellite
spacecraft that circles the Earth; some are used to help send telephone and TV signals

▲ Space shuttles

US space shuttles take humans and cargo into orbit around Earth (to circle around Earth), and then return home again. Coming back to Earth, the shuttle is the world's heaviest glider (flying without power). It comes down fast, and needs a parachute to slow down on the runway.

Saturn V moon rocket

Energiya launcher/ Buran shuttle

▶ Blast off!

To blast into space, a rocket has to travel 40 times faster than a jumbo jet. If it went any slower, gravity would pull it back to Earth. Rockets are used to send manned capsules and satellites into orbit and spacecraft to the Moon.

Spain and Portugal were invaded and settled by all sorts of peoples, including Basques, Iberians, Celts, Greeks, Romans, Germans, Moors, Jews and Roma (gypsies). In the 1500s, the kingdoms of Spain and Portugal conquered lands in the New World, making both countries rich and powerful. Spain ruled Portugal from 1586 to 1646.

▲ The navigators

This statue in Lisbon, Portugal, recalls the Portuguese explorers of the 1400s, such as Bartolomeu Díaz and Vasco da Gama. They were some of the first Europeans to carry out long sea voyages, sailing around the coast of Africa and crossing the Indian Ocean.

▶ El Cid

The Spanish knight Ruy Díaz de Vivar was a hero of the Middle Ages. He fought against, and sometimes with, the Moors who lived in southern Spain. They called him *El Cid*, which means 'the lord'. In 1094, he captured Valencia and became its ruler.

Ferdinand of Aragon

Isabella of Castile

◄ Ferdinand and Isabella

Christian knights defeated the Muslim Moors and in 1479 Spain became one country under the rule of Isabella of Castile and Ferdinand of Aragon.

◄ Spanish rebels

Between 1936 and 1939, Spain was shattered by a bloody civil war. General Franco then ruled as a dictator until 1975, when Juan Carlos I became king and a fair government was established.

Word box

Moor
a Muslim of Berber or Arab descent, who lived in Morocco or Spain in the Middle Ages

Spiders

A spider has eight legs, unlike insects, which have six legs. Nearly all spiders have a poisonous bite, using their fanglike mouthparts, but only a few are harmful to people. Most spin silk from their rear ends to make webs for catching small prey, such as flies.

tarantula

▲ Funnelweb

The funnelweb of Australia has strong fangs and powerful poison. It is dangerous because it lives in or near people's homes. It rears up and strikes quickly, unlike most spiders, which usually run away.

▼ On the prowl

Some spiders do not use webs for catching prey. They simply chase, overpower and bite their prey. The wolf spider is one of these. Like most spiders, it has eight eyes — and these are large, so it can follow its victim.

▲ Big and hairy

Tarantulas and bird-eating spiders are big, strong and hairy, and live in the tropics, mainly in the Americas. They hunt at night for small animals such as mice, shrews and baby birds.

Wow!

A web-spinning spider makes a new web almost every night — eating the old one to recycle (use again) the silk threads.

◄ House spider

The house spider spins an untidy web in a corner, and eats most small creatures that blunder into it. Spiders do not really like baths — they tend to slip in and cannot crawl out.

Spiders and their relatives

Find out more:
Animal kingdom ◄
Insects ◄ Spiders ◄

Spiders belong to a group of animals called arachnids. This group also includes scorpions, harvestmen and mites. Unlike insects, arachnids have no wings. They have four pairs of legs while insects have three. Spiders and scorpions are thought of as scary, but most do not harm humans. Mites burrow under skin, making it sore and itchy. Some pass on disease.

▼ Blood suckers

Ticks are small egg-shaped animals, and are a type of mite. They live on the bodies of other animals and feed by sucking their blood. Ticks are dangerous because they pass diseases into the blood of their victims.

this image has been magnified to show close-up detail of a tick

poisonous sting

leg

external skeleton

pincer (claw)

◄ Stinging tail

Scorpions live in warm places. They hide in the day and come out to hunt for food at night. A scorpion has a curved sting at the end of its long tail. It uses the poison in this sting to kill its prey. A scorpion sting is painful for humans but it does not usually cause death.

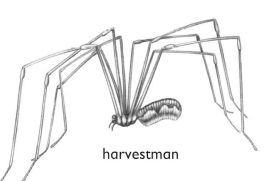

▲ Baby scorpions

Scorpions do not lay eggs – they give birth to live, fully formed young. The young hang onto their mother's back for the first two weeks after they are born.

harvestman

▲ Very long legs

The long-legged harvestman is a harmless creature. It eats small insects and fruit that it finds on the ground. Another name for it is daddy longlegs.

Wow!

Female ticks can lay as many as 18,000 eggs at a time.

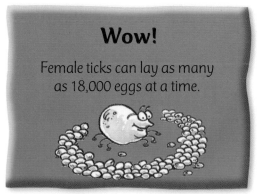

Sport

Sport provides entertainment for millions of people. Some sports involve individuals, others involve entire teams. Sport can also help to keep us fit. Many people play sport just for fun, but for others, it is their job. Great numbers of people watch athletes at stadiums (huge sports grounds), or follow them on TV or radio.

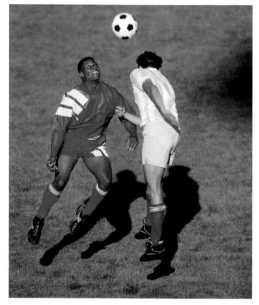

▲ Most popular

Soccer is probably the world's most popular sport. Top soccer teams play matches in stadiums in front of thousands of fans. The first rules for the game were drawn up in England in the 1800s.

Wow!

Each American football team has around 45 players but only 11 are allowed onto the pitch at one time.

▼ Up in the sky

Skydiving involves jumping from an aircraft and performing special moves in the air. Skydivers wear parachutes that help them to land safely on the ground. Teams of skydivers sometimes join hands in the air before their parachutes open up.

▼ In the basket

Basketball is played by two teams of five players each. It is the most popular indoor sport. A Canadian teacher invented the game in 1891 to keep his students busy during the long, dark winters.

▼ Steering through the water

Windsurfing is a very popular water sport even though it only started about 40 years ago. The windsurfer must balance on a sailboard while steering it through the water at top speed.

Sport in history

Find out more:
Aztecs and Mayans ◄

People have always enjoyed playing and watching sports. In the ancient world, games were sometimes part of important religious festivals. Athletics helped to train warriors for war, too, and to keep them fit. Ancient Greek weapons, such as the javelin, are still thrown by athletes today.

▼ The Olympic Games

In 1906, the first of the modern series of the Olympic Games was held in Athens, Greece. The original games had been held between 771BC and AD393. Ancient events included discus-throwing, running, jumping and wrestling.

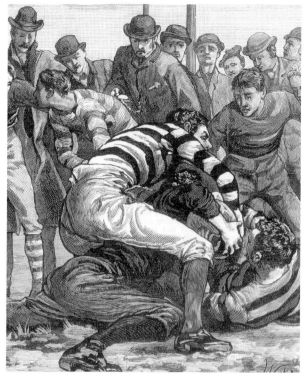

1906   771BC

▲ Making up the rules

Rugby football was invented in 1823 by a schoolboy who picked up a football and ran with it. Many other sports became popular in the 1800s and were given proper rules. These included lawn tennis, netball, badminton and baseball.

Support your team!

What is your favourite team sport and which team do you follow?

See if you can find out the facts below. Then make a chart that you can stick up on the wall, and decorate it with club colours and badges.

1. When was your favourite sport first played?
2. Where was the sport first played?
3. When was your team founded?
4. Which year was the most successful in its history?
5. Who was its best player ever?

▼ Speed sports

New machines meant new and ever faster sports were taken up in the 1900s. Racing cycles, motorcycles, cars and aeroplanes now pulled in big crowds of spectators. These racing cars date from 1953.

Stars

Have you ever seen stars twinkling?
These stars are part of the Milky Way galaxy, the family of stars that surrounds our planet. Light from faraway stars takes years to reach Earth. Light from our nearest star, the Sun, takes eight minutes to reach us.

Milky Way

▼ Star patterns

Patterns formed by stars are called constellations. Many are named after animals and people from Greek myths. The constellation of Orion is named after Orion the Hunter. A row of three stars across the middle makes up the hunter's belt.

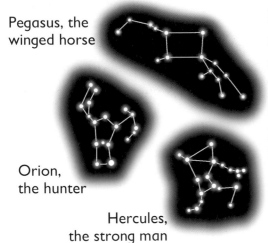

Pegasus, the winged horse

Orion, the hunter

Hercules, the strong man

▶ Star-watching

People who study stars and planets are called astronomers. Modern astronomers use very powerful telescopes. Some telescopes have been placed in space. They send pictures back to Earth. The most famous of these is the Hubble

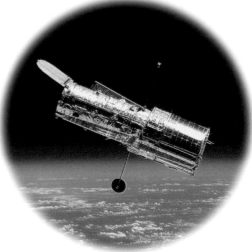

Hubble Space Telescope

▼ Different stars

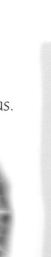

Stars give off heat and light. A blue-white star is very hot, but a red coloured star is cooler. Our Sun is a main sequence star, which means that it is medium-hot.

supergiant

main sequence star

▼ Life and death

New stars are born all the time – and old ones die. New stars are born inside clouds of dust and gas. Large stars swell before they die. Then they disappear

exploding star

Word box

constellation
a well-known pattern of stars

galaxy
a huge family of stars

supergiant
a huge red star that is beginning to cool down

Stone Age

Before people learned how to make things from metal, they made tools and weapons from stone, shell, wood, horn or bone. This period is called the Stone Age. Copper was being worked in some parts of Asia and Europe by 6000BC, but it took thousands of years for these metal-working skills to spread.

▶ Survival

The Stone Age lasted tens of thousands of years. Although people knew less than we do today, they could be just as clever. They worked out ever better ways of hunting, fishing and gathering food. In the end, they learned how to farm.

▲ Ring of stone

Towards the end of the Stone Age in Britain, some people created a ring of massive stones at Stonehenge. The stones were lined up to follow the path of the Sun across the sky. Historians think that important religious ceremonies were held here between about 3200BC and 1100BC.

▼ Homes for the dead

Between about 5,700 and 4,000 years ago, important people in northwestern Europe were buried in stone tombs, covered with mounds of earth. Some of these tombs, called barrows, can still be visited today.

▲ Cutting edge

Stone Age tools included scrapers, knives, axe-heads, spear-heads, arrows and fish-hooks. Many were made from a hard stone called flint, which could be chipped into the right shape.

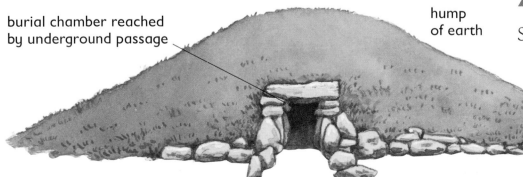

burial chamber reached by underground passage

hump of earth

Sun

The Sun is a huge ball of hot, glowing gas. It provides the heat and light that living things on Earth need to stay alive. It is our nearest star, which is why it looks bigger than other stars. The Sun is about 150,000,000 kilometres from the Earth.

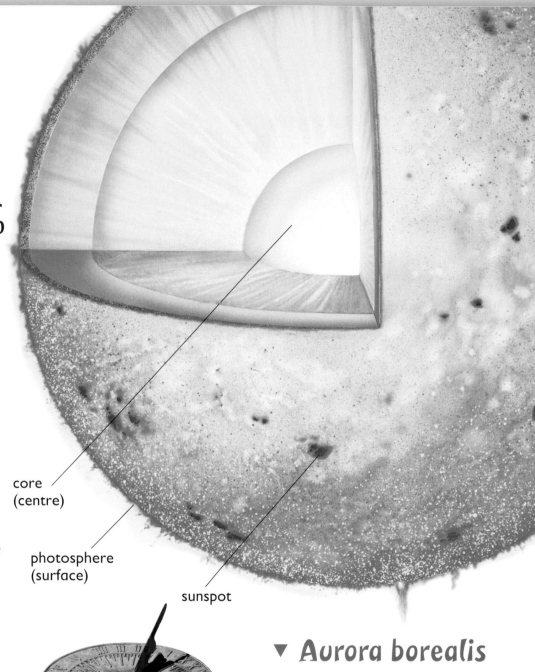

core (centre)

photosphere (surface)

sunspot

◄ Very hot

The Sun is very, very hot. The temperature on its surface is about 6,000 degrees Celsius – that's 60 times hotter than boiling water. The centre of the Sun is almost 3,000 times hotter than its surface.

▼ Spots and flares

Dark spots sometimes appear on the Sun's surface. These are called sunspots. The Sun can give off huge bursts of bright light called flares. They shoot out from its surface.

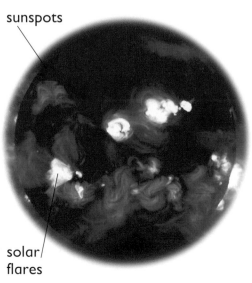

sunspots

solar flares

▲ Telling the time

You can use the Sun to tell the time. A sundial is a kind of clock that shows how a shadow changes as the Sun moves across the sky. You tell the time by looking to see where the shadow falls on the dial.

▼ Aurora borealis

Aurorae are curtains of lights in the sky. The lights may be blue, red or yellow. They occur in the far north or south of the world.

Technology

Technology is how we use science to help us.
It began many thousands of years ago, when someone discovered that stones could be broken to make a sharp blade. It has come a long way since then! Today, without technology, we could not travel long distances, surf the Internet or make phone calls to our friends.

▲ Lazy technology

This is a vacuum cleaner that does all the work by itself! It will wander about the room, cleaning away until it is switched off again. This machine contains sensors that stop it bumping into things or getting stuck in corners.

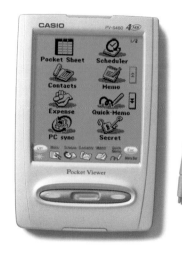

◄ Pocket PC

Powerful computers can now be packed into pocket-sized devices called Personal Digital Assistants (PDAs). They do not have a normal keyboard, and information is loaded from a large computer, or is keyed in by touching the screen with a small pen called a stylus.

Wow!
Scientists are planning to make tiny machines that can be injected into our bodies! They will be used to repair damaged body tissues. This is called nanotechnology.

► Tiny technology

A tiny chip made from silicon contains the whole 'brain' of a computer, even though it is smaller than a fingernail. It may be only 0.5 millimetres thick. The chips do not use much power and can be built into almost any machine. You will not even know they are there!

silicon 'wafer'
plastic casing
wire 'feet' link to other computer parts

► Working robots

Computer-controlled robots are used for many jobs, such as making cars and spacecraft. This robotic lifting device, called the Canadarm, was built by the Canadians for use on American space shuttles. It has been useful in assembling the new International Space Station.

Television and films

Find out more:
Communication technology ◄

Television brings many kinds of event into right into our homes. These include news from around the world, sport, music, wildlife programmes, action films and children's cartoons. In the world's wealthier countries, almost every home has a television.

◄ Early TV

Scottish engineer John Logie Baird developed an early form of TV in the 1920s and 1930s. This system used lenses set into revolving discs.

▼ Making pictures

Television programmes are sent to your home by radio waves. The aerial on your roof picks up these waves and converts them into electrical signals. Your television changes these signals into pictures and sound using electron guns and beams.

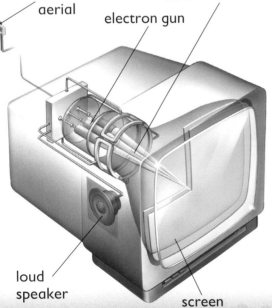

outside aerial
electron beam
electron gun
loud speaker
screen

▼ Making films

In 1911, US film makers went to a remote settlement called Hollywood, near the city of Los Angeles. They wanted to film westerns and the area was dry and scrubby. Within two years Hollywood had become the centre of American film-making, and it has dominated the industry ever since.

▲ In the studio

This picture shows a newsreader being filmed inside a TV studio as they read the news. Other parts of the news programme are filmed 'on location' – out and about wherever the story takes place.

HOLLYWOOD

Theatre

People go to the theatre to watch a play, a musical show, an opera or a ballet. The performance usually takes place on a stage at the front of the theatre. The audience sits in rows facing the stage. Thousands of years ago, plays were performed in open-air theatres in ancient Greece.

▶ In ancient Rome

Roman theatres were huge, well-built structures. One of the best-preserved is at Orange, in France. It has seats for almost 10,000 people. It was so cleverly designed that the audience could hear the actors, even from the back row.

scenery could be complicated, so it was moved around by machinery.

stage

▼ Famous writer

William Shakespeare (1564–1616) was a successful English playwright (a person who writes plays) who lived during the reign of Queen Elizabeth I. Many of his plays were performed at Elizabeth's court. Today, Shakespeare is still one of the world's best-known writers.

▶ The Globe

The plays of William Shakespeare were performed in London's Globe Theatre in the 1600s. An exact copy of the original theatre close to the same site was completed in 1996.

▲ Modern theatre

Many new theatres are modern-looking buildings, like the National Theatre in Ghana, Africa.

Time

Time can be measured in various ways. You can tell the time roughly by looking at the length of shadows. But the need for accurate time became important, in general, when railways spread around the world in the mid-1800s and train timetables were developed. Now time can be measured even more precisely with atomic clocks, which use decaying radioactive materials.

◀ Sea clocks

Harrison's 'chronometer' was invented by a clock-maker, John Harrison, in the mid-1700s. Powered by a spring, it kept accurate time over long distances. For the first time, it let sailors work out their exact position at sea, so they were less likely to get lost.

▲ Sands of time

An hourglass contains sand in a glass container. The sand runs through a small hole. It was a popular type of clock in the Middle Ages (between the years 470 and 1450), when it was used to measure short periods of time.

▼ Modern times

A digital quartz watch keeps time by using a tiny crystal that vibrates (shakes to and fro) 32,768 times a second when electricity passes through it.

▼ Giant calculator

Word box

radioactive
radioactive materials give off powerful radiation (energy). At the same time they 'decay' – change into a different form

Stonehenge, in England, is a huge circle of stones, thousands of years old. Some astronomers (people who study the stars and planets) believe it was built to tell the time of the seasons by the shadows that the stones cast.

Time around the world

Through the day, time is measured from 12 o'clock midnight. But as the Earth turns, our midnight might be midday on the other side of the world. So we have divided the world into different time zones.

Earth's orbit around the Sun takes 365 days, or 366 days every fourth year (leap year)

▼ Earth's year

The Earth takes a year to complete one orbit of the Sun. While it is orbiting the Sun, it also spins. It takes 24 hours to spin around once — one day and night.

Sun

daytime (facing the Sun)

Earth

night-time (away from the Sun)

◄ Time on Earth

What time it is depends on where you live in the world. The world is divided into 24 time zones. There is one hour between one zone and the next. Some countries are within one time zone. Others span more than one — mainland United States has five.

24-hour clock

To avoid confusion between the morning and the evening, we sometimes tell the time using the 24-hour clock. Look at the diagram on the left to find out how we do this. The 24-hour clock time is written next to each clock face.

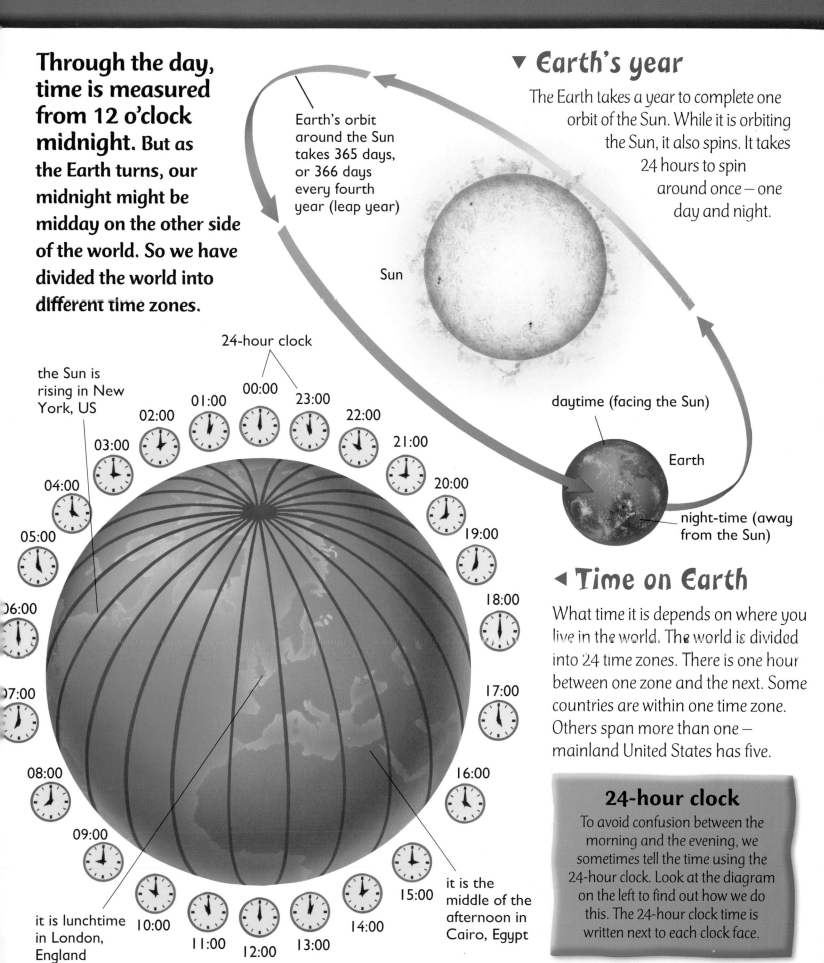

24-hour clock

the Sun is rising in New York, US

it is lunchtime in London, England

it is the middle of the afternoon in Cairo, Egypt

Town and city animals

Find out more:
Mice and rats ◄

We crowd together in cities. We cause noise and stress, and produce huge amounts of waste. Various animals share this habitat with us, too. They eat our leftover foods, nest in our buildings and enjoy our central-heating. Mammals such as rats, mice and foxes, birds like sparrows, starlings and pigeons, and insects such as flies, silverfish and cockroaches share towns and cities with people worldwide.

Word box

roost
a resting or sleeping place, usually for flying animals like birds, bats and insects

waste
rubbish that nobody wants

▼ Town birds

The starling lives in flocks, which fly out of town by day to feed. They return at dusk (early evening) to roost on roofs. As with pigeons, their droppings cause damage to buildings. Starlings and pigeons can also spread disease.

▼ City-dweller

The red fox is about at night, when there is less traffic and human activity. It learns routines quickly and visits rubbish tips, litter bins and garden heaps to sniff for any kind of food. It lives in a burrow called an earth, in a bank or under an outbuilding.

▼ Sorting the rubbish

In North America the common raccoon is a regular visitor to rubbish bins and bags. It climbs well over fences and rooftops, and sorts out edible bits using its front paws.

▶ Rats

Huge numbers of rats are found all over the world in towns and cities. They will eat almost anything and breed very quickly. Rats can cause diseases that are harmful to people.

raccoon

fox

rat

Toys

Children in the Stone Age probably played with pebbles, seeds, shells, feathers, toy spears and clay figures. Dolls, toys and other games have survived from ancient Egypt and we know that toys were sold at fairs in the Middle Ages. In the 1800s, cheap toys made of tin or wood were made in factories.

◀ Egyptian toys

Children in ancient Egypt played with colourful balls made from linen and rags, spinning tops, dolls and toy lions whose jaws snapped when they pulled a string.

▼ Yo-yo!

Some toys go through crazes at different times in history. The yo-yo, which was popular in the 1930s, 1950s and 1990s, was also a toy in ancient Greece.

▼ Dice and marbles

The ancient Romans loved playing dice and had many board games with their own pieces or counters.

▼ Rocking horses

In the days when everyone rode about on horseback, little children played with hobbyhorses and wheeled wooden horses. Rocking horses were first made in the 1600s. This one dates from the 1800s.

► Teddy

Teddy bears were first made 100 years ago. They probably take their name from an American president called 'Teddy' Roosevelt, who is said to have spared the life of a little bear when he was out hunting.

Wow!

The oldest board game surviving today was played by Sumerians at the royal court of Ur, over 4,500 years ago.

Trains

Find out more:
Trains in history ▶

Trains carry passengers and heavy loads along thick, metal tracks called rails. Passenger trains carry people on long journeys across a country or on short journeys to and from work. Some passenger trains in countries such as France and Japan travel at very fast speeds. France's *TGV* can travel at up to 500 kilometres an hour. Goods trains carry heavy loads such as coal, timber and chemicals.

▼ High speed

Japan's high-speed passenger train is known as the 'bullet train'. It can travel at speeds of up to 260 kilometres an hour.

bullet

▼ Underwater

The Channel Tunnel, which links England and France, was opened in 1994. The rail tunnels are 50 kilometres long and were built at a depth of 37 metres under the sea. The train journey through the tunnels takes just 35 minutes.

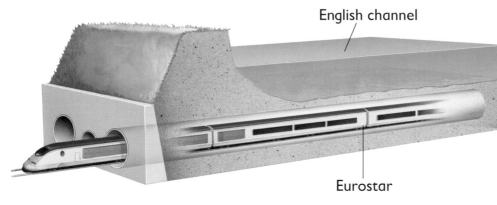

English channel

Eurostar

maglev

▲ Future trains

The maglev train is suspended by powerful magnets above a track. They can reach speeds of up to 500 kilometres an hour!

▶ Underground

In some big cities, underground trains travel along rails in tunnels built beneath city streets. The world's first underground system was opened in London in the 1860s. The first section, between Paddington and Farringdon, was opened in 1863.

Wow!

The city of New York, USA has 466 underground railway stations — that's more than any other city in the world.

Trains in history

Find out more:
Machines in history ◄

In the early 1800s, steam-powered trains were invented. The first steam locomotive pulled a train of five wagons. As engines became more powerful, longer and heavier trains were built. Locomotives were able to pull dozens of carriages containing passengers and goods.

► Early steam

In 1804, the very first steam locomotive pulled wagons along a railway track in Wales. It was built by an engineer Richard Trevithick. It began the development of the steam locomotive

Word box

locomotive
a railway engine powered by steam, electricity or diesel fuel, used to pull trains

▲ By steam

Once, all trains were steam-powered. The steam was produced by burning coal to heat water in big boilers. Some countries still have steam trains. Most modern trains run on electricity or diesel fuel.

▼ Stephenson's Rocket

In 1825, George and Robert Stephenson opened the world's first steam passenger railway, the Stockton and Darlington in England. They also built the first modern steam engine, the *Rocket* in 1829. It reached a top speed of 56 kilometres an hour.

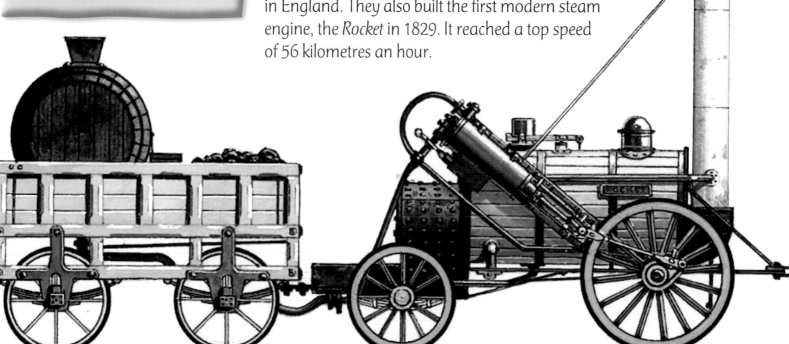

Trees

Find out more:
Air ◀ Materials ◀ Plant life ◀
Plant kingdom ◀ Rainforests ◀

Trees are the largest plants of all. The biggest tree alive today, a giant sequoia in California, USA, is over 80 metres tall. Trees provide us with wood for building and to make paper. They give us fruits such as oranges and apples, and important materials such as rubber and cork. Trees also take in carbon dioxide from the air, and give off oxygen, the gas needed by all living things.

▼ Trees in blossom

Blossom is the name for the sweet-smelling flowers of some trees. The flowers then turn into fruit that we pick to eat. Inside are seeds from which new trees can be grown.

apple blossom on an apple tree

◀ Falling leaves

These are leaves from the North American maple tree. It is a deciduous tree, which means it loses its leaves each year and is bare in winter. Its leaves are green in spring and summer and turn gold, red and brown in autumn as they fall to the ground.

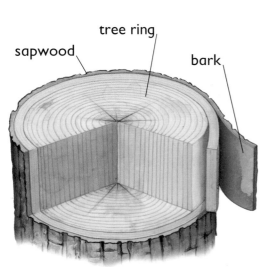

▼ Evergreen trees

Non-deciduous trees are called evergreens — they keep their leaves all year round. Some evergreens, such as pines, have needle-like leaves and woody cones. The seeds from which new trees will grow develop inside these cones.

▼ Inside the trunk

A rough, woody layer called bark protects the living parts of the tree beneath. Each year the sapwood beneath the bark grows, leaving a ring. This is how the age of fallen or damaged trees can be determined. Each ring is equivalent to one year.

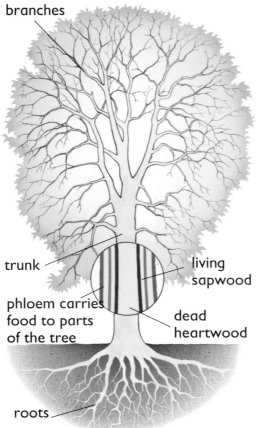

branches

trunk

phloem carries food to parts of the tree

living sapwood

dead heartwood

roots

tree ring

sapwood

bark

◀ Parts of a tree

A tree has three main parts: the trunk and branches, the leaves and the roots. The branches and leaves together are called the 'crown'. The trunk supports the crown. The roots are underground and they absorb water from the soil.

▼

Tudors and Stuarts

Find out more:
Britain and Ireland ◀ Kings and queens ◀

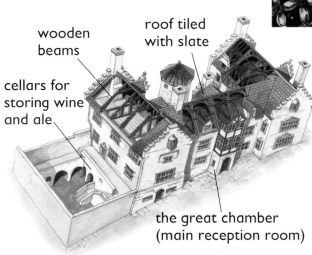

In the 1500s and 1600s, Britain was ruled by two powerful families, the Tudors and the Stuarts (or Stewarts). This was a time of bitter quarrels between Christians. The Roman Catholics supported the Pope in Rome, but the Protestants wanted to break away from the Roman Church.

▲ Henry VIII (Henry the Eighth)

The Tudors reigned over England and Wales from 1485 to 1603. Henry VIII was desperate for a son to succeed him. When the Pope refused to give him a divorce from his first wife, Henry made himself head of a new Church of England.

▼ Two queens

During troubled times in Scotland, Mary Stuart, Queen of Scots, fled to England. After being tried for plotting against Elizabeth I (below), Mary had her head chopped off.

▲ Country at war

King Charles I was unpopular. A war broke out between his supporters and the English Parliament. They cut his head off in 1649 and in 1653 handed over power to a soldier called Oliver Cromwell, who ruled the country for the next five years.

▼ King of Scotland

The Stuarts (or Stewarts) ruled Scotland for most of the time between 1371 and 1714. This is James IV (James the Fourth), one of the greatest Scottish kings. He was killed fighting the English in 1513. In 1603, the Stuarts came to rule England too.

◀ A Tudor town house

This fine house was built by a wealthy businessman in the town of Conwy, Wales, in 1577. It was built in the shape of an 'E', after Elizabeth I.

wooden beams

roof tiled with slate

cellars for storing wine and ale

the great chamber (main reception room)

Turkey

Find out more:
Byzantine Empire ◀ Cities of ancient times ◀
World War One ▶

Istanbul Black
Sea
TURKEY

A Turkish people called the Ottomans captured Constantinople in 1453. They founded a new empire which soon spread across Turkey, Greece and southeastern Europe, Arabia, Egypt and North Africa. The Ottoman Empire finally came to an end in 1922 and Turkey became a republic. It still has more people living there than any other country in western Asia.

▲▶ New Turkey

The Turks were defeated in 1918, at the close of World War One. The country was built up again by a man called Mustapha Kemal Atatürk, who was president from 1923 to 1938.

▶ Topkapi

During the 1460s and 1470s, the grand new palace of Topkapi Sarayi was built in Istanbul, looking out over the sea. At times, as many as 5,000 people lived in the palace buildings.

◀ Istanbul

The Turks turned Constantinople into the Muslim city of Istanbul. The graceful Blue Mosque was built for Sultan Ahmet I. It was finally finished in 1619.

Word box

republic
a country that is not ruled by a king or queen

sultan
the king of a Muslim country

▶ Magnificent!

The Ottoman Empire reached the height of its power under a ruler or 'sultan' called Süleyman I, the Magnificent, who died in 1566. His armies marched westwards as far as Austria.

United States of America

Find out more:
American Revolution ◄
Native Americans ◄ Wild West ►

In the 1800s, the new country of the USA grew very quickly. It gained lands in the South, the Southwest, California and Alaska. New settlers arrived from Ireland, Italy, Germany, Poland and Russia. Despite a civil war and battles with the Native Americans, farming and factories flourished. By the 1950s, the USA had become the richest and most powerful nation in the world.

▲ North v. South

In 1861, 11 southern states withdrew from the Union that made up the USA. They disagreed about the way in which the country was to be governed and they wanted to keep slavery. Many people died in this bitter civil war, which lasted until 1865, when the Union won.

► Statue of Liberty

Many Europeans came to America between 1850 and 1910 in search of a better, fairer life. The Statue of Liberty was a gift from the French people to the United States in 1884. It was a symbol of this fairness and freedom.

◄ 'I have a dream...'

One hundred years after the end of slavery, African Americans were still being treated as second-class citizens in the USA. Martin Luther King Junior led a campaign for justice. In a famous speech, he told people that he had a dream of a land in which all people were free and equal. He was killed in 1968.

▼ Abraham Lincoln

Abraham Lincoln was president of the USA from 1861 to 1865, when he was murdered. He was a great leader who helped to bring slavery to an end.

Martin Luther King Junior

Universe

The Universe contains everything that exists. This includes the Earth, other planets, and billions of stars. The Universe is about 15,000 million years old – and still growing. Scientists believe it was probably born after a very large explosion which they call the Big Bang.

Word box

elliptical
egg-shaped

▲ Cosmic rays

Stars produce huge amounts of energy. This reaches the Earth as heat, light and cosmic rays, made of tiny particles (objects). These particles travel so fast that when they hit other particles in our atmosphere they smash them, releasing bursts of radiation energy.

▼ Spins and streamers

Galaxies come in different shapes. Many of them are spinning. The stars they contain trail out to form long streamers.

▼ Galaxy clusters

Out in space there are glowing clouds made up of masses of floating dust. These are called nebulas, and they often look like smudges of light. Nebulas also contain millions of stars. Nebulas and stars form huge clusters called galaxies. Our own galaxy is called the Milky Way.

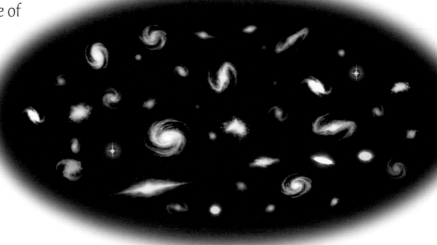

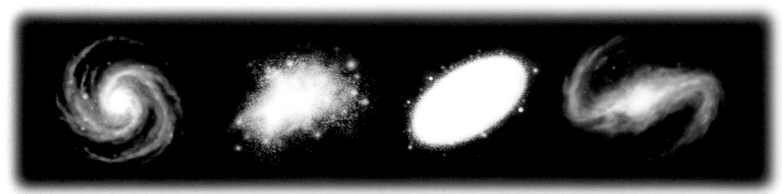

spiral galaxy   irregular galaxy   elliptical galaxy   spiral galaxy with bar across

Victorian Britain

Find out more:
Britain and Ireland ◀ Empires and colonies ◀
Industrial Revolution ◀

From 1837 to 1901, Britain was ruled by Queen Victoria. Her reign is called the Victorian Age. She ruled over large areas of the world, which made up the biggest empire in history. At this time Britain led the world in trade and in building new factories.

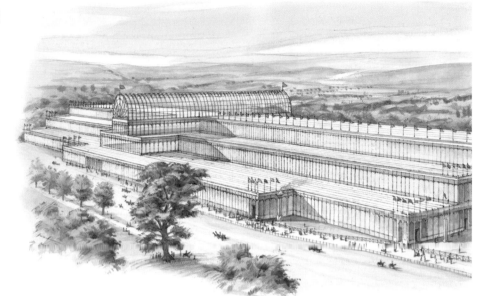

▶ Ladies of fashion

Victorian ladies wore full dresses that were stretched over a hooped petticoat called a crinoline. These 1870s models are showing off the bustle, a pad which pushed out the back of the skirt.

▼ A long reign

Queen Victoria was only 18 when she came to the throne, and she ruled for 63 years. She married a German prince called Albert. His death, in 1861, made her very sad.

▲ Crystal Palace

In 1851, a huge glass building called the Crystal Palace was put up in Hyde Park, London. Inside it was the Great Exhibition, organized by Prince Albert. It showed off produce, crafts and new machines from all over the world.

▼ The poor

Many people in Victorian Britain were extremely poor. Their lives were described in stories by the great writer Charles Dickens, who lived from 1812 to 1870.

Be a Victorian fashion designer

1. Draw a Victorian lady in a dress and bonnet, like the ones shown in the picture above.
2. Colour in her costume and add patterns, lace and bows.

Vikings

The word 'Viking' means sea raider. About 1,200 years ago, Vikings caused terror along the coasts of northern Europe. They sailed from Norway, Sweden and Denmark to attack, plunder and settle new lands. They traded as far away as Russia and the Middle East. They even sailed to Iceland, Greenland and North America.

▲ Meeting up

All free Viking men gathered regularly at a special meeting called the Thing. There they passed new laws and settled any arguments between them.

▶ Life at home

The Vikings built farming settlements, ports and towns. They were great craft workers, traders and storytellers. Family life took place around the fire.

▲ Northern fury

Viking chiefs lead a band of raiders ashore from their longboat, armed with spears, swords and axes. Viking warriors attacked towns and Christian monasteries, seizing gold, silver, cattle and weapons. Sometimes they captured people to sell as slaves.

▶ Thor's hammer

The Vikings believed in different gods and goddesses. Thor, god of thunder, had a magic hammer that he used to fight giants. His chariot was pulled by goats.

Make a Viking treasure hoard

1. Make some coins by cutting out circles of card. Viking coins might be stamped with designs of ships or swords. Cover your coins with silver foil then use a blunt pencil to make a design on them.

2. Cut out a cross and a brooch from card. Again, cover with foil and press a design on them.

Volcanoes

Find out more:
Earth features ◄ Oceania ◄ South America ◄

A volcano is an opening on the surface of the Earth. Most volcanoes are cone-shaped mountains. An erupting volcano is spectacular. Hot liquid rock pours out of the volcano and down its sides, clouds of gases and ash rise into the air and lumps of rock are blasted out.

Wow!
The biggest volcano disaster in recent times was an eruption of Mount Tambora in Indonesia in 1815 — it killed almost 100,000 people.

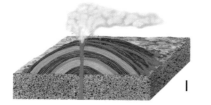

▲ Red hot lava

The fiery red liquid that pours out of an erupting volcano is called lava. It comes from deep inside the Earth. When this hot liquid cools down, it hardens and turns into dark-coloured rock.

▲ Clouds of smoke

Thick clouds of smoke, hot gases and ash stream out of this volcano. Some volcanic clouds are so thick that they block out the Sun's light. When the ash reaches the ground it covers everything around the volcano in a grey blanket of dust.

► Inside a volcano

The red-hot lava travels up through a pipe in the middle of the volcano. It pours out through the vent, the opening at the top of the volcano. Some of the hot lava leaks out through other openings in the volcano's sides.

▲ Different kinds

Some volcanoes have runny lava that runs from the vent and makes a domed shape (1). Others have thick lava that explodes, making a cone-shaped volcano (2). A crater volcano (3) occurs when the top of a cone-shaped volcano explodes and sinks into the magma chamber.

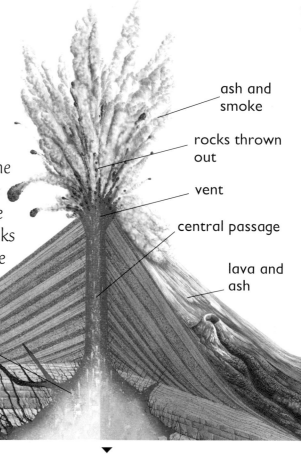

ash and smoke

rocks thrown out

vent

central passage

lava and ash

chamber

rocks

Water

Water has shaped our world. It has gradually worn down rocks and produced the soil in which plants grow. No animals or plants could survive without some water to drink. Frozen water forms the great icecaps at the North and South Poles. Most of the world's water is in the oceans, and is salty. Fresh water, with no salt, is found in rivers and lakes.

How much rain?

Use a jam jar to measure rainfall. Place the jar where the rain can fall into it. Use a marker pen to mark the water level on the outside of the jar. Keep a record of the changing levels in a notebook.

▲ Frozen drips

Icicles form when snow or ice melts and then re-freezes. The snow starts to melt during the day. Then the dripping water freezes again in the colder night temperatures.

▼ The water cycle

The water cycle involves all the water on Earth. Water droplets or vapours rise from lakes, rivers and seas to form clouds. These droplets join up to make bigger drops that eventually fall as rain. Some rain is soaked up by the land. Much of it runs back to the sea.

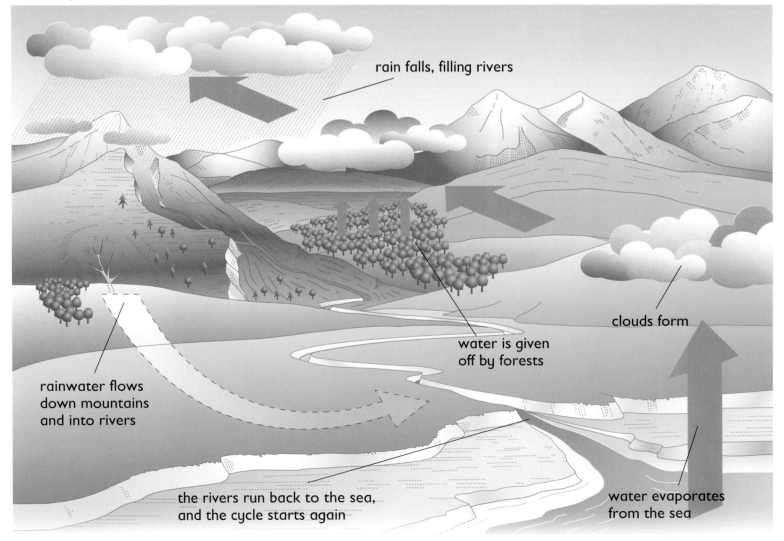

rain falls, filling rivers

clouds form

water is given off by forests

rainwater flows down mountains and into rivers

water evaporates from the sea

the rivers run back to the sea, and the cycle starts again

Water and life

All life depends on water. Our cells are made mostly from water. We carry lots of water in our blood. Like most animals, our bodies are usually able to stop us from losing too much water. But as we cannot store water, we still need to drink very regularly. Making sure that people have germ-free drinking water is vital for good health.

◄ Pot plants

Plants in pots can't get water from the ground, so they need regular watering. Too little water means they die. Too much can also kill them, by rotting their roots.

► Water holes

Oases are the few places in deserts that have water under the surface of the sand. Rainwater sinks into the sand, then collects in rock. The water moves through the rock to form a pool where the land dips down. Plants and animals can survive there.

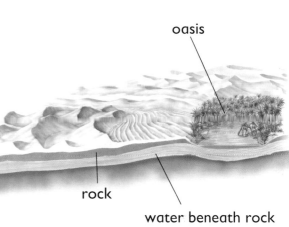

oasis

rock

water beneath rock

▼ Life in a rock pool

Rock pools contain lots of different plants and animals. All of them are adapted to withstand pounding waves and hot sun in the shallow water. Rock pools give you an idea of the huge variety of life in the sea.

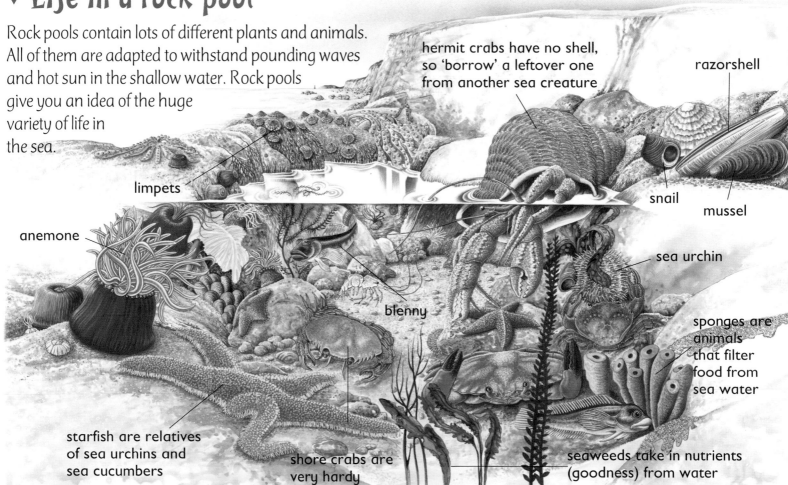

hermit crabs have no shell, so 'borrow' a leftover one from another sea creature

razorshell

limpets

snail

mussel

anemone

sea urchin

blenny

sponges are animals that filter food from sea water

starfish are relatives of sea urchins and sea cucumbers

shore crabs are very hardy

seaweeds take in nutrients (goodness) from water

Weather

Find out more:
Climate ◄ Climate change ◄ Water ◄

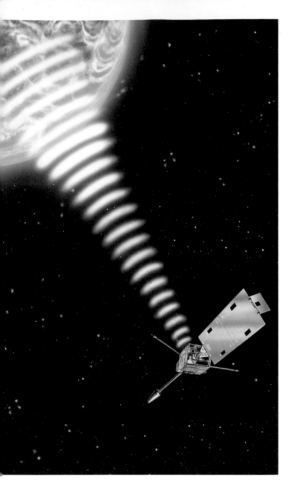

Sun, wind and water combine to produce our weather. The Sun's heat makes water from the sea evaporate (turns it into tiny droplets). These droplets rise and form clouds in the cooler upper atmosphere. Clouds are carried by the wind and deposit rain over the land.

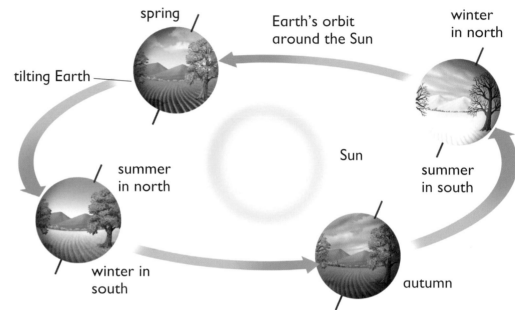

spring

Earth's orbit around the Sun

winter in north

tilting Earth

Sun

summer in north

summer in south

winter in south

autumn

▲ Sent by satellite

Clouds and storms gathering above the Earth can be seen clearly from space. Satellites photograph them and send radio messages back to Earth. The movement of the storms and clouds allows scientists to predict (guess) what the weather will be like.

► Cloud shapes

Clouds form at different heights, and in different types of weather. These things affect their appearance. Generally, the thin, wispy clouds are high up. Heavy-looking rain clouds are normally nearer the ground.

Word box

evaporate
turn into tiny droplets

satellite
a spacecraft travelling around Earth

▲ The seasons

Weather varies with the seasons. These happen as the Earth circles the Sun. One full circle takes a year. The Earth is tilted, so the poles get closer to the Sun at different times. In June, the North Pole leans towards the Sun, making it summer in northern areas.

Cumulonimbus give heavy showers of rain or storms

Cirrus clouds are very high up

contrails are white streaks created by aircraft

Cirrostratus

Cumulus clouds bring rain

Stratus clouds can bring drizzle

Whales

The blue whale is the largest mammal.
There are about 40 different types of whales.
They spend hours underwater, coming
up only to breathe. They spout out
water from a blow-hole on top.

▼ Whale with a sword

The narwhal has an amazing tusk – a very long upper left tooth. Usually only males grow the tusk. They 'fence' with rivals at breeding time, as if sword-fighting.

▲ Noisy whales

Belugas are probably the noisiest whales. They chirp, chatter, wail and moan to each other as they swim along the coasts of the Arctic Ocean. Many other whales also send out squeaks and clicks and listen to the bounced-back echoes, to detect objects around them.

▼ Sperm whale

Sperm whales can dive more than 1,000 metres into water and stay beneath for more than an hour.

▼ Blue whale

The blue whale opens its mouth wide to gulp in water. It then squeezes the water out through rows of bristly, strap-shaped plates called baleen. Small animals called krill are trapped by the baleen and get eaten.

krill

baleen

Wild West

Find out more:
Native Americans ◄ United States of America ◄

In the 1840s, the Europeans who had settled in the eastern United States began to move westwards. They settled on the prairies (grasslands) and seized land from the Native Americans. They planted crops and kept cattle, working as cowboys. Some went all the way across to the Pacific coast, in search of land or the glint of gold.

Word scramble

Can you unscramble these names? They all belong to famous people from the Wild West:

a. **MALACITY ENJA**
b. **TAWTY PERA**
c. **ENNIA KEOLAY**

answers
a. Calamity Jane b. Wyatt Earp c. Annie Oakley

▲ The Oregon Trail

Covered wagons took whole families westwards from Missouri, often as far as Oregon. It was a rough ride and many travellers died from accidents or lack of water.

▲ Buffalo Bill

William Cody was an army scout and buffalo hunter. In 1883, he set up a spectacular 'Wild West Show', which went on tour. In the 1900s, film-makers took up the same story of outlaws, cowboys and 'Indians' (as Native Americans were known).

◄ Lawless times

Gunfights and robbery were all too common. William Bonney was a cattle thief who killed 21 men before he was shot, in 1881. He was better known as 'Billy the Kid'.

◄ The 'Forty-Niners'

In 1849, gold was discovered in California. Prospectors (gold hunters) rushed to 'stake a claim', marking out their own area. They then set up camp and started searching for traces of gold in the rivers.

Women's rights

In the late 1800s, many women in Europe and North America were angry. They did not have the same rights as men and could not vote in elections. They were badly paid in factories and mills. Often they were not allowed to go to university or to be doctors or judges. They demanded better lives.

Nancy Astor

◀ Into parliament

The first nation to allow women to vote was New Zealand, in 1893. Nancy Astor became Britain's first female Member of Parliament, in 1919. Times were changing.

▲ Wars and work

Many men had to go away to fight in wars from 1914 to 1918 and 1939 to 1945. Women were taken on to do work that only men had done before. They worked on farms or in factories. They proved that they were just as good as men, but they were still not paid as much.

▼ 'Votes for women!'

Women who campaigned for the vote in the 1900s were called suffragists or suffragettes. They protested by breaking windows and chaining themselves to railings. Many were sent to prison.

◀ Bloomers

Amelia Bloomer was an American who campaigned for a better deal for women in the 1850s. She wanted them to wear more practical clothes, so she invented a new kind of trousers. These became known as 'bloomers'.

Woodland and forest

Find out more:
Air ◄ Conservation ◄ Plant kingdom ◄
Plant life ◄ Rainforests ◄ Trees ◄

Forests cover about one-fifth of the Earth's land. Every forest is filled with millions of living things, from tiny creatures that bury themselves under the leaves on the forest floor to the birds that nest high up in the branches.

the red squirrel makes its home in forest branches

Wow!

Scientists found 10,500 different kinds of living thing in a deciduous forest in Switzerland.

wild cat

deer

stoat

mouse   toad   snail   snake

tortoise

shrew

▼ Forest animals

Many animals find food and shelter in the forest. Small creatures such as squirrels and mice feed on leaves, fruits and seeds. They are eaten by larger animals such as stoats, weasels and wild cats.

▼ Changing colour

In places with warm summers and cool winters, many forests are deciduous. This means their trees have leaves that change colour and fall off.

▼ Oxygen-givers

All forests have an important job to do. Their trees take in carbon dioxide gas from the air and give off oxygen, the gas that all animals need to stay alive.

◄ Cold forests

In cool parts of the world, and in mountain areas, grow conifers — trees such as pines, firs and spruces. These trees are evergreens — they keep their leaves all year round.

World

Our world consists of the planet Earth and all the living things on it. Millions and millions of people live here. The world's land areas are divided into almost 200 separate countries, and other areas that belong to certain countries. Each country has its own government and laws, and its own national flag.

▼ Big and small

The world's biggest country is Russia. It is millions of times bigger than the Vatican City, the smallest country in the world. The Vatican City lies in the Italian city of Rome.

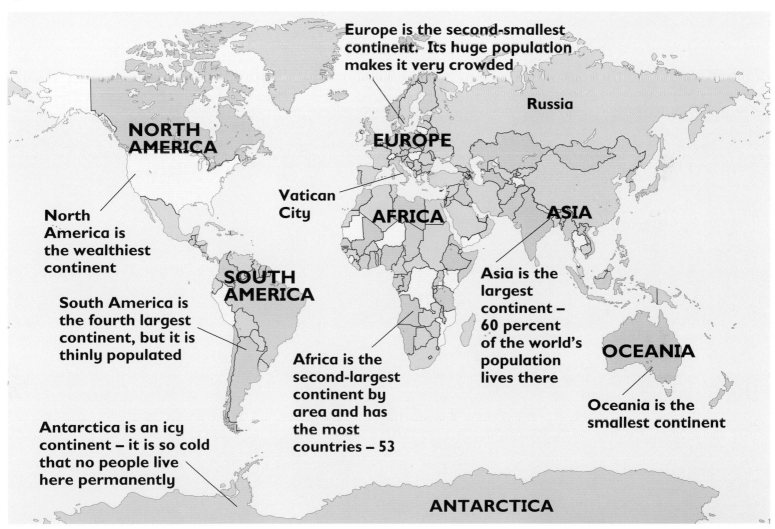

Europe is the second-smallest continent. Its huge population makes it very crowded

Russia

NORTH AMERICA

EUROPE

Vatican City

AFRICA

ASIA

North America is the wealthiest continent

SOUTH AMERICA

South America is the fourth largest continent, but it is thinly populated

Asia is the largest continent – 60 percent of the world's population lives there

OCEANIA

Oceania is the smallest continent

Africa is the second-largest continent by area and has the most countries – 53

Antarctica is an icy continent – it is so cold that no people live here permanently

ANTARCTICA

▶ United Nations

The United Nations is an organization that encourages peace between countries. Soldiers from member countries help to keep peace in troubled areas. The UN symbol shows a map of the world surrounded by olive branches, which traditionally stand for peace.

Wow!

Around the world people speak more than 3,000 different languages. The six most common ones are: Chinese, English, Spanish, Hindi, Arabic and Russian.

World War One

Find out more:
World War Two ▶

A terrible war broke out in 1914. It was fought in many different parts of the world, so it later became known as a World War. The Central Powers, which included Germany, Austria and Turkey, fought against the Allies, which in the end included the British Empire, France, Russia, Italy, Japan and the USA. Peace did not come until 1918.

▲ New weapons

Terrible new weapons were invented during World War One. The Allies used armoured tanks, like these. The Central Powers attacked their enemies with poisonous gas.

▼ War in the air

Planes were now used to fly over the enemy, spying out the land, or dropping bombs. This German plane had three wings.

▲ In the trenches

The opposing armies faced each other along a line which stretched from Belgium to Switzerland. Soldiers sheltered in long trenches dug into the ground, defended by barbed wire.

◄ So many dead

Ambulances such as this one carried wounded soldiers from the scene of battle. By 1918, ten million soldiers had been killed and many more injured.

Word box

barbed wire
tangled wire fitted with sharp spikes

poisonous gas
gas that poisoned anyone who breathed it in

tanks
armoured vehicles with moving tracks instead of wheels

trench
a deep ditch, dug to shelter soldiers from gunfire

World War Two

A second World War broke out in 1939 and lasted until 1945. In the end, armies from the British Empire, the Soviet Union (Russia) and the USA defeated those of Germany, Italy and Japan. This was the worst war in human history, leaving 55 million soldiers and civilians dead around the world.

◄ Pearl Harbor

In 1941, Japanese planes attacked an American naval base at Pearl Harbor, in Hawaii. The USA now entered the war, fighting in the Pacific islands and across Europe.

▲ Fast warfare

Germany invaded most of Europe, while Japanese troops advanced quickly through East and Southeast Asia. World War Two weapons included high-speed tanks, dive-bombers and deadly submarines.

▼ The Nazis

During World War Two, Germany was ruled by the Nazi Party. Their leader was Adolf Hitler. Anyone who disagreed with the Nazis was put in prison or killed. The Nazis hated Jewish people and set up death camps, where six million people were murdered.

Word box

civilian
someone who is not serving as a soldier, sailor or airman

► Cities bombed

Many cities all over Britain and Germany were devastated by bombs. Here, thick smoke hangs over the city of London in 1940. St Paul's Cathedral is surrounded by blazing buildings.

Writing and printing

Writing began about 5,500 years ago, in the Middle East. It allowed people to keep records and to write down their stories for the people who came after them. All sorts of scripts came into use around the world, from China to Central America. They included patterns, pictures, symbols and alphabets. These signs stood for objects, ideas or sounds.

► A B C D...

Alphabets are made up of letters that stand for different sounds. The alphabet used in this book grew from those used in southwest Asia and southern Europe. Here are the first six letters of nine different alphabets and scripts.

Phoenician

Classical Greek

Roman
A B C D E F

Cyrillic
А Б В Г Д Е

Hebrew

Arabic

Ancient Egyptian

Chinese
人 月 子 水 雨 木

Japanese
星 面 海 水 下

▲ Printed books

This Buddhist holy book was printed by hand in AD868, using carved wooden blocks to make the words and pictures.

▼ Picture writing

Between about 3200BC and AD400, Egyptian priests used a kind of writing made up of picture symbols called hieroglyphs. These can still be seen on the walls of old tombs or written out on papyrus.

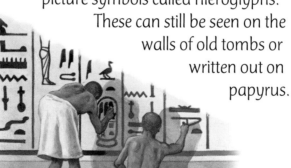

◄ At the press

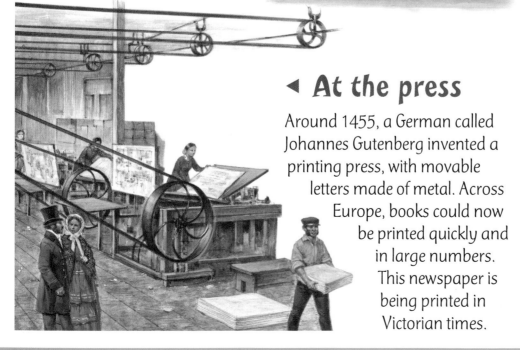

Around 1455, a German called Johannes Gutenberg invented a printing press, with movable letters made of metal. Across Europe, books could now be printed quickly and in large numbers. This newspaper is being printed in Victorian times.

Word box

papyrus
a kind of paper made from reeds

printing press
a machine in which metal shapes covered in ink are pressed against a page to print words or pictures

script
signs that are used in writing

X-rays

The invention of the X-ray machine meant doctors could see exactly what was going on inside a living body. There are now many other types of body-scanner. They 'see' inside the body by using sound waves and other forms of energy that are able to pass through living tissue.

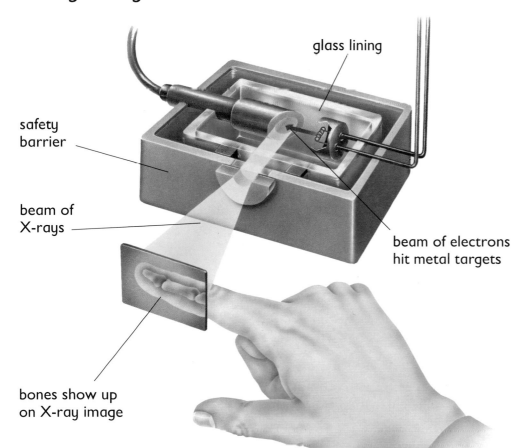

glass lining

safety barrier

beam of X-rays

beam of electrons hit metal targets

bones show up on X-ray image

▲ Airport security

To make sure that people do not carry anything dangerous on board an aircraft, their baggage is X-rayed. An X-ray can travel through most soft substances but not hard ones. This means that even the smallest objects can be seen inside a case.

Word box

discharge tube
vacuum-filled (without air) glass tube through which electricity is passed

electron
a tiny particle

▲ Inside an X-ray machine

X-rays are produced in a glass discharge tube. They pass through the body and make an image on a screen or on photographic film. As bone is harder than flesh, it leaves a shadow that can be seen very clearly.

▶ Dental X-rays

Your dentist may X-ray your teeth to find out what is happening inside a tooth. Any infection and cavities (holes) show up on the X-ray pictures, so the dentist knows what treatment to give you.

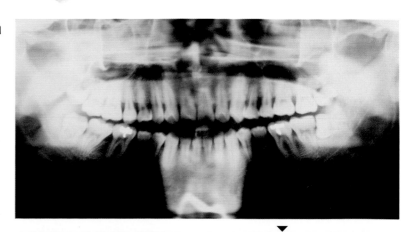

Index

The numbers in **bold** type refer to main entries in your book

The publishers would like to thank the following sources for supplying photographs for this book:

AFP: 61 (br) Roger_Viollet/AFP; 114 (bm) Roger_Viollet/AFP; 155 (br) Roger_Viollet/AFP; 233 (bl) AFP **Art Archive:** 248 (ml) British Library/Art Archive **Casio:** 175 (br); 221 (M) **Corbis:** 27 (br) Earl & Nazima Kowall/Corbis; 30 (ml) Tiziana and Gianni Baldizzone/Corbis; 46 (bm) Hulton-Deutsch Collection/Corbis; 51 (tr) James A.Sugar/Corbis; 154 (br) James L.Amos/Corbis; 196 (bl) Bob Krist/Corbis; Page 120 (mr) Charles O'Rear/Corbis; 228 (BR) Chris North; Cordaiy Photo Library Ltd./Corbis 232 (ml) Hulton-Deutsch Collection/Corbis; 249 (tr) Jacques M.Chenet/Corbis **Electrolux** 221 (m) **Nokia** 69 (br); 175 (tl) **P & O:** 204 (m) **Philips** 209 (bm) **Sanyo** 175 (tl)

All other pictures from Corel, Digital STOCK, Dover Publications, Hemera, ILN, PHOTODISC

The publishers would like to thank the following artists who have contributed to this book:

Lisa Alderson, Andy Beckett, Mark Bergin, Richard Berridge, Syd Brak, John Butler, Steve Caldwell, Martin Camm, Vanessa Card, Jim Channell, Kuo Kang Chen, Mark Davis, Peter Dennis, Richard Draper, Wayne Ford, Nicholas Forder, Chris Forsey, Mike Foster/Maltings Partnership, Mark Franklin, Terry Gabbey, Luigi Galante, Studio Galante, Shammil Ghule, Peter Gregory, Alan Hancocks, Peter Harper, Alan Harris, Ron Haywood, Steve Hibbick, Sally Holmes, Richard Hook, Ian Jackson, Rob Jakeway, John James, Aziz Khan, Steve Kirk, Stuart Lafford, Andy Lloyd Jones, Mick Loates, Kevin Maddison, Alan Male, Maltings Partnership, Janos Marffy, Angus McBride, Doreen McGuinness, Annabel Milne, Andrea Morandi, Helen Parsley, Roger Payne, Jane Pickering, Gill Platt, Jonathan Pointer, Terry Riley, Pete Roberts, Steve Roberts, Andy Robinson, Eric Robson, Eric Rowe, Martin Sanders, Desiderio Sanzi, Peter Sarson, Mike Saunders, Rob Sheffield , Guy Smith, Roger Smith, Sarah Smith, Nik Spender, Roger Stewart, Mark Taylor, Gwen Tourret, Rudi Vizi, Christian Webb, Steve Weston, Mike White, Tony Wilkins, Paul Williams, John Woodcock